1992 Annual

Kevin EuDaly

Published by Hyrail Productions, P.O. Box 55, Denver, Colorado 80201

Printed and bound in the United States of America

ISBN: 0-9628699-2-9

Editor: Mark W. Hemphill
Art Director: Dale Sanders

Cover Photo: Three Super Fleet units, General Electric 500 Class DASH 8-40BWs, lead westbound piggyback train 199 through Crozier Canyon between Valentine and Truxton, Arizona, during April 1990. The Super Fleet units returned one of the finest paint schemes, Santa Fe's red, silver and yellow War Bonnet, to railroading, starting with repainted SDFP45s in June 1985. *Colin Johnson*

Back Cover Photo: GP60M 146 was used for a one-time publicity stunt arranged by the Santa Fe for Maersk Shipping. Unlike the other GP60Ms, which were factory-painted to Super Fleet specifications, the 146 was delivered to the Santa Fe in primer. Santa Fe's Topeka, Kansas, shops applied the Maersk scheme. The 146 toured the property from August 11 through 13, 1991, in Maersk colors, spending nearly all of August 13th on Cajon Pass in southern California for publicity photos. This view shows the unit on one of the many photo runbys performed that day. The 146 was repainted into Super Fleet red and silver on August 16, 1991, and placed in regular freight service on the 24th. *Dan Munson*

Contents

Two of the hottest trains on the Santa Fe today are the 199 and counterpart 991. The eastbound 991 rounds a curve in the Tehachapi Mountains during April 1988 behind SD40-2 5133. Scheduled to run from Richmond to Chicago in 56 hours, 30 minutes, the 991 is definitely the hottest freight on Santa Fe rails in northern California. *Scott Snell*

Acknowledgements

This project was completed with extensive help from numerous sources. Employees of the Santa Fe Railway were a generous source of current and historic information, as well as being a wonderful group to work with.

Foremost among them was Homer Henry, who helped me with numerous aspects of this Annual, including a detailed look at the events that led to the formation of Transportation Training Services. He also granted me access to the business car files at Argentine, and the business car fleet itself.

Jim Wilson set up a visit to the System Operations Center in Schaumburg, where Kevin Leddy and Gregg Grabijas of Santa Fe's Scheduling Group provided information on and interpretation of Santa Fe's Transportation Service Plan, and allowed me to attend a scheduling meeting and catch a real look at their jobs. Kevin answered my innumerable questions and helped on many occasions. He also was the connection to many other Santa Fe employees, and supplied all sorts of useful information.

Ernie Ball cordially allowed me to sit in on Power Planning activities in Schaumburg, and allowed a fascinating glimpse into that aspect of daily operations.

Teresa Foy, Linda Gustis and Catherine Westphal of Santa Fe's Public Relations department lent their complete support, and set up various tours and interviews. Their patience with my many phone calls is greatly appreciated.

Rich Wessler at the Kansas City Regional Operations Center was an extremely valuable source of information, and provided a tour of the facility. Rich, along with Sam Quintana, Jesse Munoz and Dave Leininger at the Kansas City ROC were very helpful during my tours, and the evening sitting with Dave while he dispatched the Panhandle Sub-division was an unforgettable experience.

George Smallwood and John Marshall were heroes, and provided a wonderful afternoon of entertainment at the TTS. John Quilty provided a huge chunk of information including grade profiles. His "office cleaning" was a valuable asset to this project.

Janelle Gossett, John Sloan Jr., Bob Wilson and the crew at the business car facility in Argentine allowed access to business car folios and files, and arranged the cars for the interior photos. I am indebted to them for their patience.

Doug Sizemore and Dennis Derezotes allowed access to the locomotive and car files in Topeka. John Nixon and Bob Burnett provided information on the locomotive roster while John Tyburski provided the passenger car folio information in Topeka.

Eddie Defell provided materials from Santa Fe's Audio Visual Department in Public Relations. Wayne Tomasewski provided access to the disposition file on cars and locomotives, once again enabled by the Public Relations Department. And finally, Bob Lee provided folio information on the locomotives, and verified the information provided in Santa Fe's folio books.

Though I wasn't strictly a Santa Fe fan at the outset of this project, the above Santa Fe employees showed me the wonders of the railroad. Though their help was indispensable, they also opened my eyes to the many Santa Fe employees devoted to their railroad. They made this project fun.

There was also much help from the outside. Mark Hemphill and Dale Sanders at Hyrail Productions provided constant support and direction throughout the project, and never lost faith in me or in the project's ultimate success. John Hake was an almost daily reference source for numerous details, especially information on passenger operations and equipment, and provided the "experience" portion of the text on the Missouri Mainline. He also helped with proofreading and corrections, and critique on the Missouri Main article and map.

Additional support came from Larry Anderson, Alan Bradley, Dr. George Carson, George Cockle, Doug Elder, my brother Lon EuDaly, Bob Hundman, Keith Jordan, Dave Sanders, Phil Shuster, John Szwajkart, "The Group," and numerous relatives, friends, and co-workers. I also need to thank Robert Del Grosso, who helped me through the "I wonder?" phase that first-time book authors usually experience, and Harold K. Vollrath, who provided reference material and photographs from his extensive collection.

The photographers who supplied photographs and information for consideration in this Annual are listed below. The project simply couldn't have been done without them.

This book is dedicated to Dad, James EuDaly, a marvelous man who has steered me through life, and instilled a love of trains and things that are good from an early age. It is also dedicated to my family, from James McLellan Callahan (1884-1981), a machinist for the B&O and the beginning of railroading in my lineage, to my wife, Nadean, and my three children, Sarah, James and Danae, who all sat in my lap at various times during this project — some of these keystrokes are theirs.

Contributing Photographers

Jim Asplund
Richard Barnes Jr.
Bruce Barrett
Rick Bartoskewitz
John Benner
Bruce Black
Tim Black
Joe Blackwell
Eric Blasko
Don Bowen
Alan Bradley
Kyle Brehm
Greg Brown
Alan Burns
Karl Bury
Chris Butts
Ron Butts

John Carr
Thomas Carver
Thomas Chenoweth
Terry Chicwak
Gary Clark
Adam Clegg
Dave Cohen
Chuck Conway
Lon Coone
David Crammer
Paul DeLuca
Dale DeVene Jr.
Timothy Dickinson
Cliff Downey
Doug Elder
James F. EuDaly
Lon EuDaly
Don Faris
David Fasules
Andrew Filtz
Bob Finan
Frank Frisch
Chris Fry
Ed Fulcomer

Jim Gilley
Bob Gottier
Sean Graham-White
John Hake
Richard Harris
Sean Heaney
Marshall Higgins
Steve Hipes
George Horna
Brian Jennison
Gary Jensen
Colin Johnson
Ron Keller
John LaGesse
John Leopard
John Lucas
Mark Lynn

Mike Martin
Garland McKee
Jim McLane
Keel Middleton
David Miller
Hal Miller Jr.
James Mitchell
Dan Munson
J. Mussen
Dennis Mutulo
Vic Neves
Scott O'Dell
Dave Ori
Dave Oroszi
Jill Oroszi
Mac Owen
Jim Pallow
Jerry Palmer
Steve Patterson
Carl Perelman
Bill Phillips
Victor Pickle
Vincent Porreca

Steve Rasmussen
Chris Raught
Gary Rich
Jamie Schmid
Dennis Schmidt
Thomas Schultz
Robert Seale
Steve Sedaker
John Shaw Jr.
Joe Shine
Scott Snell
Brian Solomon
Gary Sugg
Warren Sunkel
John Szwajkart

John Totten
Bruce Veary
Harold K. Vollrath
Mark Wayman
Greg Weirich
Steve Wilhelm
Keith Wilhite
Don Zimmerman
Gary Zuters

Perhaps the best known of Santa Fe's modern-day images are its Super Fleet SDFP45s. A tradition of the past was revived when the classic cowls were returned to a version of their previous paint scheme in 1989. Four of the elegant units, 102, 101, 100 and 104, crest the summit of Cajon Pass with Train 1-893-18 on November 18, 1989. *Mark Wayman*

The Santa Fe Railway is a rare breed. In 1992, it's the only large Class 1 railroad remaining independent. It's easily the smallest of the "Super Seven" rail carriers. It's a sharp contrast between the Santa Fe and massive conglomerated systems such as Burlington Northern, Norfolk Southern, CSX, UP and Conrail, whose recent predecessors include dozens of railroads from small shortlines to giant Class 1s.

In keeping with most other Class 1's, the Santa Fe has recently dispensed with about one-fourth of its mileage, downsizing to remain competitive in a cutthroat transportation industry. The 1980s weren't so kind to Colonel Holliday's road. The proposed — and failed — SPSF merger remains a dark era, an era where much feverish work resulted in no gain. Yet the Santa Fe emerged a winner, calling on the determination, strength and savvy of everyone in the Santa Fe workforce to place the railway at the forefront of North American railroading.

In recent years Santa Fe has increasingly depended on intermodal traffic. In today's transportation industry, intermodal is both the most service-sensitive, and the most competitive. Santa Fe's success has produced a remarkable railroad unlike any other. A seemingly endless parade of super-hot intermodal trains flash across the system

day-in and day out, working the Chicago to Los Angeles corridor in less than 48 hours.

Standing at trackside, it seems that for every mixed freight, grain train or coal train on the Santa Fe, there are about a dozen piggy-back or stack trains, strings of trailers and containers riding the ribbon rail aboard flat cars on Santa Fe's hottest trains. There is no doubt that "Santa Fe" and "intermodal" are synonyms. In fact, if there were a definition in the dictionary for intermodal, it would surely use the Atchison, Topeka & Santa Fe Railway as a primary example.

Yet for all its modernization, the Santa Fe remains wonderfully in tune with its history. The rebuilt and expertly maintained business car fleet and the current Super Fleet red and silver paint scheme provide ample evidence that history and tradition are still in Santa Fe's vocabulary. The business cars are kept busy flashing across the system on numerous voyages, sometimes behind piggybacks on Train Q-NYLA, and other times as special trains, each tailored to the specific occasion.

The return of the red and silver warbonnet on Super Fleet SDFP45s, followed by GP60Ms, DASH 8-40BWs and DASH 8-40CWs, has brought even the most reluctant armchair railfan out into the

sunlight to capture railroading's most recognizable paint scheme on film once again. In the meantime, and hardly noticed by any, an evolution from the short piggy-back trains of the 1960s to considerably longer intermodal trains has taken place, aided by the innovation of low-tare articulated cars.

Santa Fe's motive power fleet is also evolving. The 20-cylinder SD45s and SDF45s are on the way out, as reducing fuel consumption and maintenance expenditures are critical factors in Santa Fe's formula for profitability. Super Fleet units are now a significant fraction of the roster.

There are still many older locomotives giving a spin to Santa Fe's fleet. GP20s, GP30s and GP35s are still present in large numbers years after many Class 1s scrapped them, all due to Santa Fe's rebuilding programs. Unique units such as GP40Xs

and SDFP45s run off mile after mile in revenue service. The complete eradication of switchers from the roster leaves the Santa Fe as one of the few large railroads with no switchers.

The first-generation Geeps are midway in their exodus from Santa Fe's roster. The CF7s were the first to go, and the GP7s and GP9s are steadily following. Numerous short-lines will reap benefits in the future from Santa Fe's careful rebuilding programs that put decades of new life into old Geeps.

The railroad's operating side has undergone radical change over the last two decades. Many crew change points dating to the last century have been eliminated, adding to the railroad's ability to compete with long-haul trailer-load truckers. The tower operator is all but extinct, and multi-levered dispatching boards have been replaced by the keypad, mouse and cathode ray tube.

Over the past decade, dispatching was consolidated into four Regional Operations Centers. During the next two or three years, these four centers will be consolidated again to the fourth floor of Santa Fe's new headquarters building in Schaumburg, Illinois. Dispatching will be upgraded from mid-1980s computer technology to incredibly-powerful PC-based software.

The recently occupied headquarters building is packed with state-of-the art computer networks, handling all motive power assignments, most of the scheduling functions, and the Customer Service department. Yet glass cases throughout the facility proudly display artifacts and memorabilia of an era now long-past.

Out on the railroad exciting things are happening. Amtrak's new DASH 8-32BWHs are flashing across Santa Fe iron on the *Southwest Chief* every day. Twenty-six brand new DASH 8-40CW, 6-axle, 3,800 horse-power monsters from General Electric have debuted on double-stack trains, the first three leaving Argentine on the S-CHLA1-15 of April 15, 1992. Forty more will follow in October and November this year. Anticipation is building towards the startup of Wisconsin Electric coal trains from the York Canyon Coal Mine in northern New Mexico in October 1992, reputedly to be the bailiwick of these big GEs.

Notable in the last few years has been the dramatic increase in double-stack traffic. From exactly zero dedicated stack trains just a few years ago, Santa Fe's schedule now numbers 15 dedicated stack trains. Many run several days a week, and considering there are usually five or six versions of S-CHLA and S-LACH out on the railroad at

Santa Fe still rosters a relatively large number of older four-axle units, the outcome of its rebuilding programs at San Bernardino, California, and Cleburne, Texas. GP35 2925 is just such a unit, one of 150 GP35s rebuilt at the two heavy rebuild shops, in this case Cleburne. GP20 3032 and GP39-2 3409 are likewise rebuilt units. The units are rolling the Escondido Local, train L-WB41-1, along the Pacific Ocean just south of Del Mar, California, during June 1989. Though classed as an eastbound, the local is going geographic south on the San Diego Subdivision. *Joe Blackwell*

a given instant, stack traffic is substantial, and still on the rise.

Nevertheless, Santa Fe's bread-and-butter remains intermodal. No other railroad has an intermodal operation as impressive in size or scope as the Santa Fe's, more so relative to the long mileage operated. The number of trailers moved across the system in a given week is staggering, especially considering several of the piggyback trains run in three or four sections most days. It appears not only that intermodal is here to stay, but the Santa Fe as well.

This book focuses on Santa Fe's operations — the railway, not just its hardware — and there should be something of interest for

Another blow concerned yet another attempt for access to St. Louis. The plan called for the Santa Fe to buy the Gulf, Mobile & Ohio line from Kansas City to Mexico, Missouri, and operate over the Chicago, Burlington & Quincy from Mexico to St. Louis. The CB&Q would be able to run over the former GM&O route, thereby shortening its own route between the two cities. The GM&O would retain trackage rights. Opposition to this plan came from the Rock Island, the MoPac, the Frisco and the Cotton Belt, and the ICC denied approval of the scheme.

In 1952 truck trailers began moving on flatcars, and TOFC was born on the Santa Fe. In late 1954, construction was begun on a branch to yield a better route into Dallas. It ran from Sanger through Denton to Garland, and was completed on December 1, 1955.

In 1960 an enormous grade reduction project produced a new 44-mile double-track mainline between Williams and Crookton, Arizona, at a cost of $20 million. A portion of the old line was retained to reach the Peavine line to Phoenix, and at the same time the Ash Fork to Phoenix section of the Peavine was relocated north of Skull Valley, slashing 14 miles and a tortuous mountain grade from the route.

The York Canyon Coal Mine opened in northern New Mexico in 1964. Santa Fe built a 37.5-mile, $4 million branch to serve the mine. The first train to York Canyon operated on September 28, 1966, covering 2,164 miles on its round trip to the Kaiser steel mill at Fontana, California. More coal mines opened later in this decade and the next in far western New Mexico.

In 1960 the SP announced plans to buy the Western Pacific. This was a serious threat to the Santa Fe's north-south rail

business in California, as it would give the SP a virtual monopoly on this corridor. The Santa Fe responded by acquiring WP stock, and announced its own purchase plan. The Great Northern purchased 10 percent and the Union Pacific 9.9 percent of the WP's stock, expressing their own interest.

The ICC began hearings. The GN and WP quickly lined up with the Santa Fe, while the UP, MoPac, D&RGW, Milwaukee Road and the Rock Island all supported the SP. The Justice Department opposed any outside control of the WP, and most of the affected states also opposed any merger. The ICC ruled against any takeover of the WP, and ordered the Santa Fe to divest itself of WP stock in 1965.

Meanwhile, the N&W took over the Wabash, and the C&NW acquired both the Minneapolis & St. Louis and the Chicago Great Western. The Rock Island was separately courted by the UP, SP, C&NW and Santa Fe, and after complex ICC hearings lasting seven years, the ICC announced it favored a combined C&NW and Santa Fe plan in principle, but instead preferred the creation of four "super-railroads" in the west.

Under the ICC's plan the Santa Fe would acquire part of the Rock Island and all of the MoPac, WP and D&RGW. The four-system west would remain a distant goal for years to come, and the Santa Fe is still the lone holdout in the merger department.

While this blather was going on, the Santa Fe decided to pursue both the MoPac and the Frisco. Neither deal could be closed, and neither merger was fully attempted. The MoPac then began to buy Santa Fe stock, and rather suddenly had over two million shares, making them the largest single stockholder of the Santa Fe. The Santa Fe protested to the ICC, but the ICC did not block the MoPac. The MoPac finally

The most popular F-unit by far was the F7A, its production totalling 2,366 units between February 1949 and December 1953. The Santa Fe thought it was the ideal unit, taking 476 of them. Odds are good that the unfortunate 47, rolling through western New Mexico in the mid-1950s, became one of Santa Fe's CF7 (Cleburne F7) rebuilds, a miserable fate for such a classic unit. Those days were far in the future, however, as the consist glides by the photographer towards the golden horizon. *Harold K. Vollrath collection*

gave up the fight to control the Santa Fe in 1968. The Santa Fe remained extremely opposed to outside control, and has maintained that position to this day.

Excepting a 1962 purchase in which the Santa Fe bought the Oklahoma City-Ada-Atoka Railway, a 105-mile short line that was part of the Muskogee Lines, no additional major acquisitions were attempted in the 1960s. This line was purchased from the T&P for $1 million after the T&P bought the Muskogee Lines. It gained access for the Santa Fe to Tinker Air Force Base in Oklahoma, and allowed several abandonments in the area.

Out on the railroad, speed became the emphasis. Argentine Yard in Kansas City, Kansas, received a new 48-track hump yard, capable of sorting 8,000 cars a day. One century after Cyrus K. Holliday witnessed the railway's first run, the Santa Fe was poised to run a freight train, the Super C, from Chicago to Los Angeles in under 35 hours. Trains running at speeds in excess of 100 mph probably would have blown Cyrus K. Holliday right off the tracks, but he undoubtedly would have loved to have seen it.

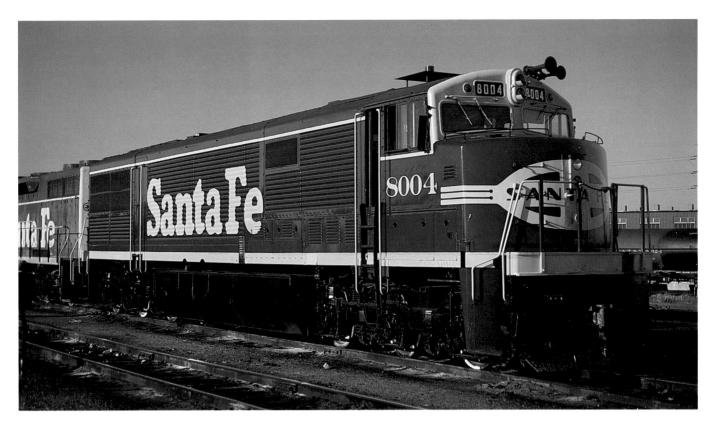

The U30CG was a truly bizarre beast, and unique to the Santa Fe. Only six of the 3,000-hp units were constructed by GE, delivered in November 1967 to Santa Fe for passenger service in the classic red and silver warbonnet paint scheme of the era. They rode on a standard U30C underframe; mechanically they were close cousins to the U30C. Unlike the U30C, their career was soon marred. An accident on Edelstein Hill involving the westbound *Grand Canyon* on February 9, 1969, focused suspicion on their tracking characteristics, as well as that of the U28CGs. Tests on March 3rd and 4th failed to pinpoint the cause of the derailment, nevertheless, the ten U28CGs and six U30CGs were shortly removed from passenger service, never to return to such august duties.

Above: At Chicago, U30CG 8004 glows in a new coat of freight blue and yellow on January 10, 1972. After Amtrak took over Santa Fe's passenger service in May 1, 1971, Santa Fe removed the steam generators from the U30CGs. The days of the *Super Chief* were indeed gone.

Top right: In freight service, but still wearing red and silver, the 8000 and 8005 rumble past the depot in Joliet, Illinois, on August 11, 1971. The U30CGs were delivered as units 400-405, and later renumbered 8000-8005. By this date their passenger colors were mirroring the dreary rigors of freight service.

Bottom right: By 1972 the new yellow and blue Warbonnet scheme was finding its way onto nearly everything in Santa Fe's fleet, including the U30CGs. In this October 9, 1972, view in Chicago, the 8005 awaits its next assignment. The U28CGs and U30CGs were retired on September 22, 1980, and traded in on B36-7s during January 1981. The 8005 fulfilled its destiny in just 13 years, passenger to freight, freight to oblivion.

Three photos, George Horna

At left: The semaphore slowly drops as a three-car northbound *Tulsan* departs the station at Cherryvale, Kansas, trackage today that's no longer part of the Santa Fe. This trackage was purchased in the massive expansion of the late 1870s under Strong, and was originally part of the Kansas City, Lawrence & Southern Kansas Railroad, which included trackage from Lawrence to Independence, Kansas (north of Bartlesville), and extended west to Hunnewell, Kansas. The era of this photo is May 1970 — the Santa Fe of today in some respects bears absolutely no similarity to the Santa Fe of 22 years ago, save for the same gauge, and the same fuel in its locomotives. *Alan Bradley*

Below: An eight-unit set of F7s drag tonnage at Fort Worth, Texas, on January 13, 1974, when time was expiring for Santa Fe's cab units. Leading the consist is "yellow bonnet" F7A 315, a model that Santa Fe purely loved. Access was originally gained into Fort Worth by merging the Gulf, Colorado & Santa Fe Railway Company into the Santa Fe on March 23, 1886. Fort Worth was the end of a 128-mile GC&SF branch which hooked up with the Santa Fe by a northward extension connecting with Santa Fe's Arkansas City line at Purcell, Oklahoma, 33 miles south of Oklahoma City. The merger of the GC&SF with the Santa Fe was the first crack in George Gould's Texas railroad empire. *Bill Phillips*

Above: A trio of Alco PAs, led by PA-1 62, handle a mail train at Williams, Arizona, in this August 1958 Kodachrome. The film has withstood the test of time, the PAs did not. Alco built 210 PA-1s and PB-1s between September 1946 and June 1950. Santa Fe took 44, becoming one of Alco's better PA customers. Mail is still a Santa Fe mainstay, though now it rides in 48-foot aluminum vans, not 80-foot steel baggage cars. The PAs began leaving Santa Fe's roster in 1967. *John E. Shaw Jr.*

At right: When new units were needed in the mid-1960s to replace ailing, ancient passenger power, Santa Fe turned to both GE and EMD. GE produced two Santa Fe-only models, the U28CG and the U30CG. The U28CGs, three of which lead this consist at the diesel shops at Argentine in April 1969, needed little modification from the standard U28C, whose design already included space for a steam generator. Add the steam generator and a "G" to the model designation and you have it. *Mac Owen*

Above left: On May 12, 1986, an eastbound Sea Land double-stack train twists through Crozier Canyon, which lies between Peach Springs and Valentine in far western Arizona. This scenic canyon offers a wealth of splendid views for the photographer that's willing to take some time and do some hiking. Curves limit train speed to 25 mph through much of the canyon, and big-time railroading makes it that much better, with dozens of freights picking their way through the canyon every day. The train is on a 1.42 percent climb to Yampai, where the mainline crests an intermediate summit and drops into Seligman. *Dave Ori*

Lower left: DASH 8-40BW 537 leads a westbound double-stack train through gorgeous scenery between West Perrin and East Doublea, Arizona, during January 1991. The 537 is one of a 60-unit order, the first GE Super Fleet units for Santa Fe. A subsequent order put another 23 of this model on the railroad, though units from the second order are rated at 3,800 horsepower rather than the 4,000 horsepower of units from the first order. The backdrop is provided by the San Francisco Mountains, ancient volcanoes whose summits reach higher into the sky than any other Arizona mountains. The train is in the middle of a 22-mile-long, 1.0 percent drop into Doublea, where a short flat section provides a momentary respite for heavy eastbounds. *Richard Harris*

Above: A westbound manifest rolls through the tremendous cut at Doublea during April 1990. Doublea lies 18 miles west of Williams, in the scenic Kaibab National Forest in north central Arizona. This is CTC fast track, but the empty gon three cars back limits this train to 55 mph. The train has been descending a 1.0 percent ruling grade from the summit of the Arizona Divide for the past 20 miles. Lead SD45 5322 was retired a little more than a year following this date. This enormous cut was dug during Santa Fe's big 1960 line reloca-tion project that greatly straightened and flattened its eastbound climb to the Arizona Divide. *Colin Johnson*

Above: The evening light at 6:35 p.m. on May 16, 1987, sets the scene for this westbound south of Matfield Green, Kansas. The train is in Mercer Creek's gentle valley, and is typical of the Flint Hills: tall grass and a nearly treeless landscape. SD45-2 5830 leads SD40-2 5155, SDF45 5974, and a trio of GP20s, 3006, 3024, and 3020, a lashup providing plenty of muscle for this manifest. Amazingly, all three of these veteran GP20s are still on Santa Fe's roster 32 years after they came out of La Grange, long after this model has vanished from nearly every other Class I. Rebuilt by Santa Fe in the late 1970s and early 1980s, they are nearing the end of their unusually long career. *Dave Oroszi*

Above right: The Flint Hills of eastern Kansas are a pleasant interruption to the monotony of one of the flatter states in the country — sort of like a sheet of plywood with a brick under one end. Four-month-old GP60M 108 leads two more GP60Ms eastbound through Matfield Green late in the afternoon on September 1, 1990, in the heart of the Flint Hills. The train will soon negotiate a pair of 3-degree, 10-minute reverse curves before crossing Crocker Creek on its way toward Ellinor. This is single track territory, and as it's part of Santa Fe's main stem between Chicago, Kansas City the west, it's an extremely busy track. *Dan Munson*

Lower right: Santa Fe's first three DASH 8-40CWs made their second westbound trip on the SCHLA1-21. On April 21, 1992, the train was rolling through Wellington, Kansas. The new six-motors were purchased to begin the replacement of Santa Fe's aging six-motor fleet. It's the beginning of the end for the 20-cylinder-powered SD45s, SDF45s and SD45-2s. Stack trains have been the normal assignment for the new GE's from day one. The new units have been arriving in Kansas City on the 213 train and are set up for service at Argentine, rather than Chicago. *John LaGesse*

Above: Train 168, with SD45 5390 on the point, waits at Ash Hill, California, for the 971 train with C30-7 8120 on the point to pass on March 11, 1987. This is the second of three trains that the 168 had to hold for due to maintenance crews that had one main track out-of-service. The 971 has a long drop into Amboy ahead, while the 168 is facing a short drop to Ludlow and then an eight mile, 1.08 percent climb up to milepost 702. Sidings off both mains at Ash Hill give the dispatcher some breathing room when traffic begins to stack up. *Jamie Schmid*

Above right: Cowls predominate in this westbound on the approach to Ash Hill during April 1990. Super Fleet SDFP45s (Santa Fe parlance for rebuilt FP45s) lead this lashup, wearing their short-lived 100 series numbers. There were so many renumberings of these units it's difficult to remember exactly which renumbering these are in; this happens to be their fourth number series on the way to their current sixth (fifth for the 101, which is now the 92). Unit 96 also only wore five different numbers. This is a poor train for this rich power, looking for all the world like a collection of leftovers from everywhere along the way. The cowl units were seldom seen on anything but hotshots earlier in their career. *Colin Johnson*

Lower right: Six units lead a westbound manifest through the big reverse curve just west of Siberia, California, milepost 678, at 2:45 p.m. on December 3, 1977. SD26 4667 with four more SD26s and an SD45 is being assisted up Ash Hill's 1.44 percent ruling grade by the following train, powered by SD40 5005, SD45 5608 (since rebuilt into 5391) and SD26 4671. The two trains were coupled together at Needles due to failed units in the 4667's consist. SD45 5539 (now the 5347) was set out at Goffs, and the two trains lost even more time when a drawbar was pulled out as the hump was crested at milepost 702. Not exactly an ideal run. *Jamie Schmid*

Above left: An eastbound double-stack train zips through the reverse curve at Noel, Oklahoma, during September 1991, with GP40X 3801 in command of the lashup. The CTC-controlled Waynoka Subdivision is classified as single track, but the 18,966-foot controlled siding here makes it resemble double track. The 3801 is one of 10 GP40Xs on Santa Fe's roster, a relatively rare model of which Santa Fe's order was the largest. These units were prototypes for EMD's 50-series, the first production models with EMD's F-series crankcase. This series also achieved significantly improved adhesion with a single-axle wheelslip detection and control system developed from a system first installed in Swedish electric locomotives. Those entranced by the arcane aesthetics of EMD design were disappointed when the GP50s emerged from La Grange without the flared radiators of the GP40X (try explaining that to a non-railfan). *Colin Johnson*

Lower left: DASH 8-40BWs 535 and 553 race eastbound through Belva, Oklahoma, on September 26, 1991. The train is a deadhead move to return the trailing passenger equipment to Argentine and Topeka, and is symbolled O-PXKC1-25. The Beginning "O" designates this as an Officer train, PXKC denotes its Phoenix origin and Kansas City destination. The all-stainless-steel passenger train has an appeal beyond any passenger train that's merely covered with glossy paint. Only Santa Fe can currently muster such an exceptional consist, and does so with great regularity for director's specials and public relations purposes. Belva lies on Santa Fe's freight main in western Oklahoma, 10.1 miles west of Waynoka on the Panhandle Subdivision. *Terry Chicwak*

Above: A mixed group of EMD high-horsepower four-motors led by GP50 3840 hustle a westbound intermodal train through Heman, Oklahoma, at 8:30 a.m. on March 26, 1992. The 3840 is the first unit of Santa Fe's second order for GP50s, which are rated at 3,600 horsepower rather than the 3,500 horsepower of the previous order. The rising sun illuminates the red clay hills that make this region distinctive. Heman is at milepost 351.8, 5.6 miles out of Waynoka on the way to Amarillo. The crew got on at Wellington, Kansas, 110 miles to the east, and will run through to Amarillo, Texas, more than 200 miles to the west. This makes the Panhandle Subdivision one of the longest crew districts on the mainline, at 312 miles. Crew changes no longer exist in Oklahoma on the freight main. *Bruce Barrett*

The 1-199-16 train winds through the curves at Marcel, California, just below the Tehachapi Loop, on March 18, 1991. A four-unit lashup of DASH 8-40BWs provides the dynamic braking for the lengthy descent. The 199, an expedited TOFC/COFC train, is one of the premier intermodal hotshots on the Santa Fe, its 2,495-mile run scheduled for just 54 hours. Santa Fe gives the 199 at least 4.0 horsepower per ton, and if this train is at its 3,800 ton limit, the four GEs up front are providing 4.2 horsepower per ton. The 199 is only allowed to "work" three places, a pickup at Kansas City, and setouts at Stockton and North Bay. Twelve crews are currently used to work the 199 train across the entire system, averaging 208 miles apiece. *Dave Ori*

Above right: A five-unit GP35 lashup takes train 869 down the Tehachapis through old Allard at 1:48 p.m. on November 13, 1983. The Santa Fe is a tenant on the SP-owned mainline over the Tehachapis, 66.9 miles from Mojave to Kern Junction in Bakersfield, and if you ask the Santa Fe crews, they're stuffed in a siding for every SP drag that happens by. Allard, a former siding, is on a fairly long stretch of double track, stretching from Tunnel #3 to Tunnel #2. It disappeared when Bealville siding was extended. The westbound train will enter Tunnel #2 in about a minute. *Jamie Schmid*

Lower right: SD45-2 5838 leads a lashup out of the Tehachapi Mountains and onto the Mojave Desert at SP milepost 374.5 during April 1988. The windmills in the background began sprouting like dandelions in spring during the 1980s, and now fill the ridgetops between the towns of Tehachapi and Mojave. The B-unit second out is one of eight SD45-2Bs rebuilt from SD45-2s at Santa Fe's San Bernardino Shops between September 1987 and January 1988. *Scott Snell*

At left: Ex-Amtrak SDP40F 622, rebuilt into Santa Fe SDF40-2 5257, leads a short 1-879-25 train through Orwood, California, at 3:32 p.m. on October 25, 1989. Orwood is located between Richmond and Stockton on the Stockton Subdivision, 15.4 miles west of Stockton. This SDF40-2 has a life that only a handful of the original 150 SDP40Fs can rejoice in. Most had a rather short, passenger career. Several questionable derailments blamed on their design resulted in their banishment from several railroads. Amtrak traded a few for Santa Fe switch engines, and a few were retained by EMD as test beds. The majority of Amtrak's SDP40Fs were gutted of their mechanical and electrical components for use in replacement F40PHs. Then they made a one-way trip to a scrap yard. *David Miller*

Above: An elephant-style lashup of new DASH 8-40BWs roll the hot 199 train westbound between Christie and Collier, California, on October 26, 1990. Their long run from Chicago is nearly complete; they're only a dozen miles from the end of their trip at Richmond. These units were delivered a few weeks earlier, and are just beginning their expected multi-million-mile career on the Santa Fe. This lashup weighs 1,156,000 pounds, and puts out 16,000 horsepower on 16 axles . . . one thousand horsepower per axle. It demonstrates the magnitude of locomotive design progression in the past three decades. The GP30's 562 horsepower per axle — which in 1961 was barely within the capabilities of traction motors and primitive wheel slip systems — is now entirely insufficient. *Eric Blasko*

Above: Twenty-seven cowls — 20 SDF45s and seven SDFP45s — received the SPSF merger paint scheme. Five SDF45s, four in the merger scheme, lead a westbound towards the setting sun at Crookton, Arizona, on October 2, 1986. Within three years all four will be back in blue and yellow, following one of the strangest non-mergers of the last two decades. *Colin Johnson*

Left: The two most prevalent Santa Fe models painted in the SPSF merger scheme were the SF30Cs and the C30-7s, of which 44 units each were repainted. Both types are represented in this view of Train 981 west of Caliente, California, in the Tehachapi Mountains on March 9, 1987. The red and yellow merger scheme units were dubbed "Kodachromes," for their similarity to the colors used on Kodak's film boxes. The Kodachromes weren't commonly seen in pure lashups, since they accounted for less than twenty percent of the Santa Fe roster. In July 1986 the merger repainting program was halted, and once again blue and yellow was the standard attire. *Dave Ori*

In February 1907, the ICC began an investigation of the railroad empire of Edward H. Harriman. At the time Harriman's domain enveloped the Southern Pacific, Union Pacific, Illinois Central and the Alton. Harriman also owned eight percent of the New York Central, 17 percent of the Santa Fe, and 18.5 percent of the Baltimore & Ohio. Only the partnership of J.P. Morgan and James J. Hill dared defy Harriman.

Harriman's power was viewed by many of his contemporaries as economically and morally bankrupt, and possibly even illegal, yet no one disputed his railroading genius and financial acumen.

When the ICC questioned Harriman about the Santa Fe, he replied that if they would let him, he'd take it tomorrow.

"Tomorrow?" they asked, to which he replied that he most certainly would, and added that he thought it was a pretty good property.

It wasn't in the cards. Harriman died in 1909 and the UP was forced to divest its SP stock in 1913. The Santa Fe remained independent.

On a Thursday morning, May 15, 1980, the Santa Fe and Southern Pacific jointly announced a memorandum of intent to merge the SP into the Santa Fe. Santa Fe Pacific Industries would be the result. Its 25,000-mile railroad would be managed by a holding company called the Southern Pacific & Santa Fe Railway Company.

Few observers of railroading had anticipated the announcement that spring day. As the 1970s drew to a close, it had seemed the SP would forever fiddle with merger schemes, and the Santa Fe would always be absent from merger speculations. In the 1970s the SP sought access to Kansas City through purchase of the Rock Island's Golden State Route, and had expressed interest in a merger involving a route to the east coast.

The surprising merger plan included enough detail for observers to conclude that the Santa Fe was the senior partner in the deal. The evidence was that headquarters of the merged roads would be in Chicago, not San Francisco; the board of directors would seat 12 Santa Fe directors, and only eight from SP; and the Santa Fe would have the ability to nominate the merged road's chairman and chief executive officer, not SP.

The best reason for Santa Fe's dominance was also the most obvious. In the years prior to the merger announcement, the Santa Fe was consistently more profitable than SP, even though it ranked second in gross revenues and net assets. In other words, the Santa Fe made more money with less investment and had a higher profit margin.

ICC chairman Darius Gaskins soon questioned in public possible anticompetitive aspects of the merger. Analysts were quick to point out that California might be adversely affected, as Santa Fe Pacific (SFP) would control 5,388 of 7,244 rail miles, about 75 percent. In Arizona, almost 100 percent of the rail miles would be controlled by the merged roads, and New Mexico was almost the same.

This wasn't entirely unprecedented, however. In Florida, the CSX combination of Seaboard Coast Lines and L&N accounted for 76 percent of 4,007 total rail miles.

It appeared the West might wind up with three major systems: UP (plus MoPac and

WP), BN (plus Frisco), and Santa Fe plus SP. BN led in route-miles, with roughly 29,200 versus 25,200 for SFP and 22,180 for UP. SFP would lead the three in revenues with about $4 billion, UP would weigh in at $3.3 billion and BN with $3 billion.

This of course left Rio Grande a dwarf in the midst of giants, and in 1980, it was not yet known where the Katy, Chicago & North Western, Kansas City Southern, Soo Line, and what was left of the Milwaukee might fit in after megamergers changed American railroading forever.

Santa Fe's 1980 attempt to take over the SP was soon thwarted due to internal problems. The concept didn't vanish, however. On September 27, 1983, Santa Fe Industries and Southern Pacific Transportation Company, the parents of the two roads, announced a proposed new merger. The two companies stated they were entering into a business agreement in which the two lines would become subsidiaries of a holding company, Santa Fe Southern Pacific Corporation.

This was a $5.2 billion transaction. It would produce the third largest railroad in the country behind BN and CSX. It was likely a reaction to the UP's continued expansion. UP was then completing its merger with the WP and the MP, and severing its remaining traffic affiliations with the SP. Of course, BN's acquisition of the Frisco had significantly enlarged the largest, but this was perhaps only a minor contributor to Santa Fe's and SP's incentive for the SFSP merger.

The new company was also willing to put one of its railroads into a trust to permit the merger of the parent companies prior to ICC approval of the merger, if that was deemed necessary.

The saga that followed this announcement was both fascinating and astonishing, and in the end had major ramifications for every western railroad.

The SFSP agreement of 1983 portrayed a different picture than the memorandum issued in May 1980. It indicated that each road would nominate half of the board of directors of the new holding company, with Santa Fe a 54 percent owner and SP a 46 percent owner. The Santa Fe was still in the lead, but only by a narrow margin.

SD45 5394 was the first unit to wear the SPSF merger scheme. Shown here in the scheme's original version, it emerged from the paint shop at San Bernardino on July 31, 1985. This August 16, 1985, view in Denver shows several of the scheme's preliminary characteristics. Most noticeable was the white "SF" lettering, which was changed to yellow. The black band at the top is even with the bottom of the flared radiators; it was later raised to about midway on the radiators, just even with the bottom of the dynamic brake blister. Less noticeable are the four red stripes on the short hood rather than the later standard of three. The 5394 left San Bernardino on its first trip on August 7th, just nine days before this shot, and by mid-September had been modified into the standard scheme. A short window of opportunity, indeed. *Bruce Barrett*

As in the earlier version, Santa Fe's John J. Schmidt would receive the title of chairman and chief executive officer, while Robert D. Krebs, president of Southern Pacific Transportation Company, would become the president and chief operating officer.

The Santa Fe and SP were curious merger partners; in many ways, its was like a marriage of the Hatfields and the McCoys. The feud between the two carriers dated to 1883, when the SP did everything it could to keep the Santa Fe out of California. They fought bitterly over acquisition of the Western Pacific in 1965, to no avail. They turned out to be unsuccessful at negotiating the Santa Fe takeover of the SP in 1980.

There was further fuel for the fire when SP accessed Kansas City by acquiring the Rock Island from Santa Rosa, New Mexico, to Topeka, Kansas, with trackage rights on the UP into Kansas City, in 1980. SP exacerbated the antagonism by obtaining trackage rights over the MoPac into St. Louis, something the Santa Fe had failed at several times.

The merger proposition was also strange, considering the huge chasm that separated the operating philosophies and physical makeup of the two roads. The Santa Fe essentially had just one transcontinental

A pair of merger-painted SF30Cs lead Train 1-305-14 through the Flint Hills south of Matfield Green, Kansas, on April 14, 1990. Within a year all active red and yellow units would be back in blue and yellow, or at least removed from the active roster. The 305 is a daily manifest from Kansas City to Temple, Texas, doing local work en route. It's scheduled to depart Kansas City at 3:00 p.m., putting it into the scenic Flint Hills in good late afternoon light. The 305's 30-hour schedule results in a 22.5-mph average, not exactly scorching hot. *Jim Gilley*

route, while SP's attention had long been splintered between two competing transcontinental routes, plus variations thereupon like the Golden State and the Modoc Line.

The Santa Fe's trademark was fast freights, personified best by its hotshots between Chicago and Los Angeles. The SP, on the other hand, was noted for its mammoth freights, and for eking out maximum ton miles from minimum locomotive miles.

The Santa Fe was synonymous with long sections of tangent double-track mainline, while SP's reputation was that of curves, snowsheds and mountain passes. The SP was primarily a single-track railroad.

Much of this disparity was inherent in the two railroads' traffic base. The Santa Fe's mainline was highly dependent on lightweight cross-country priority traffic, SP's on heavy, low-priority freight like lumber.

When one system map was laid on top of the other, the SFSP planners saw several ways to cut mileage from circuitous routes. Santa Fe's Los Angeles-Houston traffic could be routed to the SP Sunset Route, saving nearly 150 miles. SP's northern California to Dallas/Fort Worth and Memphis traffic could use the Santa Fe from Mojave, California, to Dallas/Fort Worth, saving 250 miles, and unplugging SP's Sunset Route.

High-speed intermodal traffic could take the hillier Santa Fe, the heavy boxcar non-priority traffic could take the SP's flatter

Sunset and Golden State routes. This would unplug Santa Fe's single-track territory.

No specific information as to how the railroads would be combined was presented, but the elimination of duplicative track was established as one goal. Interestingly, immediately following the SFSP merger announcement, the Santa Fe announced that they were still studying a possible purchase of Conrail — still shooting for that elusive true transcon.

An official merger plan was prepared, the Santa Fe and Southern Pacific hoping to have it submitted to the ICC by mid-1984. At this point it was assumed the ICC would be able to make a decision within two years, by mid-1986.

At the end of the business day on December 23, 1983, it became official, when Santa Fe Industries and Southern Pacific Company were merged into $6.4 billion Santa Fe Southern Pacific Corporation (SFSP). This merger involved only the holding companies, not the railroads, and not without a court battle with the UP and Katy, and after a temporary stay by the ICC was lifted.

To permit the merger of the holding companies, SFSP agreed to keep operation of two railroads entirely separate until the ICC (SFSP hoped) approved the merger. The UP had held that since the SP would be placed in a voting trust by SFSP until the ICC either approved or denied the merger, the SP's service and plant would deteriorate.

The ICC decision would have to be handed down within 31 months, due to a law instituted after the Rock Island's demise. The UP and the Rock Island had tried to merge for nearly 20 years. The lack of a timely ICC decision is believed to be one of the major factors in the crumbling of the Rock.

The possibility of a merger denial was soon brought up by the press. Schmidt had also considered that possibility. He suggested that in the event of the ICC nixing the merger there were a number of logical alternatives, including spinning off one of the railroads to the stockholders, or selling

one of the two roads.

In mid-February 1984, Santa Fe and SP dispatched a team of 14 top management people to Chicago — seven from each road — to head up what was referred to as the OR-85 team. The team's prime concern was the development of a target operating ratio of 85 percent for the new company, leaving 15 percent as operating income. Neither railroad was achieving a ratio anywhere near that at the time. It was revealed there would be three "Grand Divisions" for the new railroad, headquartered in Kansas City, Houston and Los Angeles.

On March 23, 1984, the SFSP filed its official merger application with the ICC. The application presented another strange twist, as the new railroad would be called the Southern Pacific & Santa Fe (SPSF), not Santa Fe & Southern Pacific. The Santa Fe still appeared to be in control, as according to the application the new railroad would be led by Lawrence Cena, who was then the Santa Fe's President and CEO.

The application anticipated no major line abandonments. The operating plan did include shifting traffic to more direct routes to expedite service. There were no plans revealed to cancel service to any community being served at the time by SP and Santa Fe. By law, the ICC had 31 months, until October 23, 1986, to hand down its decision.

The UP soon asked for 1,100 miles of trackage rights as a condition of the merger. This was very close to the figure the UP had to grant to other carriers, principally the Rio Grande, to gain their acquiescence when the UP merged with the MoPac and WP.

Principally, the UP wanted access to SP lines to gain access to Arizona and California's San Joaquin Valley. As part of its argument, UP claimed that SPSF would originate 90 percent and terminate 80 percent of California's rail traffic.

By March 1985 Phase II of the merger hearings were underway in Washington, D.C., wherein opponents to the merger were cross-examined by SFSP attorneys. At this point the C&NW dropped its opposition to the merger. The railroads still involved in the cross-examination included the UP, Rio Grande, Milwaukee, KCS, MKT, Texas-Mexican and Conrail.

In the meantime, the Santa Fe and SP put together a management team to guide the railroads through their transition from two roads to one, and began to plan in detail the implementation of the merger.

The possibility of a new paint scheme was revealed, with painting to be done initially at Santa Fe's San Bernardino shops. Upper management arrived at a general consensus that a post-merger scheme was not to include Santa Fe's blue or Warbonnet, nor SP's gray or nose feathering, and the new scheme was to emphasize red and yellow. Paint schemes were soon devised and applied to HO scale models. SP proposed a red and yellow warbonnet, while the Santa Fe presented several schemes using yellow and SP Daylight Orange and Red.

As of early June 1984, no paint scheme had been approved, but the selection had been narrowed to one preferred configuration. The proposed scheme would be a Warbonnet deviation, replacing Santa Fe blue with red. Black would be used from the top of the locomotive down to the bottom of the dynamic brake blister. Trucks would be silver and the fuel tank and underframe painted black.

No lettering scheme had been decided, and the whole thing still required SFSP board approval. It was planned that once the ICC approved the merger, the newly-formed system would have the entire combined locomotive fleet repainted in 14 months, a rather ambitious schedule.

As the western megamerger proceeded, several smaller railroads grew extremely uncomfortable, among them the Rio Grande, KCS, and MKT. The Milwaukee's concern diminished after their acquisition by the Soo Line on February 19, 1985.

The UP soon announced its intent to acquire the Katy. This was seen as weakening the UP's case opposing the SFSP merger. To SFSP it looked like good news, and they began to hope they could trade acquiescence to the Katy merger for keeping the UP out of the southern San Joaquin Valley, and off the Sunset Route.

Since the C&NW was locked in with the UP, and the KCS apparently was content to remain independent, it left only the Rio Grande without its dance card filled at the merger cotillion. The Rio Grande's demands were stiff: the entire Overland Route at less than scrap value, ten percent of SP's car and locomotive fleet, and access to all of northern California and Oregon.

By mid-1985, the railfan press had spewed forth an inordinate amount of speculative ink about affects of the merger. SP's Cascade Line from Portland, Oregon, to Roseville, California, was expected to stay unchanged. A reduction in traffic was perceived for SP's Overland Route to Ogden, Utah, as well as traffic between San Francisco and Los Angeles. An increase in Golden State Route traffic was predicted, and it was anticipated that the Santa Fe would really get busy between Barstow, California, and both Dallas/Fort Worth and Chicago.

The parallel routes in California's San Joaquin Valley, it was assumed, would be operated essentially as double track. More business would head over Tehachapi, and less over Cajon Pass into Los Angeles.

On July 30, 1985, the final phase of the merger's hearing process began, public hearings. SFSP officials stated their hopefulness that the merger would be consummated by late 1985 or January 1986 at the latest.

By July 1985, tentative approval of the new SPSF paint scheme was given by Santa Fe's president and CEO, Larry Cena. It was described as a yellow warbonnet, with red sides, silver trucks, black fuel tank and white SPSF lettering. A logo had been developed but it was not known whether or not this would be applied to the locomotives.

The Santa Fe had scheduled SD45 5597 for painting at San Bernardino; it was to emerge as the 5394 following its remanufacture. The SP had scheduled SD45R 7551, likewise undergoing remanufacture at Sacramento, for SPSF paint a few days after the Santa Fe unit.

On the morning of July 31, 1985, the first repainted unit, remanufactured SD45 5394, came out of the paint booth at San Bernardino for a brief round of company photos.

The yellow nose, sporting black lettering, was deemed too plain, so back into the paint booth it went for modifications. At about 1:30 that afternoon it was again brought out. Now it sported a black band with white lettering across the nose. Nope. Still no good.

Once again it was rolled into the paint booth. When it emerged the next morning the black band on the nose had become red, and red stripes had been added to the sides of its nose. Also, it now had red number boards with white numbers. Only the letters SF were painted on the sides, in white, though adequate room was left to add an SP after the merger to complete the SPSF name. Larry Cena looked it over and apparently liked what he saw.

August 3, 1985, was the scheduled day of the 5394's maiden trip, but this was delayed for the polyurethane paint to completely cure, and for final detail work to be completed. On the afternoon of August 6th, the unit was placed near the San Bernardino depot for pickup by a westbound. At 9:40 a.m. on August 7th, the 1-881-07 departed Hobart Yard in Los Angeles with the 5394 on the point, headed for an appointment with the company photographer at Sullivan's Curve on Cajon Pass. It was then released for system service following a brief break-in period between Barstow and Los Angeles.

Santa Fe then decided to repaint all locomotives undergoing remanufacturing or class III overhauls in the new scheme. This would speed up the post-merger repainting effort by several years — SFSP was still shooting for the repainting of the entire fleet in less than two years.

On August 8, 1985, SP's Sacramento Locomotive Works released SD45R 7551 painted in the post-merger scheme. It posed for company photographers, then was taken back inside for final tune-ups. The unit was then forwarded to Eugene, Oregon, for final set-up before entering system service.

On September 6th, a second Santa Fe unit, SD45 5401, was released from San Bernardino in the new paint scheme. Another unit, SD45 5400, was also released the same day, but wearing Santa Fe's standard blue and yellow scheme. On September 7th, the 5401, 5400 and two other units headed east with 1-881-07. The Santa Fe had tried to get the 5394 into the consist, but delays at Barstow had prevented the lashup from occurring until later that evening. The 918 train back to San Bernardino that evening had the 5401/5400/5394 consist. The three units

sat at San Bernardino until mid-afternoon on the 8th, then were placed on the point of a business car move from Los Angeles to Barstow.

SD45 5402 was the first unit to come out of the paint shop in the final, official, paint scheme. The principal change was the SF lettering on the long hood, which was now yellow instead of white. The 5401 was quickly sent back and modified to match the 5402. It was projected that locomotives would begin being painted into the new scheme on a regular basis on or about November 1, 1985, approximately when Santa Fe's paint shops would run out of blue paint. The 5394 remained in the first experimental scheme well into September, when it was sent back to San Bernardino for conversion into the final scheme.

Meanwhile the merger proceedings were continuing. By late September the public hearings had ended, and the review process began. There seemed to be little doubt in anyone's mind that the merger would be approved. The big question, everyone thought, was the conditions imposed on SFSP for approval of the merger. SFSP chairman John J. Schmidt had repeatedly stated that merger of the two railroads would depend heavily on these conditions. A proposed locomotive renumbering schedule was released at about this time.

On October 22nd, the U.S. Department of Justice suddenly announced it would oppose the SFSP merger. A complete surprise, the announcement shattered the calm surrounding the low-key ICC proceedings.

Charges levied by the Justice Department included a massive loss of competition, and real, direct, and non-speculative anti-

A surprising number of slugs made it into the merger paint scheme, 10 in all, and since 12 SD39s wore the red and yellow, it was inevitable that at least one slug and mother unit would shove cars over a hump in red and yellow dress. Renumbered slug 1129 (originally the 129) trails SD39 1568 in La Junta, Colorado, during November 1989. This slug began life as Union Pacific SD24B 420B, hence the three-axle trucks. The 1568 is equipped with Pacesetter controls, to suit it for the slow speeds of hump service. *Chuck Conway*

Repainting in the merger scheme ceased eight days prior to this August 2, 1986, shot of the 561 train dropping down Edelstein Hill in western Illinois. This location has long been a favorite spot for photographers, as Edelstein Hill hinders what is otherwise a very fast trans-Illinois run. The 1.1 percent ruling grade for westbounds is four and a half miles long, a little long for a "momentum" grade. The mainline crosses the hill to escape the Illinois River Valley. After the crew change at Chillicothe, seven miles to the east, this eastbound will have a quick trip to Chicago. Twenty-six GP30s wore the red and yellow paint. *Jill Oroszi*

trust problems. SFSP chairman Schmidt's reaction included "simply incredible," "radical position," and "irresponsible."

In the same announcement the Department of Justice said that it would not oppose a decision by the ICC approving the merger!

The following day, the Department of Transportation issued a statement in *favor* of the merger, saying the merger would be consistent with public interest. Schmidt claimed that the Transportation Department's stand was fundamentally sound.

The UP immediately re-emphasized its need to gain access to up to 1,500 miles of the merged system.

Meanwhile, the Santa Fe and SP paint shops had begun turning out red and yellow units in earnest. These repaints each had only half of the SPSF lettering on their sides and nose, with the other two characters to be added after merger day.

By late November, Cleburne and Argentine were producing nothing but red and yellow units, while San Bernardino held off until December 2nd because they had received the wrong shade of red DuPont Imron paint. On December 2nd, the first day of pure red and yellow production at San Bernardino, SD39 1569 was painted blue and yellow, then rolled back into the paint shop to be repainted red and yellow.

Speculation dictated that the final chapters had been written on Santa Fe's blue and yellow paint scheme, which had existed in one form or another since the early 1940s. The last locomotive receiving blue and yellow paint was SD45 5332, painted at San Bernardino. The last locomotives received by Santa Fe from the manufacturers in blue and yellow were GP50s 3840-3854 and B39-8s 7400-7402.

Engines in the new red and yellow paint scheme were soon branded "Kodachromes" by the railfan community, due to the close similarity between the colors on the units and those employed by Eastman Kodak on their Kodachrome film boxes. Another slang term for the scheme was "redbonnets," for obvious reasons.

Through December 1985 a flurry of last minute support and opposition occupied headline space, as the merger hearings were about to enter their final phase: a decision by the ICC board. Final briefs in the case were still being presented in mid-December, and were finally concluded on December 16, 1985. The Texas Mexican Railway claimed if the merger was approved they would lose 60 percent of their revenue from the combination of the Santa Fe/SP and the UP/MoPac mergers. Both the U.S. Department of Agriculture and the Mexican government stated their support of Texas Mexican's position.

SFSP had reached an agreement with BN regarding quotation of freight rates moving over post-merger SPSF lines in December 1985. This was to try to circumvent anti-competitive allegations involving the merger, and involved approximately 2.5 percent of the total traffic to be handled by the merged system. The agreement with BN caused the ICC to reopen the merger case, but only to cover the affects of the pact.

A similar agreement was reached almost simultaneously between SFSP, CP Rail and Soo Line. On December 18th, the three carriers announced that shippers in both Canada and the United States would enjoy coordinated rail service from the three

post-merger railroads.

At the same time, Rio Grande was continuing to fight the merger, stating the merger would severely damage or destroy traffic volume currently being interchanged between the SP and the Rio Grande at Ogden, Utah. Rio Grande claimed that the UP/WP/MP merger had already damaged its traffic volume (in fact, interchange carloads at Salt Lake City between the Rio Grande and the WP had dropped from several trains a day to practically nothing), and that the SPSF merger would remove up to 116,000 more carloads a year from the Rio Grande.

In 1984 interchange between SP and Rio Grande totalled 142,000 cars. The combined Overland Route-Rio Grande trackage these cars took was cited by some rail experts as the most expensive east-west rail route in the United States, as it involved four major mountain crossings requiring helpers on heavy trains. The merger, it was believed, would make the SP Overland Route redundant, and the Rio Grande mainline non-competitive. The Rio Grande would be surrounded by mega-merged rail systems.

SFSP still contended that the granting of significant trackage rights to UP, Rio Grande and/or KCS would effectively kill the merger.

By December 31, 1985, there were over 50 Santa Fe locomotives in the red and yellow merger scheme. Nearly every type of unit was represented by at least one red and yellow repaint. By late January there were nearly 75. In January a labor dispute at the paint shop at Argentine shifted its repainting work to Cleburne.

Also in January, Santa Fe crews began work on post-merger rail connections. At Colton, California, a new interchange good for 20 mph was installed between Santa Fe's south (or eastbound) track to SP's eastbound mainline. This would allow Santa Fe trains from Barstow, California, headed for Texas to bypass SP's West Colton Yard. Another 30-mph connection from the SP to Santa Fe's north track would allow SP locals from West Colton access to the Santa Fe.

Many other connections were in the plans for 1986. In California, this included new connections at Los Nietos (near Los Angeles), Stockton, Calwa (Fresno), Bakersfield, Devore (on Cajon Pass), Figarden, and Wilmington (Los Angeles Harbor). Connections planned for 1987 included an 8,700-foot, 50-mph crossover at Cajon Pass Summit (Hiland on the SP), using Martinez spur, and two in Orange County. Another Orange County connection was planned for 1988. Connections, of course, were also to be established on other parts of the system.

In mid-March 1986 a new fear crept into the minds of SFSP management. The ICC was being looked upon by the Reagan Administration as an unnecessary, over-regulating bureaucracy. Because of federal budget cuts and deregulation of the rail and trucking industries, the possibility existed that the ICC could be summarily dissolved. If that were to occur, the Department of Justice would take over the responsibility of deciding the merger case, and they had already voiced their opposition to the merger.

Through March 13th, Santa Fe had painted 140 locomotives into the new paint scheme. Cleburne announced that they were planning to rebuild 70 U36Cs by October 10, 1986, of which about 60 would be in red and yellow. This would be followed by rebuilding of Santa Fe's 3600-class GP39-2s.

In April an interesting rumor began circulating that a pair of SDFP45s were to be painted into the former Santa Fe red and silver passenger paint scheme. The rumor was just a few years too early. On April 25th Santa Fe caboose 999088 came out of the Topeka Shops with the new red and yellow scheme, and SP caboose 4726 also got the red and yellow treatment.

By May approximately 190 Santa Fe units were wearing post-merger colors. All remained quiet for the next few months, with no major headlines appearing concerning the merger.

On June 11, 1986, Santa Fe SD45-2 7219 received the full SPSF lettering on both its sides and nose for publicity photos in preparation of merger day. Later the same day, after the photos were taken, the unit went back into the paint shop so the SP lettering could be painted out.

GP38-2 2370 went from TP&W red and white 2001 to Santa Fe blue and yellow 3561 to Santa Fe red and yellow 3561 in less than two years, a lot of paint in a short period of time. As of June 1, 1986, the Santa Fe had painted 240 units in the red and yellow, and SP about 70. Cleburne was painting one unit a day at this time. .

Then it happened. The unthinkable. The unimaginable. The unprecedented. The inexplicable. The ICC voted no.

On July 24, 1986, the ICC cast their votes between 10:00 and 10:17 in the morning, ruling four to one against the SFSP merger. All who watch the railroad scene were amazed, stunned, and confused, especially when the transcript of the hearing revealed

that nearly 15 of the 17 minutes of the commission's entire meeting were spent praising the efforts of staff members who recommended that the merger be approved!

SFSP officials, SPSF management, the public, rail analysts, the media, other railroads, and government agencies were all caught by surprise. Nearly everyone recognized that there would be serious conditions imposed for approval of the merger, but the administrator of the Federal Railroad Administration perhaps put it best when he said afterwards, "Nobody expected the commission to punt!"

Only two of the 100 items on the agenda were reviewed by the commission. The first: Would the merger be in the public's interest? The vote: four noes, one yes. The second: Would the anticompetitive effects of the merger outweigh the public's benefits? The vote: four yeses, one no. The end result: A merger denied.

The UP and Rio Grande were perhaps as infuriated as SFSP, since the ICC staff members had recommended that they get almost all the trackage rights they had requested.

It was the first time in nearly two decades that the ICC had denied a major rail merger. The last denial was the BN merger proposal of 1968, a decision which was reversed two years later. Perhaps they didn't like the paint scheme.

Almost before the shock had worn off, the Santa Fe was back in the business of painting locomotives blue and yellow. A meeting the following day of Santa Fe's vice presidents and president resulted in a

directive that Santa Fe's blue and yellow warbonnet scheme was to be re-implemented that afternoon.

The last red and yellow unit out of Cleburne was SF30C 9553, with the next one, the 9554, coming out in blue and yellow. The final tally of Santa Fe repaints revealed that 320 units had received the red and yellow scheme, while SP had repainted approximately 100 units.

In a press conference on August 1st, John Schmidt vowed to fight the ICC decision, believing that the commission failed to understand the impacts to the 51,000 employees on both railroads. He discussed Santa Fe's various options, including an ICC review of its decision, taking the case to Federal Appeals Court, and introducing a revised merger proposal.

Schmidt claimed that the stockholders, the employees, the shippers and the general public did not want to pick up the pieces of a bankrupt Southern Pacific over the next several years, as it had been forced

The photographic possibilities in Arizona's Crozier Canyon are nearly endless. This one shows merger-painted SD45 5347 working east up the 1.42 percent ruling grade at milepost 481 between Truxton and Valentine. This spot is in the midst of a 40-mph speed restriction, but the previous mile is restricted to 25-mph due to curvature. By July 15, 1988, when this photograph was taken, the Santa Fe was well on the way to repainting its reminders of a frustrating era. *Mark Wayman*

SPSF Merger Painted Units

Model	Road#
10 Slugs:	109, 123, 129, 140, and 142-146
7 GP7s:	1316, 1327, 2001, 2064, 2120, 2126 and 2138
2 GP9s:	2250 and 2291
16 GP20s:	3012, 3018, 3019, 3028, 3029, 3031, 3048, 3052, 3056, 3058, 3063, 3068, 3070 and 3072-3074
26 GP30s:	2705, 2714, 2717, 2718, 2720, 2724, 2733-2736, 2745, 2748, 2750-2752, 2753, 2755, 2759, 2764, 2768, 2770, 2772, 2773, 2775, 2776 and 2780
12 GP35s:	2814, 2835, 2837, 2842, 2845, 2848, 2858, 2867, 2879, 2923, 2932 and 2946
1 GP38:	2312
6 GP38-2s:	2370-2375
8 GP39-2s:	3600, 3613, 3632, 3669, 3676, 3679, 3693 and 3696
2 GP40Xs:	3803 and 3805
1 GP50:	3828
12 SD39s:	1562, 1564-1566 and 1568-1575
16 SD40-2s:	5022, 5023, 5026, 5060, 5068, 5077, 5082, 5093, 5098, 5107, 5117, 5159, 5161, 5182, 5184 and 5192
29 SD45s:	5302, 5331, 5333, 5335, 5337-5339, 5342, 5344-5355, 5357-5360, 5362, 5364, 5394, 5401 and 5402
6 SD45-2s:	5676, 5679, 5682, 5694, 5699 and 5709
30 SD45-2s:	5800-5804, 7205 and 5806-5829
20 SDF45s:	5950, 5953-5955, 5957, 5959, 5960, 5963, 5964, 5966, 5969, 5970, 5973, 5975-5977, 5980, 5986, 5987 and 5989
7 SDFP45s:	5990-5993 and 5996-5998
9 B23-7s:	6354, 6365, 6373-6375, 6380, 6388, 6396 and 6404
2 B36-7s:	7486 and 7497
44 C30-7s:	8013, 8016, 8018, 8019, 8032, 8051, 8055, 8061, 8063, 8066, 8068-8070, 8072, 8073, 8075-8081, 8085-8090, 8104, 8105, 8133, 8139, 8141, 8142, 8146, 8148, 8150, 8154-8156, 8158, 8159, 8164 and 8165
44 SF30Cs:	9510-9553
10 U36Cs:	8736, 8739, 8741, 8744, 8746, 8749, 8750, 8752, 8753 and 8755

Notes:

1. GP20s 3019, 3063, 3068, 3073 and 3074 went to TP&W.
2. GP35s renumbered while red and yellow: 2835 to 3592, and 2837 to 3594.
3. GP39-2s renumbered while red and yellow: 2632 to 3132, 3679 to 3177, and 3693 to 3190.
4. SD45 5394 was the first Santa Fe unit painted red and yellow, July 31, 1985. It was an experimental, non-standard, version of the scheme and lasted into September 1985. SD45 5401 was the second repaint and was also non-standard for a short period of time. SD45 5402 was the first unit painted in the final standard red and yellow scheme.
5. Between August and December 1986, all SD45-2s 7200-7229 were renumbered 5800-5829. All except 5805 remained in the red and yellow. Only 7205 was not released in the red and yellow scheme.
6. SF30Cs were remanufactured at Cleburne from U36Cs between November 13, 1985, and July 24, 1986, thus falling in the range of units receiving red and yellow. SF30C 9554 was released on July 30, 1986, in blue and yellow.
7. C30-7s 8032, 8066, 8072, 8075, 8077-8079, 8087, 8133, 8139, 8141, 8142, 8146, 8148 and 8150 are now off Santa Fe and operated by GE.

Roster compiled by Kevin EuDaly

to do with Penn Central and other northeast carriers. Schmidt referred to the problems of running a moderate-size railroad in a nation overrun by UP, BN, NS, CSX and Conrail.

Over the next few days newspapers in the Southwest blasted the commission's decision. Wall Street analysts, interestingly, felt that the denial was the best thing that could happen to SFSP Corporation, citing that the company would be better off as a resource company, not a transportation company.

On September 2, 1986, SFSP filed an application with the ICC to reopen the merger case. This was based on fresh evidence that the SP would go bankrupt without the merger, and upon agreements under negotiation with other railroads for trackage rights that would minimize the anticompetition issue.

Specifically, on September 22, 1986, the Santa Fe and the Rio Grande announced they had resolved their differences by jointly issuing a letter of intent covering a settlement. If the merger was approved, Rio Grande would get trackage rights, lease rights and agency rights between Ogden, Utah, and Portland, Oregon, and between Ogden and San Francisco, Fresno and Bakersfield, California. The Rio Grande agreed to file a petition to reopen the merger proceedings, and agreed to support the merger application.

By October 1986 the ICC began to complain about the volume of letters and telegrams it had received since the July 24th denial. Almost all supported the merger. Some 1,800 shippers wrote letters to the ICC expressing their disgust with the decision, including such giants as General Motors, United Parcel Service and Sea-Land.

It was reported the ICC was also highly displeased with the public ICC-bashing dished out since July 24th by SFSP officials. But much of the bad press was not cooked up by SFSP. Perhaps the strongest statement was made by a Michigan politician, who called the ICC "brain dead" after the merger denial.

Everyone recognized, however, that the ICC didn't even have to reopen the case, and could just declare the merger off, period. It was even speculated that the ICC had made its anti-merger decision just to deliver a message to the transportation community that they were still a power to be reckoned with.

Just days after the agreement with the Rio Grande was announced, the ICC agreed to consider reopening the merger case, provided SFSP could produce new and significantly different evidence in support of the merger. SFSP was given 60 days from October 9th to present the new evidence, and to address the concerns of the Commission that centered on the anticompetitive effects of the proposed merger.

On December 1, 1986, SFSP and UP announced they had reached an agreement to provide trackage rights to both railroads over each other's right-of-ways, and that UP would drop its opposition to the merger. This came only a week prior to the deadline imposed by the ICC for submission of new evidence in the merger case.

The agreement, much like the previous one with Rio Grande, would only become effective if the merger were approved. UP would get trackage rights over the SP between Colton, California, and El Paso, Texas, and between Colton and Lathrop, California, via the Palmdale Cutoff and the Tehachapi Mountains. The UP would also get local access at Phoenix, Arizona, and Deming, New Mexico, both via SP. Access would be granted to Pittsburg and Port Chicago, California, via Santa Fe tracks.

SPSF would get trackage rights over the UP between Sierra Blanca (southeast of El Paso) and Big Sandy, Texas (near Tyler). SPSF would get local access at Pecos, Sweetwater, Ft. Worth and Dallas, Texas. Additionally, SPSF would get trackage rights on the UP between East St. Louis, Illinois, and Chicago, Bay City and Placedo, Texas, and Wichita and Benedict, Kansas.

The UP was still in opposition to the agreements SPSF had made with the Rio Grande, and indicated that it would urge the ICC to "retain competition" on the Central Corridor.

A significant and unexpected development arose when Kansas City Southern Industries, parent of KCS, announced it would seriously consider buying the SP if the merger were denied. KCS hinted at yet another railroad acquisition it also might make, but made no additional information available. Several industry sources claimed that the other acquisition was the Rio Grande. KCS Industries sent several officials to the West Coast to drum up support for their plan.

Even after all of the agreements with other roads involving trackage rights intended to preserve competition, the Department of Justice stated it was still opposed to both the merger and the reopening of the case. They based their position on the fact that the trackage rights agreements that SFSP had negotiated with UP and Rio Grande were only proposed agreements, and weren't signed and binding.

On January 26, 1987, the agreement with the Rio Grande was made binding. The Department of Justice was still of the opinion that the anticompetitive issues were not resolved. Interestingly, the Departments of Agriculture, Transportation and Defense all supported the merger.

On February 5, 1987, SFSP Corporation signed supplemental agreements with UP and Rio Grande. Early the same month the ICC gave SFSP Corporation a 30-day extension to provide evidence regarding the reopening of the merger case. The KCS continued to push for denial of the merger, and still wanted to buy the SP, admitting it had a silent partner in the deal.

BN, which previously was in support of the merger, reversed its stand and voiced opposition to the merger due to the agreements SFSP made with the Rio Grande and UP. By May much effort was being put forth by both sides. SFSP launched a media campaign to try to impress upon the ICC the quantity of support it had for the merger, while KCS and BN continued their fight against it.

On April 19, 1987, SFSP Chairman John Schmidt resigned. John S. Reed came out

of retirement to replace him on a temporary basis. Reed, previously Chairman and Chief Executive Officer of Santa Fe Industries, had retired in April 1983. Although no one involved would comment, many observers concluded Schmidt's resignation was at least partially attributable to the unhappiness SFSP's directors had with Schmidt's reportedly poor handling of the merger and what the ICC reportedly viewed as Schmidt's arrogance.

The ICC, in the meantime, heard arguments on the reopening of the merger case on May 14th. If the case were not reopened, SFSP was allowed 90 days to divest itself of at least one of its railroads.

On June 30, 1987, the ICC voted four to one against reopening the merger. The suspenseful drama which spanned nearly four years had drawn to a close. Reasons cited were Rio Grande's offer to match anyone else's bid, that Rio Grande's offer was backed by owner Philip Anschutz's reputation and management style, that Rio Grande's operating technique and experience closely resembled SP's, that Rio Grande agreed to honor existing SP labor agreements, and finally, that a Rio Grande-SP combination would offer better diversity and competition in the west.

The KCS offer was rejected by the ICC due to an enormous antitrust judgment against KCS regarding a stillborn coal-slurry pipeline.

The last phase of the ill-fated merger was the repainting of the SPSF merger units into traditional blue and yellow. It took considerably longer to get the units back into the blue and yellow scheme than it had to get them into red and yellow. Typically, Santa Fe waited until SPSF-painted units

entered its shops for heavy shopping or overhauls to repaint them.

By October 1, 1990, several classes were completely back to blue and yellow, including the SDF45s, SD39s, GP40Xs, GP39s, GP38-2s, GP20s and slugs, and only 57 Kodachromes were still in service. By January 1, 1991, there were no operating units in red and yellow on the Santa Fe, thus ending the SP merger era on the Santa Fe.

Quite a few Kodachromes still exist. Most of SP's, of course, are still so painted, though looking rather horrid. Several former Santa Fe merger units inhabit shortlines which purchased units retired by Santa Fe. A few Kodachromes remain in storage, and merger-painted C30-7s that GE is now leasing to other railroads still wear the scheme as well.

As for a three-system West? We may have quite a wait.

Merger painted SF30C 9543 leads unit sulfur train S-RSGV1-18 past the east end of Dermott, Texas, en route to Galveston on September 20, 1989. This is on the line from Clovis to the Gulf of Mexico, between Slaton and Sweetwater, Texas. The train originated at Rustler Springs, New Mexico, two days prior. The original plan with the repaints was for Santa Fe to paint its units with the letters SF, and SP to paint theirs with the letters SP. The two missing letters would be added after merger day. As shown here the cramped nose of the rebuilt U36Cs didn't allow for this, and the scheme would have required a revision after the merger was finalized to accommodate the SF30Cs. As it was it didn't matter, and the SF30Cs were all back in blue and yellow soon enough. *Jill Oroszi*

The Quest For Speed

The obvious question here is which weighed more, the units pulling the train or the train? Ten trailers on five flats with a caboose surely weigh considerably less than 800-odd tons of SD45-2 up front. The train is approaching the Colorado River bridge at Topock, Arizona, on February 24, 1975. This train's horsepower-per-ton ratio is just simply too ridiculous to calculate. It's no wonder the Super C didn't last. *Steve Patterson*

Santa Fe's association with speed goes back into the previous century. One of the Santa Fe's first high-speed runs took place in 1890, when New York reporter Nellie Bly set out to beat the fictional record of Phileas Fogg in Jules Verne's *Around the World in Eighty Days*.

Like Fogg, she departed from New York heading east, across the Atlantic. She arrived San Francisco on January 21, 1890, where the Santa Fe had a special train waiting. The special averaged a staggering (for the time) 37 mph over the 2,577 miles to Chicago, reaching Chicago in 69 hours. Nellie Bly's trip was a success; she travelled around the world in 72 days.

Interestingly, in the 1870s and 1880s Santa Fe's passenger trains were treated as second class. Short, slow locals predominated in the passenger schedules.

Santa Fe's first "luxury" train was inaugurated on November 27, 1892, when the *California Limited* departed Chicago's Dearborn Station. In 1896 the train was scheduled from Chicago to Los Angeles in 72 hours, a whopping 31.4 mph, quite fast for the era. Service expanded quickly. The

record was set one day when the *California Limited* ran in an amazing 22 sections westbound and 23 eastbound.

Another high-speed run occurred in 1895 when Santa Fe director Benjamin Cheney's son became ill while in California. The run left Colton, California, on July 23, 1895, and covered the distance to Chicago in 79 hours, 2 minutes. This time was substantially lengthened by numerous washouts encountered en route, and a lengthy detour off the main line.

The next record-breaker was the Peacock Special, which carried A.R. Peacock, Vice-President of Carnegie Steel & Iron Company, to Pittsburgh, Pennsylvania. The special left Los Angeles at 10:00 a.m. on March 27, 1900, and reached Chicago at 9:56 p.m. on March 29th. Total time was 57 hours, 56 minutes.

The train consisted of just a Pullman and a buffet-smoking-baggage car. The fastest long-distance portion of this run was between La Junta, Colorado, and Emporia, Kansas, 429 miles in 447 minutes, for a 58 mph average.

In the early 1900s Santa Fe's locomotives

began to grow in size and capability, and the old records began to fall. In 1903 a new record was established on a special run for H.P. Lowe of the Engineering Corporation of America, which ran from Chicago to Los Angeles in 52 hours, 49 minutes.

This run was part of a transcontinental trip, the first portion of which was on Lake Shore & Michigan Southern's *Twentieth Century Limited*. The special left Dearborn at 10:17 a.m. on August 5th, and arrived in Los Angeles at 1:06 p.m. on August 7th.

The special's ocean-to-ocean time was 73 hours, 21 minutes. The crews that handled

One of the first record-shattering runs on the Santa Fe was the Coyote Special of July 9-11, 1905. It ran 2,251 miles from Los Angeles to Chicago (via Topeka but not Great Bend) in 44 hours, 54 minutes, averaging 50.4 miles per hour. This replica of the special was posed for company photographers — if you hadn't guessed by the power towers in the background. The 1010 was built by Baldwin in 1901 with 79" drivers. Originally a compound, it was converted to simple in November 1923 at La Junta. The 1010 is now at the California State Railroad Museum in Sacramento. *Santa Fe Railway Photo*

Steam-era speed records were annihilated by the diesel, a machine that made no stops for water. Arriving from Electro-Motive Corporation in August 1935, boxcabs 1 and 1A produced a Chicago-Los Angeles test run of 39 hours, 34 minutes. The two pioneer units are leaving Los Angeles with the last trip of heavy-weight cars on the *Super Chief*, on April 22, 1937. *Harold K. Vollrath Collection*

the special were rewarded with $50 each time a divisional or subdivisional speed record was broken. Needless to say, most of the records fell: $50 was mighty big money in 1903.

This was followed by one of the most amusing tales in Santa Fe history. July 8, 1905, a Saturday morning, was at first no different than any other Saturday for John Byrne, the general passenger agent at Los Angeles for the Santa Fe west of Albuquerque.

Into the office walked a plain-looking cowboy. He introduced himself as Walter Scott, and asked if the Santa Fe could take him to Chicago in 46 hours. Byrne thought Mr. Scott was both strange and demented, but without hesitation replied "Absolutely!"

When Scott asked the price, Byrne did some quick figuring and replied "Fifty-five hundred dollars." To Byrne's amazement, Scott peeled the cash off of a tremendous roll of bills on the spot. The train would leave from the La Grande depot at one o'clock the next afternoon. It would be called, variously, the Scott Special or the Coyote Special.

It turned out that Scott was "Death Valley Scotty," a well-known miner and prospector in California, well-known as an eccentric, that is. Scott had traveled the Santa Fe between southern California and Chicago several dozen times. He decided he needed to set a record, and Byrne recognized that a golden publicity opportunity was at hand.

The next 24 hours were spent establishing the schedule, lining up crews, and selecting locomotives for the special. The train was comprised of diner 1407, Pullman *Muskegon*, and baggage car 210, 170 tons in all.

The press was alerted, and by Sunday afternoon an estimated 20,000 spectators jammed the streets around the depot to see the train off. Passengers included Scott, his wife and reporter C. Van Loan.

The run began at 1:00 p.m. behind 4-6-0 442, which raced over the 141 miles to Barstow (including a 25-mile helper push up Cajon Pass) in 2 hours, 55 minutes, averaging 48.3 mph over some of the roughest terrain on the entire run. Van Loan dashed out report after report on his typewriter, dropping them off on the fly at telegraph stations en route, informing the world of the train's progress.

The crews in California set a new speed record, and other records fell as the train sped east. In Glorieta Pass a crew member stumbled as the train swung from curve to curve, and broke a window with his shoulder. The chef saw at least one meal splattered on the floor as the train careened through mountain curves.

Raton Pass slowed the train. But across the high, empty plains east of La Junta, the Coyote Special seared the right-of-way with speeds of 85 to 90 mph. Divisional speed records were broken all the way across Kansas. Engine 530, a 4-4-2, lost a cylinder head and had to be rescued. More divisional records fell between Kansas City and Chicago, where the special was pulled by more high-stepping 500-class Atlantics.

Between Shopton Yard at Fort Madison, and Chillicothe, Illinois, Scotty rode in the cab of the 510. The special's fastest speed was recorded between Cameron and Surrey, reportedly 106 mph over three miles. The 239 miles between Shopton and Dearborn were covered in 239 minutes.

Van Loan's reports were front page news coast-to-coast. The Coyote Special pulled into Dearborn at 11:54 a.m. on July 11th. It had covered 2,265 miles in 44 hours, 54 minutes, for an average of 50.4 mph.

The truth is, "Death Valley Scotty, the

On Santa Fe's east end, train 199 streaks west at Streator, Illinois, on July 5, 1986. Lead SD40 5014 is one of 18 SD40s still rostered by Santa Fe, remanufactured and obviously capable of long-haul, high-speed duty. The 199 is currently scheduled to leave Chicago at 2:00 p.m., and arrive in Kansas City at 11:00 p.m., 448 miles in 540 minutes. *Jill Oroszi*

Speed-Mad Miner," led a largely mythical life. Actually, Scott never owned a gold mine in Death Valley, nor anyplace else, but it sounded good to the flacks of the era. The trip — which Santa Fe records verify — was actually financed by an E. Burdon Gaylord, a Los Angeles real estate speculator who was promoting a Mojave Desert mining concern. The $5,500 receipt bears his name.

Santa Fe's passenger trains were soon associated with speed. On December 12, 1911, the weekly *De Luxe* was inaugurated. It ran from Chicago to Los Angeles in 63 hours, pushing the average speed up to 36 mph. It was short-lived, however, as World War I placed restrictions on luxury travel.

The *Chief*, an all-Pullman train, was inaugurated on November 14, 1926, to replace the prewar *De Luxe*. It also ran on a 63-hour schedule. In 1929 its schedule was trimmed to 58 hours, and in 1930 cut even further to 56 hours, giving it an average speed of 40.4 mph.

The diesel era allowed for even more speed. Santa Fe motive power expert John Purcell

and Vice President W.K. Etter were the prime instigators of diesel power for Santa Fe's passenger trains. The Santa Fe's first diesel passenger units, Boxcabs 1 and 1A were received from Electro-Motive in August 1935. The second week of October they produced a test run of truly record-shattering proportions. The two units, hauling nine standard heavyweight passenger cars (approximately 720 tons), averaged 56.5 mph between Chicago and Los Angeles, for a time of 39 hours, 34 minutes. It purely obliterated all past Santa Fe records.

The name of the new train said it all: *Super Chief*. On May 12, 1936, the *Super Chief's* inaugural run departed Dearborn on a regular schedule of 39 hours, 45 minutes.

New equipment, lightweight stainless-steel cars, and big improvements in diesel motive power prompted another high speed test run, on May 15, 1937, three days prior to the scheduled revenue service inauguration date for the new equipment. Referred to in the press as the "second *Super Chief*" or the "*Super-2*," to distinguish it from its heavyweight predecessor, the train departed Los Angeles at 8:00 p.m. for Dearborn station on a good-will trip. It covered the mileage at an average speed of 60.8 mph, reaching a top speed of 108 mph in eastern Colorado.

The new record: 36 hours and 49 minutes. The E1s had burned out a traction motor en route, however, and the train's first revenue run had to be made behind boxcab 1A and EMC demonstrator 512.

The new equipment revolutionized rail travel. Passenger trains in general were placed on the fastest schedules possible, and to avoid conflicts with freights, many freights had to be speeded up as well. Some freights often operated as second sections of passenger trains. Track improvement projects were implemented to cope with the new schedules. This era faded, however, by the 1960s, as jet aircraft replaced Pullmans and Budd coaches.

In any presentation of Santa Fe hotshots, the Super C is soon woven into the discussion. Perhaps this is due to the Super C's blazing times across the Chicago-Los Angeles corridor, or perhaps for its often exotic power: U28CGs, U30CGs, F45s, FP45s and red-white-and-blue SD45-2s.

In the mid-1960s, the Santa Fe was looking for ways to capitalize on the intermodal market, which looked ready to develop into a massive traffic base. Santa Fe's original concept was coast-to-coast intermodal service, to be offered in conjunction with the New York Central on existing mail trains.

The NYC was already running a mail and express train, #3, which left Manhattan at 1:40 a.m. and arrived Chicago at 8:15 p.m., a schedule of less than 24 hours. At 11:55 p.m., Santa Fe's *Fast Mail Express*, #7, left Chicago for a Los Angeles arrival at 6:30 p.m. the second day. The combination of these two trains could easily trim a day off then-existing coast-to-coast schedules. Since it's typically of no benefit to customers if their cargo arrives at two a.m. instead of eight a.m., service would have to be improved by 24 hours, or not at all.

Santa Fe ran the first test run without the New York Central's participation, an omen of things to come. Referred to as Test Run 1, it departed Corwith Yard in Chicago at 10:00 a.m. on May 26, 1967. Four U28CGs, 352, 355, 356, and 359, hauled 20 flat cars loaded with 40 trailers, plus dynamometer car 5015 and business car 20.

The train's total weight was 1,744 tons; the horsepower-per-ton ratio 6.4. Initially, the top speed was held to 70 mph in order to observe the stability of the TOFC cars. The limit was then boosted to 79 mph, and finally to 90 mph west of Belen. The train was fueled at Argentine Yard in Kansas City, Belen, New Mexico, and Winslow, Arizona. Six 500-mile inspections were performed.

Only one unscheduled delay occurred, a short pause to pick up a brakeman near Emporia, Kansas. Test Run 1 arrived Hobart Yard in Los Angeles on May 27th at 9:33 p.m. The average speed was 58.7 mph. Its time, 37 hours, 33 minutes, was 44 minutes short of the record set by the goodwill run of the first lightweight *Super Chief* on May 15, 1937.

Deemed a success, it was announced on June 1, 1967, that the Santa Fe would begin a 40-hour Chicago-Los Angeles freight run.

A second test run followed. It began on June 8th, this time in conjunction with the NYC. The train, powered by four NYC GP40s, departed Manhattan at 10:24 p.m. with 18 loaded Flexi-Van flats and a coach, weighing in at 1,235 tons. The target was Chicago in 14 hours. The run turned into an embarrassing 18-hour, 51-minute, 51.1 mph trek due to numerous delays and problems.

The Santa Fe took over the train and slapped the same four U28CGs that powered Test Run 1 on the head end. The train was 20 cars and a caboose, 1,389 tons. One of the U28CGs, the 352, experienced ATS (Automatic Train Stop) failure and was replaced in Kansas City by the 358.

The train streaked across the railroad and into history: Chicago to Los Angeles in 34 hours, 46 minutes, averaging 63.2 mph and breaking the *Super Chief* record of 36 hours, 49 minutes by more than two hours. It also broke the 56 hour, 55 minute transcontinental record set by UP's M-10001 in October 1934. The test train's total run, including the frustrating NYC portion, ran coast-to-coast in 54 hours, 21 minutes, for a 58.2 mph average.

Unfortunately, the NYC pulled out of the deal. Santa Fe continued on, and ran Test Run 3. This train operated via Raton Pass from Kansas City to Winslow, Arizona, to explore the potential of this route. It also employed four U28CGs. Test Run 3 turned in a disappointing 59.1 mph average. Winds on the western Kansas and eastern Colorado

plains were partially to blame. A larger contributor was the route's 20.1-mile greater length and slow track in Raton and Glorieta Passes, handicaps which couldn't be overcome despite high speeds achieved on certain portions of this route. The net lost time was calculated to be one hour, 12 minutes.

The high-speed project faltered for a few months. Finally on September 22, 1967, a memorandum was circulated pushing the operating people to develop the train. A 40-hour schedule was the result, to be operated Monday through Saturday.

The selection process for a name for the train narrowed to two choices; the Super Freighter or the Super C. The winner, obviously, was Super C. Billed as the "World's Fastest Long-Distance Freight Train," the initial run was scheduled for January 17, 1968.

On that date, the first Super C departed Corwith behind new FP45s 100 and 102, dynamometer car 5015, sleeping car-lounge *Denehotso*, business cars *Topeka* and *Mountainair*, seven TOFC cars with 14 loaded trailers, and a caboose. The horsepower-per-ton ratio was a staggering 8.3.

The train was timed to the second. The result was another page in the history books: Chicago to Los Angeles in 34 hours, 35 minutes, 40 seconds. It beat Test Run 2 by 10 minutes. This record still stands.

Initially no eastbound Super C's were operated due to lack of business, and westbound traffic wasn't much better. The train operated as #99 westbound and #100 eastbound throughout 1968, failing miserably to make a profit.

The U.S. Mail rode to the Super C's rescue, with a parcel post contract beginning on April 17, 1969. Suddenly the Super C was a $1 million-a-month, high-stakes train. The schedule was adjusted to meet the Postal Service's requirements, and daily trains began running in both directions for the first time.

In 1971 train symbols were revised, the Super C becoming 891 eastbound and 198 westbound. The glory years for the Super C, however, were short. By 1976 the U.S. Postal Service re-bid its Chicago-Los

Angeles parcel post contract. The UP and C&NW, though offering slower service, substantially beat the Santa Fe's price.

With the loss of the Super C's primary customer, the train's future was bleak. Santa Fe's conventional intermodal trains were running on increasingly faster schedules across the same route. The Super C's premium rates, as a result, were buying less than they had previously.

The Super C's schedule was canceled on May 4, 1976, but occasional business resulted in a few more runs. The final arrival, the 891 of May 18th, pulled into Chicago on time at 3:30 a.m. on May 20th.

A look at Santa Fe's current freight schedules reveals no match for the Super C. Santa Fe's highest-priority trains are those in the 9-series, 11 trains in all, plus the Q-LANY and the Q-NYLA.

Five of these trains, the 194, 391, 394, and 197/791, average less than 40 mph over their entire run, and have a horsepower-per-ton ratios less than 4.0. This leaves eight "hot" trains to evaluate.

The 991 has the highest horsepower-per-ton, 4.4. It's the only train in excess of 4.0. Is it the hottest? Look closely at the table in this article.

The fastest average speed belongs to 891 at 46.5 mph — at least Tuesday's and Wednesday's 891. Thursday, Friday, Saturday and Sunday the average drops to 45.0 mph. Its counterpart, 198, averages 45.1 mph over the same route. If the averages are weighted and an overall average is calculated, the average speed for all 198/891 trains is a respectable 45.3 mph.

The 199/991 pair must be credited with the longest run, and a combined average speed of 45.4 mph puts them into the same category as 198/891.

The 398/893 pair are odd in that their scheduled times are different as well as their average speeds. The much faster 398 posts a relatively fast time, but the slower 893 drops the cumulative average to a speed of 42.0 mph, clearly not quite as fast as the previous two train pairs.

This leaves the Q-LANY and its westbound counterpart, the Q-NYLA. By sheer average speed they are the hands-down

A pair of F7s accelerate the Super C out of Chicago three days after the Super C's inaugural run on January 17, 1968. The third Super C (none was operated on January 18th) has six boxcars and a lone piggy-back flat for the revenue portion of the train, not even enough to pay the fuel bill, much less the rest of the train's operating costs. Fifteen months later Postal Service vans began filling the Super C's flatcars. *John Szwajkart*

winners, averaging 46.0 mph over 2,207 miles. They also spend the least amount of time in terminals, when total terminal time is spread out over total mileage. But they only spend six percent less time in terminals per mile of route than Tuesday's and Wednesday's 891.

Clearly all of the trains discussed above are operating marvels, scorching the ballast to achieve the scheduled times. But none compare to the original 198 and 891, the Super C, scheduled between Chicago and Los Angeles in 40 hours: seven hours, 30 minutes faster than today's 198.

Amtrak's *Southwest Chief*, #3 and #4, by comparison, are scheduled from Chicago

The second section of the 198 sweeps through the big two degree curve at mile-post 844, near Willard, New Mexico, on July 27, 1990, behind three DASH 8-40Bs. The 198 is scheduled to leave Clovis, New Mexico, at 2:45 p.m., and arrive in Belen, New Mexico, at 7:10 p.m.. This curve has a posted speed limit of 65 mph, after which the engineer will step on it, for the next speed restriction is more than 10 miles away at Mountainair. At Belen the train will get a fresh crew, fuel for the thirsty units, and an inspection. The inspection is one of only three for this train; the other two are at Kansas City and Barstow. *John Lucas*

to Los Angeles in 41 hours, 10 minutes, and from Los Angeles to Chicago in 41 hours, 20 minutes. This is via the longer, hillier, Raton Pass route.

Leaving the statistics behind, Santa Fe's System Operations Center in Schaumburg, Illinois, sheds some light on Santa Fe's hottest trains. Discussions with Kevin Leddy and Gregg Grabijas of the scheduling group reveals that all trains with a "9" in the middle of their symbol are hot, and all are equal, regardless of average speed or terminal times. They also verify that the Q-NYLA and Q-LANY have equal stature to the "9" series trains. Therefore, in the truest sense all these trains are equally the hottest.

Santa Fe employees remain both intrigued by and interested in speed to this day. A recent example of the railroad's interest in speed occurred on March 31, 1992, when a special was operated from the depot in Galesburg to Kansas City. The special was powered by BN F9-2s BN-1 and BN-2, Burlington Northern's 2,000-hp Executive F-units.

The train consisted of ten cars, which included Santa Fe's *John S. Reed* and *Cyrus K. Holliday*. Symbolled O-GBKC1-31, it ate up the 266.7 miles from Galesburg to Congo, on the outskirts of Kansas City, in three hours, 54 minutes and 49 seconds, for an average speed of 68.15 miles per hour.

The train was limited to a speed of 79 mph.

"This was the fastest time any of us can remember in recent years," said Rich Wessler, Santa Fe's Manager — Operations Planning. For comparison, Q-NYLA averages about 50 mph between these two points.

Comparing the O-GBKC1-31 with Super C's record breaking inaugural run yields some interesting statistics. First, comparing the makeup of the two trains shows Super C had 867 tons and two FP45s, for a horsepower-per-ton ratio of 8.3, while the O-GBKC1-31 had 825 tons and two F9-2s for a horsepower-per-ton ratio of 4.8, 58 percent of Super C's.

Comparing Super C's time from Chillicothe, Illinois, to Argentine, with O-GBKC1-31's time from Galesburg, Illinois, to Argentine, reveals that Super C averaged 64.96 mph while O-GBKC1-31 averaged 63.83 mph. Not much difference. But it's important to note that Super C's mileage between Chillicothe and Galesburg is fairly fast track, which pushed its average up slightly. It's also important to note that the O-GBKC1-31 took a delay at Congo, on the outskirts of Kansas City. The Super C's inaugural run took no delays east of Kansas City.

Santa Fe Engineers R.E. Lauber, running between Galesburg and Fort Madison, and M.D. Stone, running between Fort Madison and Kansas City, definitely put

Q-LANY2-14 roars eastbound at milepost 444, just east of Pica on the Seligman Subdivision in Arizona, on June 15, 1990. The "2" in the train symbol denotes this as a second section, an increasingly common occurrence. Q-LANY and its westbound counterpart, Q-NYLA, usually have quite a few J.B. Hunt trailers in their consist, which alone identifies them as hot trains. Early morning sun on this portion of the railroad makes this a good train to shoot, as it's scheduled out of Needles at 4:30 am. Four high-horsepower units are typical power on these two Q-trains. *Mark Wayman*

the O-GBKC1-31 into the big leagues. Lauber recorded the fastest sprint on the O-GBKC1-31 over 10.0 miles from Stronghurst to Lomax, Illinois, at an average speed of 80.0 mph.

Looking at timetable versions of the same run reveals that several passenger trains have accomplished nearly the same times over this trackage, but none were regularly scheduled at quite this speed. The *San Francisco Chief's* westbound run over this trackage from the 1965 timetable reveals a posted time of exactly four hours from Galesburg to Congo, five minutes longer than the O-GBKC1-31 took.

The *San Francisco Chief's* only two stops were at Fort Madison and Shopton. The Shopton stop was a crew change, which O-GBKC1-31 had as well. This indicates that the *San Francisco Chief* and the O-GBKC1-31 ran the route at nearly identical speeds. It could well be that the passenger trains of old often ran this section somewhat faster than the timetable showed.

In comparison, Amtrak's *Southwest Chief* posts a regularly scheduled westbound time of four hours, 39 minutes between Galesburg and Union Station. This is 4.8 miles shorter than the O-GBKC1 run. The *Southwest Chief's* average speed from Galesburg to Union Station in Kansas City is 58.84 mph, clearly well below the O-GBKC1, the *San Francisco Chief* and Super C, but one has to remember that the *Southwest Chief* stops at Fort Madison, La Plata, Missouri, and Marceline to take on and discharge passengers. The *Southwest Chief's* eastbound run over the same territory is a little faster, with a timetable run of four hours, 26 minutes, for an average speed of 61.71 mph.

Another recent high-speed train was a RoadRailer test performed by Amtrak on the Santa Fe, symbolled T-CHAQ1-28 (Test Train, Chicago to Albuquerque). The train departed Chicago at 9:30 a.m. on April 28, 1992, and consisted of Amtrak DASH 8-32BWH 509, Santa Fe business car 58, Santa Fe test car 83, and three empty RoadRailers, a total weight of 200 tons. The train's purpose was to study the stability of RoadRailers at high speeds, so the train was authorized to run at 90 mph, just like the *Southwest Chief*.

The special ran with Amtrak crews, and operated via Raton Pass. The passenger train speeds, a horsepower-per-ton ratio of 16, and no stops allowed this train to average 67.91 miles per hour between Chicago and Union Station, Kansas City, Missouri. This is 2.95 miles per hour faster than the inaugural run of Super C. Unfortunately the RoadRailers exhibited instability on jointed rail at high speeds west of Newton, Kansas.

The Super C, nevertheless, remains a cut above them all, truly the hottest, and the undisputed champion between Chicago and Los Angeles.

From Nellie Bly to the O-GBKC1-31 and the T-CHAQ1-28, Santa Fe's quest for speed is woven into the fabric of the railroad, a railroad constantly in search of speed. The Coyote Specials and Super C's of the future should be interesting to behold. The lightweight *Super Chief's* record held for 30 years and 24 days. Super C Test Run 2 held the record for a short seven months and nine days, and then was beaten by 10 minutes by the Super C's inaugural run.

The Super C's inaugural run has been on the books for 24 years and six months at this writing. It stands alone at the top: Chicago to Los Angeles in 34 hours, 35 minutes, 40 seconds. Time will tell how much longer the Super C will own the Santa Fe speed record.

The Santa Fe runs an enormous quantity and variety of trains, ranging from coast-to-coast premium-service TOFC trains Q-NYLA and Q-LANY, to coal trains, to mundane locals. To track, manage and schedule its important trains, the Santa Fe has developed the Transportation Service Plan.

At present the TSP is dominated by piggy-back TOFC, conventional COFC, and double-stack trains. If you've ever stood at trackside on Santa Fe's Chicago to Los Angeles main, you can see why, as there's ample evidence that in the dictionary of railroading "Santa Fe" and "intermodal" are synonymous.

The TSP includes two basic types of train symbols, one numeric, the other alpha-numeric. The first type is based on a three-digit numeric sequence. Each number in turn designates a specific train's origin, its priority, and lastly its destination. The first number, the origin code, uses nine location designations:

1 — Chicago area
2 — Illinois and Iowa
3 — Kansas City area
4 — Colorado, Kansas and Oklahoma
5 — East Texas
6 — West Texas
7 — New Mexico and Arizona
8 — Southern California
9 — Northern California

The second number in the sequence is a priority designation for the train, as follows:

0-4 — Local and carload freight
5-7 — TOFC/COFC/carload freight
8-9 — High-priority TOFC/COFC

The third digit is the destination code for the train. The destination codes are identical to the origin codes. Using this system, the 198 train is thus a Chicago to southern California, i.e., Los Angeles, high-priority TOFC/COFC train.

Since many of these trains are daily trains, the three-digit code has a two-digit suffix number indicating the train's date of origin. For example, a 198 originating on Wednesday, January 18th would be the 198-18. Twenty-four hours to the west another 198 is on the railroad, but since it originated on Tuesday, it's carrying a designation of 198-17. In this way several trains of the same number in progress across the railroad at any particular time can be distinguished, not inconsequential as it takes two to three days for even the hottest of hot Santa Fe trains to cross the system.

Some days more tonnage is presented than a given train can haul. In this case, two or more sections are run. A one-digit prefix number is used to indicate the section number.

Section numbers are used to designate multiple trains running on the same schedule. For example, suppose Sears and Toys 'R Us have delivered 11,000 tons of expedited TOFC/COFC at Santa Fe's ramp in Chicago on December 15th, all of which is supposed to travel to Richmond on 199's schedule. This frequently happens

due to seasonal fluctuations, in this case Christmas.

Since the 199 is limited to 3,800 tons, it will require three trains to move the 11,000 tons that day. The first section is designated 1-199-15, and hauls 3,800 tons west, leaving about noon, two hours ahead of 199's scheduled departure of 14:00. The second trainload, also 3,800 tons, pulls out about 13:30, and is designated as 2-199-15. The last section, 3-199-15, leaves with the remaining 3,400 tons at 14:00, running on 199's schedule.

In this example the sections left in order, but it's not uncommon for the sections to get shuffled at the departing terminal, the second section departing before the first section. Shuffling en route is even more likely.

In the TSP the prefix number has special significance for ten trains operating in southern California, where Santa Fe runs more trains than it has combinations of origin/destination numbers and second

A quartet of six-motor EMDs roll the S-CHLA1 around the curve west of Holliday, Kansas, leaving the Kansas River Valley for Mill Creek Valley on a sunny day during December 1991. This westbound double-stack operates out of Chicago Tuesdays through Sundays, and is scheduled out of Kansas City at 12:20 p.m. It's usually filled with conventional intermodal equipment. A solid double-stack consist indicates a second section is probably following. The S-CHLA1 connects from Conrail train TV-201 Mondays through Thursdays, and from Conrail's TV-203-C on Fridays. *Keith Wilhite*

digits. Train 1838 is a Barstow to San Bernardino local manifest, and train 2838 is its opposite counterpart running from San Bernardino to Barstow.

There are five trains currently listed in the TSP with a "2" prefix, the 2818, 2828, 2838, 2868 and 2888. For these five trains and their "1" counterparts, the "1" and "2"

are not true section numbers. For the rest of the Santa Fe system, however, the prefix number is the section number. Confused? For clarity, hyphens are used to separate the prefix and suffix numbers, e.g. 1-198-18, but only if the prefix is a section number. So the 1838-18 has only one hyphen.

The second type of train symbol in the TSP uses five-letter designations and a numeric suffix. The first letter is the train type, the next two letters the alpha code designation for the origin city, and the last two letters the alpha code for the destination city. The number suffix following the five letters is used to designate section number.

The exceptions to this rule are the S-LACH5 and S-LACH8 trains, where the "5" and the "8" are not section numbers, but are used to distinguish those trains from the S-LACH1. Lord knows what might happen if the S-LACH8 ran in two sections one day!

Using this alpha-numeric system the Q-AQEP1 is a "Q", or Quality Service Network TOFC train, Albuquerque to El Paso, 1st section. This system is often hyphenated, and includes the date of origin just like the numbered trains. Thus a Q-AQEP1 departing on August 3rd would be Q-AQEP1-03. City, railroad and prefix codes currently used by Santa Fe are presented after the schedule.

Most alpha codes are followed by origin and destination cities, such as G-HUHO1-22 for a grain train from Hutchinson, Kansas, to Houston, 1st section, originating on April 22nd. Amtrak trains, however, use their Amtrak train numbers instead. For example, the eastbound *Southwest Chief*, Amtrak train #4, is designated A-41, for Amtrak number #4, 1st section. The *San*

Diegans Amtrak numbers have the first number dropped by the Santa Fe, thus Amtrak #572 is Santa Fe A-721. Like any pigeonholing system, sooner or later there are too many pigeons and not enough holes. Or fat pigeons.

The TSP is extremely detailed, with far more information than can be presented here. It describes a complex transportation network, with one train dependent on several other trains. It includes information on all blocking, and destinations of all the blocks in a given train.

For example, the TSP reveals even a relatively uncomplicated train like the 315 carries blocks for El Dorado, Winfield, Oklahoma City and Fort Worth when it leaves Kansas City. The entire train is reclassified at Temple, Texas, and leaves with a new block for Rosenberg. The train terminates at Houston Belt & Terminal's New South Yard, where its power is transferred to train 524.

Furthermore, the 315 picks up two blocks at Oklahoma City, one for Fort Worth and one for Temple. Another Temple block is picked up at Fort Worth, and a final block is picked up at Mykawa destined for the HBT.

You can imagine the havoc that begins to happen when something ties up Santa Fe's mainline for even a few hours. Since everything effects everything, especially true for intermodal traffic, a relatively minor derailment, equipment malfunction or grade crossing accident sends ripples through the entire system which might take days to sort out.

For example: on February 18, 1983, the Emporia Subdivision's CTC (Computerized Traffic Control) system went down when a

A second section of the flagship of the fleet, Q-LANY2-26, climbs towards the Arizona Divide between Crookton and Seligman, Arizona, on July 27, 1990. This premier intermodal train runs from Los Angeles to New York, operated east of Chicago by Conrail as train TV-10. The Q-LANY only works three places on its run across the Santa Fe: San Bernardino, Barstow and Kansas City. It gets fueled and inspected at Belen and Kansas City.
Mark Wayman

backhoe knocked down power lines near Olathe, Kansas. With all signals dark, all trains were restricted to five mph over most of the subdivision for several hours until power was restored. Although it allowed the opportunity to chase hot trains from one grade crossing to the next — on foot — it made a mess out of Santa Fe's schedules, and several people probably went home with headaches that day, particularly the unfortunate backhoe operator.

This incident illustrates the vulnerability of schedules to accidents, weather or human error. The next time Q-NYLA doesn't show up when it's supposed to, and you're about to cuss the schedule, remember that somewhere on the Santa Fe, someone is having a day much worse than yours.

It's important to realize not all trains run on time, and many of the hotter trains regularly run *ahead* of schedule by two or three hours. Also, a train that doesn't run daily, such as the S-LACH8, which leaves Los Angeles only on Tuesdays, will show up in Missouri on Thursday or Friday, illustrating the need to extrapolate the schedule to the area of interest.

Santa Fe Freight Schedule Summary
January 1991 to March 1992

Trains Originating Chicago Area

Train	Days	Orig	Leave	Dest	Arrive	HPT	Max. Tons	Avg. Speed
103	Mon-Sat	CH	09:30	KC	05:00	1.1	None	23.2

Local manifest. Performs local work entire route. TOFC for points west of Clovis, NM will connect to 169 at Fort Madison, IA.

151	Tue-Sat	BC	02:30	CH	08:00	4.0	None	30.9

Mixed train via GTW. Manifest is mostly auto parts and connects to 165 at Chicago.

165	Tue-Sat	CH	13:01	DA	20:00	2.9	4,000	32.7

Intermodal, auto parts and Dallas manifest. One block picked up from 443 at Kansas City. Power reduced to 2.0 HPT Oklahoma City to Dallas.

168	Wed-Sat	CH	07:00	LA	04:15	2.4	5,500	31.0

Handles conventional overflow traffic from S-CHLA. Picks up at all stations tonnage and room permitting. Does not handle double-stacks or San Diego TOFC. Connects from TP&W at Fort Madison, IA. Picks up two blocks at Kansas City when 368 not operated.

169	Thu-Sat	CH	03:00	RI	03:00	3.0	5,500	35.0

Non-premium intermodal. May consolidate with train 189 at Chicago. Connects with BN #103 from Galesburg, IL at Fort Madison, IA. May include southern California overflow traffic for connection at Clovis, NM. Train will not hold in Clovis for Q-BHLA when that train is late, or when Richmond arrival would be in jeopardy. Connects to 578, Q-FWLA, and 268 at Clovis. Picks up six blocks from 578 and Q-BHLA at Clovis. 5,100 Tons maximum Barstow to Richmond.

171	Sunday	DT	00:01	CH	10:00	4.0	None	30.1

Intermodal via GTW.

181	Tuesday	CH	22:00	DT	10:00	4.0	None	25.0

Intermodal via GTW.

183	Mon-Sat	CH	22:00	KC	07:55	2.8	4,000	45.3

TOFC and autos. May consolidate with train 185 at Chicago on Sunday. One block autos to V-KCPX at Kansas City.

185	Daily	CH	21:00	DA	02:15	2.9	4,000	32.3

TOFC and auto parts for Dallas and Oklahoma City. Includes UPS and USPS. One block picked up from 133 on Eastern Region. One block picked up from 443 at Kansas City on Saturday and Sunday. One block to 195 at Dalton Jct., TX. Power reduced to 2.0 HPT Oklahoma City to Dallas. Split into 1185A and 185B.

Train	Days	Orig	Leave	Dest	Arrive	HPT	Max. Tons	Avg. Speed
185A	Mon-Fri	CH	21:00	DA	02:15	2.9	4,000	34.6

Intermodal handling Oklahoma City auto parts. Connects from Q-CHHO on Chillicothe Subdivision. One block to V-KCHO at Dalton Jct., TX. Power reduced to 2.0 HPT Oklahoma City to Dallas.

185B	Sat-Sun	CH	20:00	DA	02:15	2.9	4,000	34.0

Intermodal handling Oklahoma City auto parts. Picks up Dallas manifest in Kansas City Saturday, and protects Kansas City TOFC Sunday. Connects from Q-CHHO on Chillicothe Subdivision. One block to V-KCHO at Dalton Jct., TX. Power reduced to 2.0 HPT Oklahoma City to Dallas.

188	As Req.	CH	05:30	LA	05:00	4.0	3,800	44.6

All TOFC. No flat on the deck, COFC or Econopac unless authorized. On Monday traffic will move on Q-NYLA from Chicago. Protects UPS traffic.

189	Daily	CH	22:00	RI	07:40	4.0	4,000	41.8

Expedited TOFC. Handles traffic for El Paso, TX, only when 197 is not operated. Connects to Q-FWLA and 398 at Clovis, NM. One block to 777 and one block to Q-BEEP at Belen, NM. Three blocks picked up from Q-EPBE, 747, 767, 781 and 791 at Belen. One block to V-KCPX on Central Region. Connects from 708 on Needles Subdivision.

194	Tue-Sun	CH	05:00	OK	02:40	2.9	3,800	36.5

Expedited auto parts, autos, and TOFC destined Kansas City and Oklahoma City. Protects UPS Fort Worth and Houston traffic from Chicago to connection with V-KCHO at Kansas City. Limited to 70 cars out of Kansas City; overflow Oklahoma City manifest will go to 305. Four blocks to V-KCHO and one block to 344 at Kansas City. Connects from 893 and 951 on Emporia Subdivision.

197	Tu,Th,Sa	DT	00:01	EP	03:00	4.0	4,000	35.7

Expedited all-TOFC train handling Ford parts, racks and other premium TOFC. Operates via GTW between Detroit and Chicago. One block picked up from 893, Q-AQBE, and Q-NYLA at Belen, NM, and one block from S-LACH at Belen. Power reduced to 3.0 HPT and tonnage increased to 5,000 tons maximum Belen to El Paso.

198	Daily	CH	16:45	LA	15:40	4.0	3,800	45.1

Premium all-TOFC. Includes UPS and USPS. Fills four blocks in Kansas City when 398 not operated. One block to 189 at Clovis. Two blocks picked up from 747, 767 and Q-EPBE at Belen, NM. One block to V-KCPX Monday-Tuesday and 787 Wednesday-Sunday on Seligman Subdivision.

199	Daily	CH	14:00	RI	18:00	4.0	3,800	46.2

Expedited premium TOFC/COFC train. Includes UPS and USPS.

The hottest northern California pair, the 199 and 991, meet just west of Caliente, California, in a photograph taken from the cab of the 991. SDF45s lead both trains, the 991 east to Chicago, and the 199 west to Richmond, California, on April 11, 1984. *Kyle Brehm*

A GP39-2 and a GP30 power the westbound 305 train near Matfield Green, Kansas, in the Flint Hills of eastern Kansas at 3:15 p.m. on April 15, 1990. The 305 train is now scheduled to originate at Kansas City at 3:00 p.m. It handles excess cars from train 194 when 194 exceeds its 70-car limit. The 305's destination is Temple, Texas; it normally works at Emporia, Arkansas City, Guthrie, Oklahoma City, Fort Worth, Cleburne, and Temple, but can work other locations enroute. In other words, it's a dog.
Jim Gilley

Trains Originating Illinois and Iowa

Train	Days	Orig	Leave	Dest	Arrive	HPT	Max. Tons	Avg. Speed
213	Daily	SR	22:45	KC	12:30	1.1	None	26.7

Conrail-Santa Fe through train from Elkhart, IN, to Streator, IL, as Conrail train ELSF. Handles all traffic for Kansas City and beyond. Automobiles and auto parts to 195, V-KCPX and 168 at Kansas City. No oversized loads.

233	Daily	ES	16:00	KC	12:00	1.0	None	15.8

Manifest via Gateway Western. Auto connection from Alton & Southern.

268	Daily	ES	21:00	LA	04:15	1.5	None	25.5

Manifest and intermodal. Operates via Gateway Western between East St. Louis, IL, and Kansas City. USPS connects to 398 at Kansas City, otherwise one block connects to V-KCPX and one block stays on 268. Connects to 1-828 on San Bernardino Subdivision.

Trains Originating Kansas City

Train	Days	Orig	Leave	Dest	Arrive	HPT	Max. Tons	Avg. Speed
301	Daily	KC	19:00	CH	19:00	1.0	None	18.5

Local manifest. Performs local work entire route. One block connects to TP&W and KJRY at Fort Madison, IA.

305	Daily	KC	15:00	TE	21:00	1.0	None	22.5

Manifest. Fills at Kansas City when 194 exceeds 70 car limit. Connects from 813 at Emporia, KS. One block picked up from 425 on Ft. Worth Subdivision. One block to 605 at Temple, TX.

322	Daily	KC	04:00	ES	23:30	1.2	None	16.2

Manifest operating via Gateway Western. Train length restricted to 5,000 feet.

326	Daily	KC	10:00	AM	20:00	1.0	None	19.9

Manifest via Topeka and Newton, KS. Protects Boeing traffic. One block to 733 and one block to 318 at Mulvane, KS.

332	Daily	KC	12:30	ES	10:30	2.0	None	14.3

Manifest and intermodal via Gateway Western. Train length restricted to 5,000 feet.

338	Daily	KC	11:00	BA	04:00	2.0	None	24.0

Manifest. One block picked up from 326 at Mulvane, KS.

339	As Req.	KC	21:00	RI	11:00	2.4	None	32.0

Non-premium intermodal and manifest. Overflow traffic from 169.

344	Daily	KC	05:00	DE	03:30	1.0	None	15.1

Intermodal and manifest. Performs local work enroute. Connects to 425 at Newton, KS. Connects to 194 and 435 at La Junta, CO. Connects from 534 and 844 at La Junta. 1.5 HPT provided Pueblo to Denver, CO.

Train	Days	Orig	Leave	Dest	Arrive	HPT	Max. Tons	Avg. Speed
365	Tuesday	KC	00:45	DA	20:00	2.9	4,000	25.4

Intermodal and auto parts. Will also handle Dallas manifest. One block picked up from 443 at Kansas City. 2.0 HPT provided from Oklahoma City, OK, to Dallas.

391	Tue,Thu-Sat	KC	07:30	CH	19:30	2.5	4,500	37.4

Operates from westbound yard Argentine handling trailer dock traffic. Two blocks picked up from 443 and 893 at Kansas City. One block to TP&W at Fort Madison, IA.

394	Monday	KC	17:05	OK	02:40	2.9	3,800	31.3

TOFC and automotive. Limited to 70 cars out of Kansas City, overflow Oklahoma City manifest will go to 305.

398	Tue-Sun	KC	02:00	LA	16:00	4.0	3,800	44.0

All TOFC premium service. Includes UPS and USPS. One block to 189 at Clovis, NM. Two blocks picked up from 747, 767, 781, 791 and Q-EPBE at Belen. One block to V-KCPX Monday-Tuesday and 787 Wednesday-Sunday on Seligman Subdivision.

Trains Originating Colorado, Kansas and Oklahoma

Train	Days	Orig	Leave	Dest	Arrive	HPT	Max. Tons	Avg. Speed
425	Daily	NW	17:00	TE	20:30	1.0	None	19.1

Local manifest. Performs local work en route.

435	Daily	LJ	22:00	TE	13:30	1.3	None	18.2

Manifest. Performs local work entire route. Includes west TOFC, connects to west train at Amarillo, TX, for furtherance to Clovis, NM and subsequent fill on proper symbol to final destination. Connects from 344 and 443 at La Junta, CO. One block to 668 at Amarillo. One block to 875 at Lubbock, TX. One block to 625 at Brownwood, TX.

443	Daily	DE	19:00	KC	22:00	1.5	None	14.7

Intermodal and manifest. Performs local work en route. One block to 448 and one block to 435 at La Junta, CO. 1.0 HPT from Pueblo, CO, to Kansas City.

448	Daily	LJ	23:00	BA	05:00	3.3	9,999	19.9

Manifest. Performs local work La Junta to Trinidad, CO. Connects from 443 at La Junta, CO. One block to 627 at Gallup, NM. One block to 726 and 718 at Winslow, AZ. One block from 627 and 817 at Winslow. 2.0 HPT and 8,000 tons maximum Albuquerque, NM to Barstow, CA.

476	Mon-Fri	OK	08:00	WA	16:00	1.0	None	19.8

Manifest and intermodal. Operates via BN Enid to Avard, OK. Two blocks to Q-BHLA and one block to 668 at Waynoka, OK.

Trains Originating East Texas

Train	Days	Orig	Leave	Dest	Arrive	HPT	Max. Tons	Avg. Speed
503A	As Req.	TE	20:00	KC	23:00	N/A	None	25.1

Manifest. Operates with overflow from Q-HOCH.

| 503B | As Req. | PE | 18:00 | KC | 11:00 | 1.5 | None | 21.5 |

Manifest. Operates with overflow from Q-HOCH.

| 505 | As Req. | TE | 22:00 | GA | 08:00 | 1.1 | None | 21.9 |

Local manifest. Performs local work entire route.

| 506 | Daily | SI | 02:30 | TE | 13:00 | 1.5 | None | 21.7 |

Manifest. One block to Q-HOCH and one block to Q-HOBA at Somerville, TX.

| 513A | Mon,Fri,Sat | DA | 07:30 | KC | 12:15 | 1.5 | None | 19.7 |

Manifest. One block to 524 at Gainesville, TX.

| 513B | Tue-Thu | DA | 07:30 | KC | 08:00 | 1.5 | None | 23.1 |

Manifest and intermodal. Protects UPS traffic Zacha Jct., TX, to Kansas City. One block to 524 at Gainesville, TX.

| 515 | Daily | SI | N/A | BM | N/A | 0.7 | None | N/A |

Texas Division local Silsbee to Beaumont, TX, and return. Performs local work entire route. Connects from 605 at Silsbee, TX.

| 524 | Daily | HO | 15:00 | NE | 15:00 | 1.0 | None | 15.7 |

Houston-HBT to Needles, CA, manifest. Power received from 315 at Houston. Train reclassified at Temple, TX, connects from 565. Two blocks to 555 and one block from 535 at Cleburne, TX. One block from 513 at Gainesville, TX.

| 525 | Mon-Sat | FW | 01:00 | BD | 09:00 | 1.0 | None | 18.2 |

Moves intermodal and manifest traffic from Fort Worth to 578 and Q-DABA. One block to 578, one block to 534 and one block to Q-DABA or Q-HOBA at Brownwood, TX.

| 534 | Daily | TE | 20:00 | LJ | 11:00 | 1.2 | None | 18.9 |

Manifest. Performs local work entire route. Connects from Q-HOBA at Brownwood, TX. Train reclassified at Amarillo, TX. Connects to 344 at La Junta, CO.

| 535 | Daily | DA | 16:00 | CL | 21:00 | 2.0 | None | 12.6 |

Moves north and south traffic to Cleburne, TX, for connection. One block to 524 and two blocks to 425 at Cleburne, TX.

| 545 | Daily | GA | 01:30 | TE | 13:30 | 1.2 | None | 18.2 |

Manifest. One block to 503 and one block to Q-HOBA at Somerville, TX.

| 555 | Daily | BD | 15:00 | DA | 04:00 | 2.0 | None | 15.2 |

Manifest. Connects from 435 and Q-BAHO at Brownwood, TX. Two blocks picked up from 425 and 524 at Cleburne, TX.

| 563 | Sunday | DA | 20:00 | KC | 17:20 | 2.0 | None | 26.5 |

Intermodal and manifest. One block to 524 at Gainesville, TX. One block to 891 at Kansas City.

| 578 | Tue-Sun | DA | 05:00 | LA | 12:30 | 3.0 | None | 28.7 |

TOFC service originating at Zacha Jct., TX, and points out of the southeast with connections from KCS at Dallas. May handle Long Beach, CA, double-stack block from Dallas on Tuesday-Wednesday which connects to S-HOLB at Brownwood, TX. Train reclassified at Clovis, NM. Connects to 589 at Clovis.

| 581 | Mon-Sat | DA | 20:00 | CH | 06:30 | 2.0 | None | 29.4 |

Intermodal. One block to 195 at Dalton Jct., TX. One block to 344 at Emporia, KS. One block to TP&W at Fort Madison, IA. 2.5 HPT Kansas City to Chicago.

| 588 | Wed-Fri | PE | 02:15 | LA | 13:45 | 2.7 | None | 29.0 |

Intermodal. May operate on Saturday. Three blocks picked up from 545 at Alvin, TX. One block to V-KCPX at Belen, NM. One block to 1-868 at Barstow, CA.

| 589 | Tue-Sat | PE | 00:15 | RI | 21:00 | 3.0 | 5,000 | 29.3 |

All TOFC/COFC. Overflow traffic may be handled by 588. Four blocks picked up from 545 at Alvin, TX. Connects to 578 and one block to Q-FWLA at Clovis, NM. Train reclassified at Clovis.

Trains Originating West Texas

Train	Days	Orig	Leave	Dest	Arrive	HPT	Max. Tons	Avg. Speed
605	Daily	TE	03:00	SI	14:00	1.3	None	20.7

Manifest.

| 606 | Daily | BO | 19:00 | AM | 04:00 | 1.0 | None | 6.2 |

New Mexico Division local. One block to 866 and two blocks to 623 at Pampa, TX. Symbol 2-606 may be used for New Mexico Division local operating Lubbock to Whiteface, TX, and return.

| 615 | As Req. | AM | 18:00 | TE | 17:00 | 1.3 | None | 20.9 |

Manifest. Handles overflow traffic from 435. One block to 875 and one block to 805 at Dallas.

| 616 | Daily | AM | 06:00 | BO | 09:00 | 1.2 | None | 18.7 |

Central Region local. Two blocks picked up from 534 at Amarillo, TX. One block picked up from 326 at Panhandle, TX.

| 617 | Daily | AM | 13:00 | BE | 06:00 | 1.3 | None | 19.2 |

Local manifest. Performs local work entire route.

| 623 | Mon-Sat | AM | 21:00 | KC | 02:00 | 1.5 | None | 19.8 |

Manifest via Newton and Topeka, KS. One block picked up from 733 at Amarillo, TX.

| 625 | Daily | BD | 09:00 | FW | 17:00 | 1.5 | None | 43.6 |

Manifest. Connects from 435 at Brownwood, TX. One block TOFC picked up from S-RIDA and one block autos picked up from 975 on Dublin Subdivision.

| 627 | Tue-Sun | GP | 08:00 | WI | 18:00 | 2.0 | None | 12.7 |

Local Manifest. Performs local work entire route.

| 636 | As Req. | SA | 00:00 | SA | 00:00 | 1.0 | None | N/A |

New Mexico Division local operating Slaton to Lamesa, TX, and return.

| 646 | As Req. | SG | 00:00 | PD | 00:00 | 1.2 | None | N/A |

Texas Division local operating San Angelo to Presidio, TX.

| 656 | As Req. | PD | 00:00 | SG | 00:00 | 1.2 | None | N/A |

Texas Division local operating Presidio to San Angelo, TX.

| 668 | Wed-Mon | WA | 05:00 | BA | 12:00 | 2.5 | 5,500 | 22.4 |

Run through BN and Santa Fe mixed intermodal and manifest from Memphis, TN. Connects from BN #175 at Avard, OK. Two blocks picked up from 476 at Waynoka, OK. One block picked up from 435 at Amarillo, TX. One block to 578 and 589 at Clovis, NM. One block to 879 at Barstow, CA.

| 674 | Tue-Sat | WA | 01:00 | OK | 08:30 | 1.0 | None | 21.1 |

Manifest and intermodal. Operates via BN between Avard and Enid, OK. Four blocks picked up from 674 at Enid previous day. Connects to 305, 315 and 425 at Guthrie, OK.

Trains Originating New Mexico and Arizona

Train	Days	Orig	Leave	Dest	Arrive	HPT	Max. Tons	Avg. Speed
707	Daily	EP	13:00	BE	23:59	1.5	None	20.4

Manifest. Performs local work entire route.

| 708 | Daily | PX | 01:00 | BA | 15:00 | 1.8 | None | 24.6 |

Runthrough with Arizona & California. Manifest and intermodal. Three blocks to 189 on Needles Subdivision. Includes UPS.

| 715 | As Req. | BE | 16:30 | TE | 23:30 | 2.5 | None | 23.0 |

Manifest. Handles overflow from 805. One block to UP at Sweetwater, TX.

| 716 | As Req. | BE | 16:30 | AM | 11:00 | 1.3 | None | 19.7 |

Local manifest. Performs local work entire route.

| 717 | Daily | BE | 08:00 | EP | 18:00 | 1.0 | None | 22.4 |

Manifest. On Monday only will depart Belen, NM, at 18:00, and arrive El Paso, TX, at 02:30 handling traffic normally on Q-AQEP including UPS from Albuquerque, NM. Performs local work entire route.

| 718 | Mon-Sat | WI | 11:00 | SG | 21:00 | 2.0 | None | 14.3 |

Local manifest. Performs local work entire route.

| 726 | Mon-Sat | WI | 10:00 | GP | 20:00 | 2.0 | None | 12.7 |

Local Manifest. Performs local work entire route.

| 733 | Daily | BE | 04:00 | KC | 18:00 | 2.0 | None | 23.7 |

Manifest. One block picked up from 866 at Belen, NM. One block picked up from 606 at Pampa, TX. 1.0 HPT Clovis, NM, to Kansas City.

| 737 | Daily | BE | 09:15 | AQ | 10:15 | 0.5 | None | 31.0 |

Local manifest. Handles intermodal traffic from 991 on first trip to Albuquerque, and from Q-NYLA on second trip. Performs local work as required. Connects from 991 and Q-NYLA at Belen, NM.

An all-EMD consist works eastbound up Cajon Pass between Alray and Summit, California, with the 2868 train on January 23, 1992. This manifest and intermodal train is a Monday through Saturday run from San Diego to Barstow, California, and is normally powered at 2.0 HPT. Its scheduled time out of San Bernardino is 2:15 p.m., making it an ideal schedule for Cajon Pass on the occasional non-smoggy winter day. *Joe Blackwell*

Train	Days	Orig	Leave	Dest	Arrive	HPT	Max. Tons	Avg. Speed
747	Daily	AQ	11:00	BE	12:15	0.5	None	24.8

Local manifest. Handles intermodal traffic from Albuquerque, NM, ramp. Performs local work entire route. TOFC connects to 198, 189 and Q-LANY.

757	Daily	PX	21:00	BE	23:59	2.0	None	20.9

Manifest.

767	Tue-Sun	AQ	00:01	BE	01:15	0.5	None	24.8

Local manifest. Handles intermodal traffic from Albuquerque ramp. Second trip handles Kansas City and Chicago UPS for connection to 991 and Q-LANY. Performs local work as required.

771	Tue-Sat	PX	06:00	CH	11:45	2.5	None	35.8

Intermodal. One block to 875 on Seligman Subdivision. Train 771 may be annulled at Winslow, AZ, due to insufficient traffic. Blocks will then be picked up by 875, 891, 893 and 976

777	Mon-Sat	BE	22:15	AQ	23:15	0.5	None	31.0

Local manifest. Handles intermodal traffic for Albuquerque and north on first trip and from 189 and 893 on second trip. Performs local work as required. (This symbol was previously an Arizona Division local).

781	Mon,Wed	EP	23:15	DT	10:00	3.0	5,000	32.0

Premium intermodal train handling Ford auto parts destined Kansas City, St. Louis, Chicago and Detroit. Operates via GTW between Chicago and Detroit. One block to 332 at Kansas City. One block to TP&W at Fort Madison, IA. 4.0 HPT and 4,000 tons maximum Belen, NM, to Detroit.

785	Thu-Mon	BE	12:15	HO	21:15	2.5	None	28.6

Intermodal and auto. Connects from 875 and 976 at Belen, NM. One block from S-RIDA on Lampasas Subdivision on Wednesday only. One block to 505 on Galveston Subdivision. One block to UP via HBT.

787	Wed-Sun	WI	01:00	PX	12:30	3.0	6,000	25.7

Intermodal. Protects UPS traffic from Chicago off 198 and Kansas City traffic off 398. Connects from 198, 398, 668 and 991 at Winslow, AZ.

791	Tue,Thu,Sat	EP	22:30	DT	05:00	3.0	5,000	34.6

Premium intermodal handling Ford auto parts from El Paso to Kansas City, St. Louis, Chicago and Detroit. Operates via GTW Chicago to Detroit. One block to 332 at Kansas City. 4.0 HPT and 4,000 tons maximum Belen, NM to Detroit.

Trains Originating Southern California

Train	Days	Orig	Leave	Dest	Arrive	HPT	Max. Tons	Avg. Speed
807	Daily	BA	10:00	PX	07:00	1.5	None	16.4

Run through with Arizona & California Railroad. Performs local service enroute to Phoenix, AZ. Connects from 951 at Barstow. One block picked up from 885 on Needles Subdivision. One block to 708 at Rice, CA.

813	Daily	BA	19:15	KC	07:00	2.0	None	27.8

Manifest. Connects to 305 on Emporia Subdivision.

817	Tue-Sun	SE	08:00	WI	18:00	2.0	None	14.3

Local manifest. Performs local work entire route.

1818	Daily	BA	01:30	LA	11:30	2.0	None	15.2

Barstow to Los Angeles-Los Angeles Junction Railway manifest via San Bernardino Subdivision. One block to Pico Rivera road switcher at Pico Rivera, CA. Terminates at LAJ A-yard.

819	Daily	BA	00:01	BK	06:00	2.5	None	23.1

Local manifest.

1828	Tue-Sun	BA	06:00	WT	23:00	2.0	None	10.6

Manifest via San Bernardino Subdivision. Uses symbol LCA63 between Los Angeles and Watson.

1838	Daily	BA	16:00	SB	21:00	2.0	None	16.2

Local manifest. Handles local traffic for San Bernardino and Pasadena Subdivisions. Also handles intermodal traffic from various connections.

839	Daily	BA	18:30	RI	10:00	2.5	None	28.4

Manifest.

844	Daily	BA	17:00	LJ	21:00	2.0	None	21.3

Manifest. Performs local work Barstow, CA, to Winslow, AZ, and Albuquerque, NM, to La Junta, CO. Connects from 2-828 at Barstow. One block to 726 and 718 and one block picked up from 726 and 718 at Winslow. Connects from Q-EPAQ at Albuquerque, NM. Train classified on arrival at Albuquerque. Two blocks to 344 at La Junta. 3.3 HPT from Albuquerque to La Junta.

A trio of Dash 8-40BWs charge east with the second section of the 891 train at Dawn, Texas, on December 5, 1990. Imagine how frustrating it must be for the truckers on parallel Highway 60, who are watching seventy trailers they're not hauling speeding past at 70 mph. Dawn lies in the Texas Panhandle, between Amarillo, Texas, and Clovis, New Mexico, on the Hereford Subdivision of the Central Region. *John Lucas*

Train	Days	Orig	Leave	Dest	Arrive	HPT	Max. Tons	Avg. Speed
849	As Req.	BA	23:45	RI	23:00	2.5	None	18.9

Manifest.

Train	Days	Orig	Leave	Dest	Arrive	HPT	Max. Tons	Avg. Speed
861	Thu-Sat	LA	09:30	CH	10:30	2.5	5,500	31.1

Intermodal. Will pickup at all stations. One block picked up from 2-868 at Corona, CA.

| 866 | Daily | BA | 17:00 AM | 05:10 | 2.0 | None | 31.4 |

Manifest. One block to 733 and two blocks to 976 at Belen, NM. One block to 623 at Amarillo, TX. (This was previously a run-through Santa Fe-BN train connecting to BN #174 at Avard, OK, to Tulsa, OK. Destination changed to Amarillo, TX.)

| 1868 | Sun-Fri | BA | 08:00 | SD | 19:30 | 2.0 | None | 20.0 |

Manifest and intermodal. Connects from S-CHLA at San Bernardino, CA.

| 869 | As Req. | LA | 20:00 | RI | 21:00 | 2.5 | None | 23.7 |

Intermodal repositioning train.

| 875 | Mon-Sat | LA | 01:30 | ZJ | 14:00 | 3.1 | 5,000 | 28.3 |

Intermodal, includes double-stacks. One block picked up from 771 on Seligman Subdivision. Connects to 785 at Belen, NM. One block to 975 at Clovis, NM. Connects from 975, Q-BAHO and Q-LAFW at Clovis. One block picked up from 435 at Lubbock, TX. One block to 555 at Cleburne, TX. 2.4 HPT from Belen to Zacha Jct., TX.

| 879 | As Req. | BA | 12:01 | RI | 02:00 | 3.0 | None | 31.5 |

Protects loads arriving Barstow, CA, not covered by Clovis, NM, intermodal switching hub destined Fresno, Modesto, Stockton and Richmond, CA. Connects from Q-BHLA at Barstow, CA.

| 881 | Fri-Sat | LA | 10:00 | CH | 18:00 | 3.5 | 4,200 | 40.9 |

Handles double-stack and articulated equipment for Chicago. Conventional equipment may be added as fill, train room permitting. Connects from 2-868 at San Bernardino, CA.

| 885 | As Req. | LA | 01:00 | HO | 21:15 | 3.5 | None | 27.1 |

Intermodal and auto includes double-stacks. Connects from 976 at Belen, NM. One block picked up from S-RIDA Wednesday only on Lampasas Subdivision. One block to 505 on Galveston Subdivision. Delivered to UP via HBT. 2.5 HPT from Belen to Houston.

| 1888 | Mon-Sat | BA | 20:00 | LA | 04:00 | 2.0 | None | 19.0 |

Manifest and intermodal via San Bernardino Subdivision. Connects from 668 and 991 (991 Monday only) at Barstow, CA.

Train	Days	Orig	Leave	Dest	Arrive	HPT	Max. Tons	Avg. Speed
891	Tue-Sun	LA	04:00	CH	07:00	4.0	3,800	45.0

Expedited TOFC/COFC handling Chicago TOFC including Chicago UPS. May consolidate with 893 at Los Angeles on Sunday. On Tuesday and Wednesday 1-891 will operate 30 minutes early and 2-891 will operate one hour, 30 minutes later. Split into 891A, B, C and D.

| 891A | Tuesday | LA | 05:30 | CH | 07:00 | 4.0 | 3,800 | 46.5 |

Expedited fully-articulated train handling TOFC and UPS and USPS. One block picked up from 771 on Central Region. Three blocks to Conrail at Chicago. Will not fuel at Barstow, CA.

| 891B | Wednesday | LA | 05:30 | CH | 07:00 | 4.0 | 3,800 | 46.5 |

Expedited fully-articulated train handling TOFC and UPS and US mail. One block picked up from 771 on Central Region. Will not fuel at Barstow, CA.

| 891C | Thu-Sat | LA | 04:00 | CH | 07:00 | 4.0 | 3,800 | 45.0 |

Expedited TOFC handling Chicago TOFC including Chicago UPS. One block picked up from 771 on Arizona Division. Will not fuel at Barstow, CA.

| 891 | Sunday | LA | 04:00 | CH | 07:00 | 4.0 | 3,800 | 45.0 |

Expedited TOFC handling Chicago TOFC including Chicago UPS. One block to 807 on Needles Subdivision. Three blocks to Q-BEEP and 777 at Belen, NM. One block to 674 at Waynoka, OK.

| 893 | Tue-Sat | LA | 00:00 | KC | 04:00 | 4.0 | 3,800 | 40.0 |

Expedited intermodal. Handles Phoenix, AZ, UPS and US mail destined Kansas City and UPS originating Albuquerque, NM, for Kansas City. Train is consolidated with 891 at Los Angeles on Sunday. One block to 807 on Needles Subdivision. Three blocks to Q-BEEP and 777 at Belen, NM. One block to 194 on Emporia Subdivision. One block to 391 at Kansas City. 3.5 HPT from Belen, NM, to Kansas City.

| 2818 | Daily | BA | 07:00 | BA | 14:00 | 2.0 | None | 21.7 |

Manifest via San Bernardino Subdivision from Los Angeles Junction.

| 2828 | Tue-Sun | WT | 23:59 | BA | 12:30 | 2.0 | None | 14.5 |

Manifest via San Bernardino Subdivision. Uses symbol L-CA64 between Watson and Los Angeles. One block to 893 at Los Angeles.

| 2838 | Daily | SB | 13:30 | BA | 21:00 | 2.0 | None | 10.8 |

Manifest.

| 2868 | Mon-Sat | SD | 06:00 | BA | 17:00 | 2.0 | None | 20.9 |

Manifest and intermodal. One block to Q-LANY Monday-Saturday, one block to Q-LAFW, and one block to Q-LABH at San Bernardino, CA.

| 2888 | Daily | LA | 20:00 | BA | 04:00 | 2.0 | None | 19.0 |

Manifest and intermodal via San Bernardino Subdivision. Connects to 899 at Barstow, CA.

Trains Originating Northern California

Train	Days	Orig	Leave	Dest	Arrive	HPT	Max. Tons	Avg. Speed
928	Daily	RI	18:00	BA	21:30	2.5	None	16.0

Local manifest and intermodal reposition train. Picks up at Pittsburg, CA, picks up and sets out at Stockton, Fresno and Bakersfield, CA.

Train	Days	Orig	Leave	Dest	Arrive	HPT	Max. Tons	Avg. Speed
938	Daily	BK	11:00	BA	20:00	2.5	None	15.3

Local manifest. Protects miscellaneous TOFC for connection at Barstow, CA. Connects from SP at Magunden, CA.

| 948 | Daily | RI | 07:00 | BA | 10:30 | 2.5 | None | 16.0 |

Local Manifest.

| 951 | Tue-Sat | RI | 11:00 | CH | 11:30 | 3.5 | None | 35.4 |

Intermodal and manifest, handling Kansas City TOFC, reposition equipment, loaded autos and expedited manifest. Includes overflow from 971 at Richmond, CA. One block to 807 at Cadiz, CA. One block to 194 on Emporia Subdivision.

| 952 | Mon-Sat | RI | 05:00 | SR | 21:30 | 2.0 | 6,000 | 27.8 |

Richmond to Streator, IL, Conrail manifest. Train delivers to Conrail on arrival. Protects Belen, NM, manifest, train room permitting (866 outlet for overflow).

| 961 | Tue-Sat | CA | 02:00 | CH | 15:15 | 3.7 | None | 38.8 |

Calwa (Fresno), CA, intermodal train, handling Plan III TOFC.

| 965 | As Req. | CA | 01:30 | HO | 21:15 | 2.5 | None | 28.3 |

Intermodal and auto train. Connects from 875 at Belen, NM. Connects from Q-LAFW at Clovis, NM. Delivers to UP via HBT at Houston.

| 968 | As Req. | RI | 06:00 | LA | 18:00 | 2.5 | None | 16.4 |

Empty intermodal equipment repositioning train.

| 971 | Mon-Sat | RI | 22:00 | CH | 15:00 | 4.0 | None | 39.6 |

Intermodal handling primarily Plan III TOFC and other intermodal traffic, train room permitting. One block picked up from Q-EPAQ at Belen, NM.

Train	Days	Orig	Leave	Dest	Arrive	HPT	Max. Tons	Avg. Speed
975	Tue-Sat	RI	02:00	DA	05:00	3.1	5,000	26.5

Intermodal and manifest run-through with KCS at Dallas. Transit time on KCS Dallas to New Orleans 23.0 hours. Train reclassified at Fresno, CA, to line up in original block order. One block to Q-LAFW on Needles Subdivision. One block to 875 and one block picked up from 875, Q-LAFW and S-RIDA at Clovis, NM. One block picked up from 435 at Lubbock, TX. Connects to 625 at Brownwood, TX. 2.0 HPT from Belen, NM, to Dallas.

| 976 | Tue-Sat | RI | 13:00 | WA | 10:00 | 4.0 | None | 25.7 |

Intermodal and manifest via BN, Avard, OK. May operate daily from Belen, NM. Train may split at Fresno, CA, volume permitting with 965 (two blocks) protecting south Texas traffic. Connects to 785 and picks up two blocks from 866 at Belen. May connect to Q-BHLA at Clovis, NM, as required, train room permitting. Operates through to Tulsa, OK, as BN #178. St. Louis traffic to BN #172 at Tulsa.

| 991 | Daily | RI | 03:00 | CH | 14:00 | 4.4 | 3,800 | 43.9 |

Expedited all TOFC/COFC. Train departing Richmond on Monday terminates at Barstow, CA, with traffic connecting to Q-LANY. Handles Dallas UPS from Barstow Tuesday and Wednesday. One block to 787 on Seligman Subdivision. One block to 737/Q-AQEP at Belen, NM. One block to BN at Amarillo, TX. One block to 674 at Waynoka, OK. Handles UPS traffic. Split into 991A and 991B, see below.

| 991A | Tue-Sat | RI | 03:30 | CH | 14:00 | 4.4 | 3,800 | 44.2 |

Expedited intermodal. One block to 787 on Seligman Subdivision. One block to 737 or Q-BEEP at Belen, NM. One block to BN at Amarillo, TX. One block to 674 at Waynoka, OK. Includes UPS.

| 991B | Sun-Mon | RI | 03:30 | CH | 14:00 | 4.4 | 3,800 | 44.2 |

Expedited intermodal. Train departing Richmond on Monday may terminate at Barstow, CA, with traffic connecting to Q-LANY, Monday departure also includes Quantum reposition equipment for Los Angeles. One block to 888 at Barstow, CA. One block to Q-LAFW on Needles Subdivision. One block to 787 at Seligman, AZ. One block to 737 or Q-BEEP at Belen, NM. One block to S-LADA or S-LBDA at Clovis, NM. One block to BN at Amarillo, TX. One block to 674 at Waynoka, OK. Includes UPS.

The 2818 train slogs up Cajon Pass at Sullivan's Curve on September 29, 1984. The power consist includes an SP tunnel motor and a B36-7; there's a high/wide six cars deep as well. The 818 is a daily manifest from Los Angeles to Barstow, running from Los Angeles Junction Railway's A-Yard to Barstow via the San Bernardino Subdivision. It's currently scheduled to leave Los Angeles at 7:00 a.m.
Thomas Carver

The S-CHLA1-07 hustles west just east of Chelsea, Kansas, on July 7, 1990. The time is 5:31 p.m., and the sun is still high in the sky on this baking mid-summer day on the Emporia Subdivision. Chelsea is at the southern extreme of the nearly treeless Flint Hills, 72.5 miles west of Wellington, Kansas. S-CHLA1 is one of the most consistent double-stack trains on the railroad, usually running within an hour or two of its schedule. *Jim Gilley*

Alpha Coded Trains

Train	Days	Orig	Leave	Dest	Arrive	HPT	Max. Tons	Avg. Speed
Q-BAHO1	Tue-Sun	BA	02:00	HO	15:00	2.5	None	19.7

Expedited manifest to Port Terminal Railroad Association. Connects from 928, 938, 948, 2888, 2828 and 2868 at Barstow, CA. One block to 975 at Belen, NM. One block to 875 at Clovis, NM. Terminates at PTRA North Yard. Power forwarded to Houston Belt & Terminal Basin Yard for Q-HOBA.

Train	Days	Orig	Leave	Dest	Arrive	HPT	Max. Tons	Avg. Speed
Q-BEEP1	Tue,Thu,Sat	BE	19:15	EP	03:00	N/A	None	28.9

Intermodal. Connects from Q-NYLA, S-LACH and S-LAKC.

Train	Days	Orig	Leave	Dest	Arrive	HPT	Max. Tons	Avg. Speed
Q-BHLA1	Wed-Mon	WA	21:00	LA	09:15	4.0	4,000	37.4

BN-Santa Fe run-through from Birmingham, AL, to Los Angeles via Avard, OK. Connects to 169 at Clovis. If connection jeopardizes 169's Richmond, CA arrival, connection reverts to 879 at Barstow, CA. Connects from BN train #75 at Avard. Connects from 476 at Waynoka, OK. Connects from BN at Amarillo, TX. One block (two blocks on Wednesday-Sunday) to 169 and one block to V-KCPX at Clovis, NM. Connects from 589 and 578 at Clovis, NM. Connects to V-KCPX (Monday and Tuesday origination only) at Belen, NM. Connects to 879 (Monday and Tuesday origination only) at Barstow, CA.

Train	Days	Orig	Leave	Dest	Arrive	HPT	Max. Tons	Avg. Speed
Q-CHHO1	Daily	MC	19:00	HO	20:00	2.5	3,800	18.3

Indiana Harbor Belt to Houston Belt & Terminal manifest. Will handle overflow from V-KCHO at Kansas City. Train restricted to no more than 6,000 feet with 30 or more bi/trilevels in train. One block to 185 at Joliet, IL. Picks up at Dalton Jct., TX, when V-KCHO restricted. Setout at Alliance, TX, overflow from V-KCHO. Picks up at Cleburne, TX, when V-KCHO restricted. Train reclassified on arrival at Temple, TX. 2.0 HPT and 5,500 tons maximum from Oklahoma City to Houston.

Train	Days	Orig	Leave	Dest	Arrive	HPT	Max. Tons	Avg. Speed
Q-DABA1	Daily	DA	15:30	BA	05:00	1.5	8,000	23.1

Expedited manifest. Connects from KCS #56 at Dallas. Connects from 525 at Dublin, TX. Connects to 839, 1888, 849, 1818, 1828, 868 and 838 at Barstow, CA. 2.0 HPT and 6,000 tons maximum from Belen, NM, to Barstow, CA.

Train	Days	Orig	Leave	Dest	Arrive	HPT	Max. Tons	Avg. Speed
Q-EPBE1	Friday	EP	22:30	BE	05:45	2.5	None	35.2

Intermodal. Two Blocks to 737, two blocks to 991, and one block to 189, 398, 785, 875, 975 and 976 at Belen, NM.

Train	Days	Orig	Leave	Dest	Arrive	HPT	Max. Tons	Avg. Speed
Q-FWLA1	Tue-Sun	FW	04:45	LA	22:30	3.8	5,200	36.5

Premium intermodal. Connects from 168, 169, 268 and S-CHLA at Clovis, NM. One block to 189 at Clovis.

Train	Days	Orig	Leave	Dest	Arrive	HPT	Max. Tons	Avg. Speed
Q-HOBA1	Mon-Sat	HO	04:00	BA	04:00	1.5	8,000	22.2

Expedited manifest connects from PTRA. Power from Q-BAHO at Houston. Two blocks to Q-HOCH at Pearland, TX. Connects from 506 and 545 at Somerville, TX. Two blocks to 534 at Brownwood, TX. Connects from UP at Sweetwater, TX. Overflow traffic for Barstow, CA, may be reduced to Q-DABA at Belen, NM. Connects to 839, 1888, 849, 1828, 1868 and 1838 at Barstow, CA. 2.5 HPT and 6,000 tons maximum from Belen, NM, to Barstow, CA.

Train	Days	Orig	Leave	Dest	Arrive	HPT	Max. Tons	Avg. Speed
Q-HOCH1	Daily	PE	09:30	MC	07:00	1.5	None	29.8

Houston to IHB intermodal and manifest. Connects from Q-HOBA at Pearland, TX. Connects from 506 at Somerville, TX. One block to 581 at Emporia, KS. Train delivers to IHB on arrival. 2.0 HPT from Kansas City to McCook.

Train	Days	Orig	Leave	Dest	Arrive	HPT	Max. Tons	Avg. Speed
Q-LABH1	Mon-Sat	LA	21:00	WA	18:15	4.0	4,000	33.1

Intermodal to Birmingham, AL. Handles 875 and S-LACH1 fills from San Bernardino and Barstow, CA, to Clovis, NM, for classification. Connects from 938 at Barstow. Connects from 785, 875, 976 and S-LACH1 at Clovis. Connects to BN train #74 at Avard, OK, departing Waynoka at 20:45.

| Q-LAFW1 | Mon-Sat | LA | 23:50 | FW | 22:00 | 3.8 | 5,200 | 36.2 |

Premium intermodal. Connects from 991 on Monday and Tuesday, and from 975 on Wednesday-Sunday on Needles Subdivision.

| Q-LANY1 | Daily | LA | 18:30 | CH | 20:30 | 4.0 | 3,800 | 46.0 |

Premium Los Angeles to New York run-through via Conrail at Chicago, handling TOFC only. Handles USPS and LTL TOFC connecting with Conrail train TV-10, departing Ashland Ave. Yard (Chicago) at 01:30. One block from 2868 at San Bernardino, CA. Includes UPS and USPS.

| Q-NYLA1 | Daily | CH | 10:30 | LA | 08:30 | 4.0 | 3,800 | 46.0 |

Premium New York to Los Angeles run-through via Conrail at Chicago, handling TOFC only. Connects from Conrail train TVLA/MAIL-9 (TV-9). One block to 737 and one block to Q-BEEP at Belen, NM. One block to 1868 at San Bernardino, CA. Includes UPS and USPS.

| S-BDFW1 | Wednesday | BD | 20:00 | FW | 04:30 | 2.7 | None | 41.1 |

Double-stack train for "K"-Line.

| S-CHLA1 | Tue-Sun | CH | 01:00 | LA | 13:00 | 2.7 | 5,500 | 35.6 |

Handles double-stack and articulated equipment exclusively, except conventional intermodal traffic may be added when 168 not operated. Connects from Conrail train TV-201 Monday-Thursday and TV-203-C on Friday. Picks up at Kansas City when 368 not operated. Connects to Q-FWLA at Clovis, NM.

| S-ESLA1 | Wednesday | ES | 12:01 | LA | 02:00 | 2.7 | 5,500 | 32.4 |

Mitsui double-stacks for Los Angeles.

| S-HOLB1 | Wednesday | PE | 10:00 | LB | 03:00 | 2.7 | None | 27.1 |

Handles double-stack traffic for "K"-Line destined for Port of Los Angeles. Will not be filled en route.

| S-KCLA1 | Thursday | KC | 23:30 | LA | 23:45 | 2.7 | 5,500 | 42.0 |

Run-through double-stack from C&NW at Kansas City, to Los Angeles for "K"-Line.

| S-LACH1 | Daily | LA | 23:00 | CH | 17:00 | 2.7 | None | 34.5 |

Handles double-stack and articulated equipment exclusively except that conventional intermodal traffic may be added as fill, train room permitting. Will operate Sunday if sufficient traffic. Connects to Q-BEEP or 197 at Belen, NM. Connects from Q-FWLA at Clovis, NM. One block to 332 at Kansas City. Connects to TP&W at Fort Madison, IA. Three blocks connect to Conrail TV-262 at Chicago.

| S-LACH5 | Sunday | LA | 23:30 | CH | 17:00 | 2.7 | None | 34.8 |

Handles all double-stack and articulated equipment destined Chicago and beyond. Conventional intermodal traffic may be added as fill, train room permitting. At McCook, IL, delivers to NS. At Chicago delivers to Conrail (connects to TV-262) and CSX.

| S-LACH8 | Tuesday | LA | 18:00 | CH | 10:00 | 2.7 | None | 35.6 |

Handles double-stacks for Hyundai originating Hobart Yard. Also will handle COFC traffic for steel wheel interchange Chicago to NS via Belt Railway of Chicago. Operates Tuesdays unless Hyundai traffic is off schedule.

| S-LADA1 | Sunday | LA | 20:30 | ZJ | 06:00 | 3.1 | 5,000 | 29.9 |

Double-stack and intermodal. May fill with regular intermodal, train room permitting. Connects to S-BDFW at Brownwood, TX.

| S-LAES1 | Sunday | LA | 23:00 | ES | 13:15 | 3.8 | 5,500 | 34.4 |

Mitsui double-stack destined Memphis, TN, and Marysville and Columbus, OH. Memphis connects to ICG train I-11, and Columbus/Marysville is handled in run-through on Conrail train TV-600 departing at 16:00.

| S-LAKC1 | Sunday | LA | 21:00 | KC | 01:00 | 2.7 | None | 35.2 |

"K"-Line double stacks. Train delivers to C&NW on arrival Kansas City.

| S-LAZJ1 | Monday | LA | 08:00 | ZJ | 21:00 | 2.7 | 5,000 | 28.1 |

Double-stack, may fill with regular intermodal traffic, train room permitting. Connects to V-KCHO at Cleburne, TX. 2.4 HPT Belen, NM, to Zacha Jct., TX.

| S-LBDA1 | Sunday | LB | 17:00 | ZJ | 14:00 | 2.7 | None | 25.2 |

"K"-Line double-stacks. Connects to 785 at Belen, NM. Connects from 991B as required at Clovis, NM. Connects to S-BDFW at Brownwood, TX. 2.0 HPT Belen, NM, to Zacha Jct., TX.

| S-LBKC1 | As Req. | LB | 17:00 | KC | 01:00 | 2.7 | None | 33.2 |

"K"-Line double-stacks. Train is alternate to S-LAKC for operating convenience. Connects to Q-BEEP at Belen, NM. Train delivers to C&NW on arrival.

| S-RIDA1 | Sunday | RI | 23:00 | ZJ | 01:20 | 3.0 | None | 26.9 |

Intermodal handling Maersk Lines traffic. If train is late at Stockton, CA, one block goes to 991B. One block to 781 at Belen, NM. Connects to Q-LABH (or 2-976), 785, Q-LAFW and 975 at Clovis, NM. 2.5 HPT from Belen to Zacha Jct., TX.

| V-KCHO1 | Daily | KC | 22:30 | HO | 05:45 | 2.0 | 5,500 | 28.4 |

Expedited TOFC and auto train destined Alliance, Fort Worth and Houston, TX. Train is restricted to 6,000 feet out of Kansas City when handling 30 or more bi/trilevels. One block picked up from 581 and 185 at Dalton Jct., TX. If overflow, pick up with Q-CHHO. Connects from S-LBDA or S-LADA at Cleburne, TX. May handle traffic from Quanex Industrial park from Buckholts to Belleville, TX. Also may handle empties from Quanex to Houston.

| V-KCPX1 | Daily | KC | 19:30 | PX | 01:00 | 2.8 | None | 26.5 |

Intermodal and auto. Connects from NS, 213 and 133 at Kansas City. Two blocks picked up from 668 at Amarillo, TX. Connects from Q-BHLA Tuesday-Sunday at Clovis, NM. Connects from 189, 448, 578 and 589 on Arizona Division.

| V-OKKC1 | Tue-Sat | OK | 04:00 | KC | 15:30 | 1.2 | None | 29.9 |

Auto and manifest to move GM traffic. Two blocks to 952 at Kansas City.

Santa Fe Alpha Codes:

AM — Amarillo, TX		LU — Lubbock, TX	
AQ — Albuquerque, NM		MC — McCook, IL	
BA — Barstow, CA		MD — Modesto, CA	
BC — Battle Creek, MI		NE — Needles, CA	
BD — Brownwood, TX		NW — Newton, KS	
BE — Belen, NM		NY — New York, NY	
BH — Birmingham, AL		OK — Oklahoma City, OK	
BK — Bakersfield, CA		PB — Pueblo, CO	
BM — Beaumont, TX		PC — Port Chicago, CA	
BO — Borger, TX		PD — Presidio, TX	
CA — Calwa, CA		PE — Pearland, TX	
CH — Chicago, IL		PR — Pico Rivera, CA	
CL — Cleburne, TX		PX — Phoenix, AZ	
CV — Clovis, NM		RI — Richmond, CA	
DA — Dallas, TX		RR — Red Rock, OK	
DE — Denver, CO		SA — Slaton, TX	
DG — Daggett, CA		SB — San Bernardino, CA	
DJ — Dalton Jct., TX		SD — San Diego, CA	
DT — Detroit, MI		SE — Seligman, AZ	
EM — Emporia, KS		SG — San Angelo, TX	
EP — El Paso, TX		SI — Silsbee, TX	
ES — East St. Louis, IL		SJ — San Juan Capistrano, CA	
FR — Fresno, CA		SL — St. Louis, MO	
FW — Fort Worth, TX		SR — Streator, IL	
GA — Galveston, TX		ST — Stockton, CA	
GP — Gallup, NM		TE — Temple, TX	
HB — Hobart Yard (LA), CA		TP — Topeka, TX	
HO — Houston, TX		TR — Trinidad, CO	
KC — Kansas City, KS		WA — Waynoka, OK	
LA — Los Angeles, CA		WI — Winslow, AZ	
LB — Long Beach, CA		WT — Watson, CA	
LJ — La Junta, CO		ZJ — Zacha Junction, TX	

Miscellaneous Abbreviations

BN — Burlington Northern	KCS — Kansas City Southern
BRC — Belt Railway of Chicago	KJRY — Keokuk Junction Railway
CR — Conrail	LAJ — Los Angeles Junction Rwy
CSX — CSX Transportation	NS — Norfolk Southern
GTW — Grand Trunk Western	PTRA — Port Terminal RR Assoc.
HBT — Houston Belt & Terminal	UP — Union Pacific
HPT — Horsepower Per Ton	UPS — United Parcel Service
IC — Illinois Central	USPS — U.S. Postal Service
IHB — Indiana Harbor Belt	

Santa Fe's new headquarters building is at Schaumburg, Illinois, a suburb of Chicago. The building houses Santa Fe's System Operations Center, the control center of the railroad. The SOC handles all locomotive assignment functions, most of the scheduling, and customer relations. *Kevin EuDaly*

Santa Fe's System Operations Center (SOC), located in Santa Fe's new head-quarters building in Schaumburg, Illinois, is the railway's operational center. The facility was occupied by Santa Fe in January 1991. Santa Fe's Power Office, which handles locomotive assignments, moved in the weekend following the headquarters move. Fleet Management, which handles Santa Fe's car distribution, moved from Kansas City to the new facility the following month.

The most visually impressive aspect of the Schaumburg headquarters is the SOC, as it's dominated by a six-segment, 60-foot-long video projection showing the entire railroad. The display is constantly updated with overlays showing the location of every train on the railroad.

Computer terminals in front of each power planner show the location and status of every locomotive on the Santa Fe. The system was developed in conjunction with IBM to replace the power office at Santa Fe's old Chicago headquarters, which used magnetic tags on an immense metal system map to identify the location of each locomotive. The tag system was used between 1970 and 1991.

The primary job of the power planners is to assign locomotives to trains. There are normally two power planners on duty, one responsible for Santa Fe's Eastern and Southern Regions, the other for the Central and Western Regions. Each power planner has an assistant to keep track of a multitude of details, and to coordinate power assignments with Santa Fe's scheduling group. The power planners work directly with a host of personnel on the railroad, including superintendents, trainmasters, supervisor — train operation (STOs), and mechanical department personnel.

The power planners also have to make sure all locomotives are in the right place at the right time for mechanical inspections. (Locomotives are required by FRA regulation to undergo 92-day, 180-day and yearly inspections.) Locomotives overdue for inspection cannot be operated.

Planning to have locomotives in the right place at the right time for inspections becomes extremely complicated, and involves a great deal of long-range thinking and an intuitive grasp of how the railroad operates in all traffic and weather conditions.

The locomotive displays use symbols and color codes to indicate when inspections are due, the nature of any and all reported defects, and details such as which units are radio control leaders (RCE) and which are radio controlled receivers (RCR).

For example, a quick check at 10:50 a.m. on March 23, 1992, revealed that of the RCE and RCR-equipped units the 9521, 9535, and 9543 had bad-order RCE equipment, and thus should not be used in that service. The 9521 was at Galveston, Texas, the 9535 at Pueblo, Colorado, on the 1-344-21, and the 9543 was at Carlsbad, New Mexico. The 9543 was due for an inspection at the General Electric mechanical shop on April 2, 1992.

Other details the power planners are responsible for include when and where locomotives are to be sent off-line or are coming on-line, and units with minor defects, such as cab problems that restrict a unit to trailing status. They must balance power across the railroad to ensure the proper number and type of units are available for the trains scheduled. A major part of their job is verification of which units are where.

Another position in the SOC is the Fuel Conservation desk. This job is responsible for day-to-day management of all measures that will conserve fuel and save the Santa Fe money. One aspect of the job is to identify when deadheading locomotives will become necessary, and ensure the deadheading units are shut down in transit. Another important function is to slow down trains that are running well ahead of schedule, as a train running 70 mph will consume roughly three times as much fuel as a train running at 45 mph.

The railroad's scheduling group, also at the SOC, is responsible for maintenance, updating and monitoring of the Santa Fe's Transportation Service Plan. The TSP is the detailed instruction book for operating the railroad's intermodal and manifest freights. The TSP is a fluid document, and is updated on a weekly basis or better to improve both customer service and operating efficiency.

Changes in the TSP are recommended or requested by the four Regional Operations Centers (ROCs), and Santa Fe's superintendents. There are also customer-requested

changes, and changes requested by Santa Fe's marketing group and Intermodal Business Unit.

Each Monday, the scheduling group meets to address requested changes in the TSP, plus problems that have cropped up. The topics are widespread, from delays encountered while blocking a train at one location, to excess crew costs at another, to power imbalances, to train-handling difficulties. Sometimes difficult problems remain on the agenda for months until the scheduling group can determine a solution.

Even seemingly minor changes such as revising a departure to meet a customer's shipping schedule can result in big, unforeseen problems elsewhere. A change can ripple outwards without effect, or it might cascade into a big headache. When major changes are in the offing everyone gets involved, including customers. Often there is no perfect solution, and the scheduling group will experiment with various schemes until the best alternative is discovered. From the outside it may look like they just run trains when the yard gets full, but it's not even remotely that simple.

The SOC is equipped with a rear-screen projection system displaying every train on the railroad. Each train is designated in a lit strip on the screens. Computer terminals at the hands of the power planners identify every unit, where it's at, when it's due for inspection, any mechanical problems it's experiencing, and a slew of other information necessary for the constant power planning process. The next time you see a trio of SDFP45s, remember the lashup was put together here long before it was put together out on the railroad. *Kevin EuDaly*

The TSP has quickly evolved from a crude reference book into an exacting schedule. Currently the TSP contains only numbered trains, Q-trains, S-trains and V-trains, but eventually it will include all coal trains, locals, and many other regularly scheduled movements.

In the future Santa Fe's new headquarters building will become much more important. The four Regional Operations Centers will soon be consolidated to Schaumburg, along with all other major operating functions.

It's 12:30 on a Saturday morning. While Kansas City sleeps, Santa Fe's Eastern Region ROC (Regional Operations Center) is humming. Dispatchers are talking to trainmen, trainmen calling dispatchers, dispatchers talking to dispatchers, and clerks keeping track of a thousand details.

The Eastern Region dispatching center began operation in March 1989. Tonight, Sam Quintana is dispatching the Topeka and Western Kansas branchlines, all non-CTC territory. He gives us a general explanation of how things work. His section is very quiet this evening, the only activity a grain train that's trying to get out of Topeka before the westbound *Southwest Chief* gets hung up behind him.

Sam enters a track warrant on the computer, allowing the Houston-bound grain train to occupy the railroad south of Topeka. At Topeka the train crew gets the warrant that starts their run, calling Sam when they are moving.

"We're out of Topeka at 12:40."

Sam writes it down on the train sheet. After a few minutes of shooting the breeze he takes us over to the next panel, labelled "Arkansas City", "Newton" and "La Junta." The Kansas City ROC has none of the large track diagrams on the walls, lit-up with thousands of lights and studded with rows of knobs, buttons and levers that dispatching centers once featured. Instead, banks of computer screens and keypads fill the semi-circular room. The dispatchers for each section of the Eastern Region are arranged in areas, much like spokes on a wheel.

Behind the dispatchers, and elevated slightly above them, is a semicircular row of open desks where "Communication Coordinators" work. They're tasked with tracking the details of Santa Fe's 24-hour operations. They keep up with everything, from where each signal maintainer is working, to what pickups and setouts need to be made by each train. In essence, they're the link between train operations and the Supervisors — Train Operation (STOs).

The STOs are back one more tier, and up another level. The three Eastern Region STOs are the eyes and ears for both Santa Fe's System Operations Center (SOC), in Schaumburg, Illinois, and Santa Fe's entire Eastern Region. An analogy is the Santa Fe's nerve center is the SOC, and the four ROCs are the muscles that run the railroad. The STOs in each of Santa Fe's four regions monitor train performance, file accident reports and generally keep things running as smoothly as possible.

The next panel to the east of the Arkansas City panel displays "Panhandle" in large stainless steel letters. It's one of eight dispatching jobs currently working on the Eastern Region. This position's 11 computer screens display an amazing quantity of detail concerning the operations of one small segment of Santa Fe's Chicago-Los Angeles mainline.

The names of the sidings are displayed across the track plan on six computer screens, from west to east, and left to right: Kings Mill, West Pampa, Pampa, East Pampa, Hoover, Codman, Miami, Lora, Mendota,

Canadian, Clear Creek, Glazier, Coburn, Higgins, Goodwin, Shattuck, Gage, Fargo, Tangier, Gerlach, and Woodward. More screens to the right of this group display the territory covered by the Waynoka dispatcher, who sits to the right of the Panhandle job, and controls the territory beginning at Mooreland, the next siding east of Woodward. More screens to the left display the territory covered by the dispatcher to the west. These let the Panhandle Dispatcher know what to expect at a glance.

On the screens, territory not under the Panhandle Dispatcher's control appear with the identifier code numbers for the switch and signal locations in red. White identifier code numbers show the section of track under the Panhandle Dispatcher's jurisdiction. These parameters can be quickly modified to reduce or expand any dispatcher's territory.

Dave Leininger, the third trick dispatcher for the Panhandle Subdivision this night, sits back to study his screens for a brief moment, makes his decision, and punches in the number 177, the identifier code for the west end of the siding at Coburn, Texas. He hits the Switch Reverse key, and then the East Signal Clear key, and finally the Transmit key, all in under two seconds. A moment later the screen flickers, and the switch graphic changes to show the switch's new position.

Meanwhile, 437 miles from the ROC, the switch motor at the west end of Coburn powers up, and the points move over until they contact the stock rail with a metallic clunk. The eastbound signal at the west end of Coburn lights up red over green, the following signal shows red over yellow, and there's a double red at the east end of the siding. A bright light stabs through the

darkness to the west as the 941 train appears over the western horizon.

On Dave's screen, a red line on the track diagram expands to include the block ending at the west switch of Coburn. The number "941" above it indicating its tenant is train 941, a Richmond, California, to Chicago manifest.

The 941's crew spots the red over green and calls Dave.

"Panhandle Dispatcher to 941, you'll be in the hole for two," he replies. Meanwhile, two red bars, one right behind the other, show that westbound train Q-NYLA2 is closing fast on the east switch of Coburn, and the 188 is right behind it at Higgins. That's not all. Eastbound 733 is about five blocks behind 941, and within six blocks of 188 are two more westbounds, 169 and V-KCPX.

The screen covering territory to the west shows westbound S-CHLA1 is passing eastbound 623, which is in the siding at Canadian. The east end screen shows eastbounds 991 and Q-LANY are about to leave Dave's territory at Woodward, and enter the Waynoka Dispatcher's territory.

At Coburn, 941 pulls into the siding. Q-NYLA2 has made a brake application to conform with its approach signal east of East Coburn. Dave squirms just a little, knowing it doesn't look good to slow the Q-NYLA for even a minute, as it's one of the hottest trains on the railroad.

Working ahead, Dave has "stacked" several commands. These will automatically clear the west end of the siding the moment the 941 OS's (clears) the switch. His intuition proves correct, for the 941's red line blips into the siding a few seconds before the Q-NYLA2's red line moves to the west.

The screen flickers, and shows the switch at the west end of Coburn has gone back to normal. Green signals flip on ahead of the Q-NYLA2, and soon it's accelerated to track speed. Dave records the time the 941 entered the siding, since the dispatchers keep track of all train delays. Now moving past Coburn is the 188, hot on the heels of Q-NYLA2. Dave again records 941's time as he clears the siding at Coburn, a delay of 31 minutes to the 941 for the double meet.

Now, the 733 is in the siding at Glazier for Q-NYLA2 and 188, so Dave turns his attention to the next problem, getting the 941 past 169 and V-KCPX. His fingers fly on the keypad as he lines 941 out the east end of Coburn and routes him into the siding at Goodwin. He stacks commands again to let V-KCPX follow on 169's blocks, and to let 941 out of the siding at Goodwin the instant the two westbounds clear. Since there's nothing else closing from the west, it's time to get rid of the S-CHLA1, now clearing Canadian.

He changes keypads and turns his attention to two lower screens, one of which shows all the trains on his subdivision. He arrow-keys down to the line showing S-CHLA1 and types an "A" in front of the train, and the F15 key for transmit. A small "a" appears on the screen next to the train.

This has put the CTC system in "Auto-clear," which tells the computer-driven system to automatically change the signals to green from their red, default position, four blocks ahead of the S-CHLA1. Each time the train enters a block, the fourth block ahead will clear up, allowing the dispatcher to concentrate on more pressing tasks.

Trains on the lower screen appear in one of six colors: blue if they're an hour or more ahead of schedule, a color which the Q-NYLA2 so far enjoys tonight; light gray for 16 to 59 minutes ahead of schedule, green if a train is within 15 minutes of schedule, yellow for 16 to 59 minutes late, and red if it's more than an hour late. Trains not running on a schedule show as white.

As soon as the "a" turns to an "A" Dave knows he can forget about S-CHLA1. Well, almost.

As the S-CHLA1 nears Hoover, Dave looks at the clock. "Better call him for about . . . 02:30," he says, mostly to himself. He turns to yet another screen and keypad, selects the S-CHLA1, and types in commands to call a crew for the train at Amarillo for 02:30. Amarillo is an hour and a half away. The crew caller in Albuquerque now has the information to call the next crew for the S-CHLA1.

"On several subdivisions where crew change points have been eliminated, we call crews as much as three and a half hours in advance, in order to give them enough time to drive to their new crew change point," Dave explains. "In winter weather we give them even more time." Typically, each dispatcher only has to notify crew callers for one direction of movement, as the dispatcher's territory typically doesn't include a complete crew district. The Panhandle Dispatcher, for example, notifies only the crew caller at Amarillo for westbounds.

More typing, and the 623 leaves the siding at Canadian headed for the siding at Clear Creek, where it will meet Q-NYLA2 and 188.

"I've got to get 623 moving, he's been out eight hours already, and he has work to do at Shattuck. Twelve hours and he goes dead on the law," Dave says.

The 623's in at Clear Creek and none too soon, as Q-NYLA and 188 are eating up the railroad through Glazier, where 733 is patiently waiting. A few more Autoclear commands and Q-NYLA2 and 188 are history, except that the crew caller still has to be called at Amarillo. Now the 733 is lined east to the siding at Coburn and 623 to the siding at Glazier, where they'll wait for 169 and V-KCPX. V-KCPX has cleared Goodwin, so 941's red line blips east, headed off the screen on Autoclear. As soon as 169 and V-KCPX clear 733 at Glazier, 733 also heads east behind 941.

The 169 blasts through Clear Creek with V-KCPX hot on his tail, clearing Glazier, and 623 can finally make it to Shattuck to do its work.

Dave looks up at the clock. It's two-thirty in the morning. The last two hours have gone by in a flash.

"Some times," Dave says, "you get in here and work like mad, and by the time you look up its 6:45, the day shift is coming in, and you realize you've forgotten to eat supper. Other times, like tonight, its not so busy."

Not so busy? Ten trains have run across the screens in the last two hours! And the Panhandle job is only one of eight such jobs in the Eastern Region alone.

Halfway across the room Jesse Munoz is busy getting the Sibley Coal Train onto the railroad at Eton, from its interchange with the Union Pacific. The Marceline Dispatcher, Jesse's job tonight, is more complicated than Dave's, but is blessed with double-track except for the bridge over the Missouri River at Sibley. The Marceline Dispatcher handles the railroad from Congo Junction, just east of Rock Creek Junction in Kansas City, to Fort Madison, Iowa. The section's double track, however, must also accommodate Norfolk Southern traffic for 30 miles between CA Junction and WB Junction in western Missouri, and Union Pacific and Cotton Belt traffic for seven miles between Eton and Rock Creek.

The 199 and the Q-LANY, which has already gone halfway around the room from Dave's position, are both closing on Eton from opposite directions, which is holding up the coal train.

Jesse looks back to one of three Chief

Dispatchers overseeing the whole affair.

"Has there been a restriction put on Q-LANY?" he asks the chief.

"Sometimes when a train is way ahead of schedule," he explains to us, "we'll cut down his speed to save on fuel. Since Q-LANY is nearing Sibley, I need to decide whether to let 199 across the bridge. If Q-LANY is restricted to 50 mph, I have time to get 199 across the bridge without stopping Q-LANY, but if he's running at track speed, I'll have to hold 199."

The chief dispatcher replies that there is no restriction, so Jesse gives Q-LANY the bridge. The restriction is a decision that comes from the Fuel Conservation position at the SOC in Schaumburg.

Three more Santa Fe ROCs — Euless, Texas, which handles the Southern Region, Albuquerque, New Mexico, which covers the Central Region, and San Bernardino, California, which covers the Western Region — repeat this activity every day, every hour, every minute, all year.

The amount of information entered, transmitted and evaluated is mind-boggling. Somewhere deep in the circuits of Santa Fe's computer network there's information on every car in every train, what's in the car, train tonnages, times of trains at key locations on the railroad, who's put Q-NYLA in the siding . . . the information age, indeed.

Yet the future is already changing. New and bigger advances in dispatching are fast approaching. Computers are already setting up meets, making minor dispatching decisions, and controlling the switches and signals out on the railroad. It's merely a matter of more comprehensive software and faster microprocessors before computers begin running the railroad. The dispatcher will still be necessary, but only to solve the problems the computer can't anticipate.

A few years ago the Santa Fe had 11 dispatching centers. Of the four current ROCs, only San Bernardino was previously a dispatching center. Fresno and San Bernardino, California, were consolidated into the current San Bernardino ROC. The territory handled by the dispatching offices at Winslow, Arizona, Clovis, New Mexico, plus part of La Junta, Colorado's territory and part of Amarillo, Texas's territory, were combined into the Albuquerque ROC. Temple and Fort Worth, Texas, were combined into the Euless ROC. The remaining portions of Amarillo and La Junta were consolidated at Newton, Kansas. Finally, Newton and Emporia, Kansas, and Fort Madison, Iowa, were consolidated into the Kansas City ROC.

More consolidations will occur as soon as software is written to accomplish more tasks. Eventually, Santa Fe's four regional dispatching centers will be compressed to one center at Schaumburg. The crew calling functions are the first scheduled for the move, on or about January 1, 1993. The dispatching functions are not scheduled to move until well into 1994.

Until then, the Eastern Region ROC dispatchers in Kansas City will continue to ensure the Q-NYLA always gets a clear block.

GP60 4001 is the mock-up unit used for Santa Fe's full-motion simulator. The Santa Fe also has two simulators which do not include motion simulation. They're modeled after two different prototypes, GP60M 100 and SD40-2 5124. The hydraulic system used to create the motion is shared for the SP and Santa Fe simulators, significantly lowering the cost for each railroad. The 4001 once came off its hydraulic system during a hair-raising run (there's a large dent in the corner dating to this occurrence), resulting in a more realistic wreck simulation than anticipated. Fortunately no one was hurt. *Kevin EuDaly*

The Tech Center — Transportation Training Services

"Dispatcher to Extra 4001 West, train Q-FWLA, you're cleared to depart West Flagstaff. Your train today is 54 cars, 4,220 tons, 5,240 feet, all articulated equipment, with four 4000s up front." A glance at the watch reveals its 2:02 p.m. on February 6, 1992. The deep snow on the Arizona Divide is brilliant white in the afternoon sun. The engineer picks up the radio.

"Q-FWLA departing West Flagstaff at 14:02."

The engineer gets up, and Lon EuDaly sits down at the controls. The engineer tells Lon to go ahead and take 'em ahead. It's not every day a railfan gets the chance to run a hotshot. He gives Lon a quick explanation of the controls and Lon slowly notches out the throttle.

By milepost 349 the train is motoring along smartly at 45 mph, held back by the curves between MP 348.2 and 350.2. The 1.42 percent climb is using up most of the power available. We crest the hill at milepost 351, and get a clear block in this CTC double-track territory, the Seligman Subdivision.

Lon drops the throttle into idle, waits a few seconds and moves the dynamic brake lever up into notch 2, making a slight dynamic brake application. With this little bit of dynamic braking the slack runs in, and with a well-felt bump the unit rocks back and forth.

We round a sharp curve to the left. The engineer tells us this is "Turpentine Curve," the site of an accident which spilled turpentine on Interstate 40 several years ago. We round the curve at 44 mph, barely under the posted 45 mph speed limit. As we clear the curve Lon kicks off the dynamic and the engineer simultaneously punches a button on the console. He explains that the counter will begin to run off the feet we've traveled since he hit the button. This way we'll know when the rear of the train is off the 45 mph curve.

The speed limit increases to 55 mph, but since our train is all articulated equipment, we can run at 70 mph. As soon as the meter passes the 5,200 foot mark, Lon notches out the throttle, and the units roar and vibrate as they strain against the train's dead weight.

We're soon up to 68 mph, and blasting through a clear block at Bellemont. Two miles west of Bellemont the next signal pops out from around a curve, yellow over

A high tech, state-of-the-art facility, the Transportation Training Services (TTS), also known as The Tech Center, is an operation run jointly with the Southern Pacific. It's located in Lenexa, Kansas, a suburb of Kansas City. The instructor in the foreground monitors engineer performance from behind the locomotive simulator, which is located behind the screens at the top of the photograph. The instructor has the ability to throw a huge number of different scenarios at an engineer. This provides careful training for real emergency situations, training that's been proven to reduce train operating failures. This particular simulator is Santa Fe's full-motion simulator, which rocks, sways, pitches and accelerates, mimicking the feel of a real train. *Kevin EuDaly*

red. Lon drops the throttle into run 4 and makes a slight air reduction, which slowly drops the speed down to 40 mph. Soon the throttle is in idle and he's using the dynamic brakes again, the engines rocking back and forth and the dynamic brakes whining. The slack runs in again, with a slight jolt.

This is undulating territory, and it takes finesse to keep the train moving without excess buff forces. Dropping down past milepost 361 with the dynamic brakes on, the alarm bell goes off, the lead unit gasps slightly, then dies. A quick check reveals we've lost all power on the lead unit, killing the dynamic brakes as well. The engineer immediately sets the air slightly. Lon pushes the selector out of dynamic braking and into idle , and suddenly everything stops. No more motion, no more throbbing engines . . . just silence.

A voice comes in over a speaker in the cab.

"Just because the lead unit dies doesn't mean you've lost all your dynamic brakes," it points out somewhat petulantly. "You've only lost the lead unit. The other three units will easily hold the train on this grade." Immediately the sound and motion returns and suddenly we're rolling down

the mountain again.

So we've made our first mistake on this run, a run simulated with state-of-the-art software and a locomotive cab that looks, feels, and even operates exactly like a real one . . . well, almost. The cab is mounted on hydraulic actuators, which imitate the motions and feel of being in a real locomotive cab by accelerating it on all three axis at once. The hydraulic system is driven by a computer program that mathematically models what the locomotive should "feel" in practically any situation.

The scene that's been unfolding before the windshield is a movie of the Seligman Subdivision west of Flagstaff, over a thousand miles to the west. We're in Lenexa, Kansas, on the southwest side of Kansas City, at Santa Fe's and Southern Pacific's Transportation Training Services (TTS) facility. The mission of the TTS is to train locomotive engineers, dispatchers, brakemen, conductors, yardmasters — just about anyone involved in train operation.

The need for a training facility came about in 1986, when the Santa Fe was looking for a way to eliminate wrecks on the Seligman Subdivision.

Prior to 1984 trains on this district averaged 40 to 50 cars, with plenty of

Another interesting aspect of the training capabilities at the TTS facility are its dispatcher training courses. John Marshall, at left, who assembled these courses, demonstrates the capabilities of the systems to "student" Lon EuDaly. The computer screens arc nearly identical to the setup in Santa Fe's Regional Operations Centers. Any number of trains, routes and scenarios can be programmed into the system, allowing the re-creation of actual railroad schedules and events.
Kevin EuDaly

power up front. In 1985 train lengths and tonnage began to increase, and increase, and increase. The crew change at Seligman was eliminated, and crews began running 292 miles from Winslow to Needles in one jaunt. With the advent of "black box" speed recorders, there was increased pressure on crews to run trains as close to speed limits as possible, in order to expedite traffic across the system, yet without exceeding speed limits.

The Santa Fe had no makeup restrictions on the trains, and as train lengths and tonnages grew, the long crew district and a lack of experience in the proper handling of long trains caught up with the Santa Fe.

"This particular territory had the worst accident record on the entire Santa Fe, and averaged 10 to 12 major derailments a year in the period from 1984 to 1986, and nearly all were attributable to human error," says George Smallwood, TTS's manager, and a Santa Fe employee.

"This section west of Flagstaff is un-doubtedly the toughest run on the entire railroad," says Homer Henry, Santa Fe's Director Operating Practices and Manpower Planning. Henry oversees the TTS.

"Train physics had narrowed the margin for error significantly, and we had another

major pile-up, the type where trailers were spinning off into the fields. Both an operat-ing officer and a representative of the Brotherhood of Locomotive Engineers called me up and told me that the engineer in that particular wreck was one of the best. His track record was without a mark against it. He told me that the engineer involved was not one who should be faulted, and that perhaps something needed to be done."

Henry first considered more training on the Santa Fe simulator in Topeka, but decided that its 1969-era technology was inadequate. Henry contacted SP's Gary McLain to discuss Santa Fe's use of SP's state-of-the-art locomotive simulator in Cerritos, California.

They struck a deal, and the engineer involved in the wreck went to SP's facility for some simulator time. They programmed the same train he had wrecked into the simulator, replicating the tonnages and train dynamics car-for-car. Though the exact Santa Fe trackage was not available on the SP system, a similar SP segment with an undulating profile much like the Needles-Winslow run was chosen.

In his first hour on the simulator the engineer scattered his train all over the right-of-way three times. In every case the derailment occurred at two empty 89-foot flats in the middle of the train. The engineer was then sent to a classroom course on train dynamics and train handling, called "Theory of Long Train Handling." On his next try at the simulator, his performance was flawless.

"With those results in hand we instituted a training program in 1987 in Cerritos, California, using the SP facility already in place. The crews on the Winslow-Needles run had all become quite worried, and we wondered how we could possibly force them all to go through the training program," says Henry.

"There were 110 engineers running between Winslow and Needles, and we set up an elaborate scheme to get them to go. We encouraged them to take their families, and paid all expenses. When we circulated the sign-up sheet, we had 110 volunteers!" The coursework was specifically designed to meet the operational difficulties of the Seligman Subdivision.

The next year proved this wasn't just a whitewash. The Seligman Subdivision went from the worst wreck record on the Santa Fe system, to the best. Only one major derailment occurred the following year, and it was unrelated to train handling.

Since derailments cause a dollar loss from the bottom line, any demonstrable method of decreasing accidents increases the profitability of the railroad. A quick study showed it would require seven years to get all of Santa Fe's engineers through SP's Cerritos simulator. Santa Fe's management wasn't willing to accept more train-handling wrecks that would probably occur in the interim.

After further discussions with the SP, the two railroads agreed to build a joint Santa Fe-SP facility with joint training programs, both to reduce costs, and to draw upon the experiences of both railroads.

The center was soon opened, and within a year, every Santa Fe engineer went through the TTS. For the Seligman Subdivision alone, the results have been impressive: zero derailments due to train-handling errors in the five years after the TTS opened.

There is an astonishing unification of energy and effort between the two otherwise fiercely competitive railroads at the TTS.

"We decided early on that safety benefits everyone, and both the SP and the Santa Fe agreed to help each other out," Smallwood explains.

Anyone going through a training program at the TTS surely comes away with the belief that both the Santa Fe and the SP are deeply committed to improving safety through training.

There are four locomotive simulators at the TTS. The SP has one, a full-motion simulator based on SD40 8799. The Santa Fe has three. Two of these are not hydraulically actuated, and have no motion capability. One is modeled after GP60M 100, and the other after SD40-2 5124. The 100 simulator is equipped with modern desktop controls, the 5124 with a traditional AAR control stand.

The third Santa Fe simulator has full motion, and is based on GP60 4001. The hydraulics that actuate the two full-motion simulators is shared to reduce the cost of this very expensive and sophisticated system.

The system accurately replicates the motions that one feels in a locomotive cab: side-to-side rocking, slack running in and out, braking buff forces, low-frequency vibration during hard pulls, and even a realistic change in sound when the "locomotive" passes under a bridge or through a tunnel.

Another component of the TTS facility is its dispatcher training center. The screens it uses are identical in all respects to the screens in Santa Fe's four Regional Operation Centers.

"The dispatcher training will duplicate nearly any situation a dispatcher could possibly be faced with anywhere on the entire system," says John Marshall, who's in charge of TTS's dispatcher training programs. "We've slowly managed to accumulate enough terminals to reproduce what's actually in the four Regional Operations Centers, with enough software set up to run any area on the whole system."

Dispatchers are faced with the same sequences and decision-points as a dispatcher on the real railroad. One major difference between the TTS and the actual dispatching centers, however, is that at the training center all the trains move at the same rate, and each train is very short.

"I'm hoping in the near future to add the capability to alter train speeds, and so be able to replicate, for example, a Q-NYLA gaining quickly on a 103 train," John says.

Several functions exist that are rarely used in practice, such as the Meet/Pass function. This allows the dispatcher to set up a meet on single track ahead of time by specifying which train goes into the siding. With a few simple commands to the computer the meet is set up, and all switches and signals operate as if the dispatcher had done it with previously "stacked" commands.

"The next step will have the computer making many of the operating decisions, freeing up the dispatchers to do many other functions," explains John Marshall.

The dispatchers out in the real world are still a little dubious of letting the computer handle a complete meet, and so most still stack the commands by hand.

We sit down and John quickly demonstrates how trains are added to the system. Any quantity of eastbound or westbound trains can be programmed for a session. The territory on the screens happens to be a portion of the Clovis Subdivision, single-track CTC from Vaughn to Mountainair, New Mexico. At once we're engrossed in moving trains across the screens. It happens incredibly fast, much faster than on the real railroad, and constant attention is necessary.

After twenty minutes we've cleared nearly all the trains off, and set up a Meet/Pass between the last two, 991 and 339. They're still many miles apart. John asks; "Where do you want to set up the meet?" I pick a

spot halfway in between and tell him, "Silio." He glances at the screen, nods his approval, and asks, "who goes into the siding?" I respond that obviously the 339 is the inferior train and should go into the hole. He grins and types in a series of commands that set up the meet, and we sit back and watch.

The 339 gets to Silio well ahead of 991, and the computer automatically routs it into the siding. As soon as it clears the east end, the switch goes back to normal. "You probably could have gotten 339 to Willard without slowing down the 991, but better safe than sorry," he says. A few minutes later the 991 moves east across the screen and clears Silio. Seconds after it clears, the west switch throws and the signals light up green for the westbound. Train 339 continues on its imaginary run westward.

The TTS not only handles training for the Santa Fe and the SP, but offers courses to all other railroads. Recent users include Amtrak, Kansas City Southern, FNM, and several shortlines and operating railroad museums. The TTS also has a complete series of videos to assist in training programs, and can provide specialized services, such as videotaping of railroad territories for specific clients.

Both the SP and the Santa Fe have built-in sequences which lead to possible accidents. SP's is a head-on collision, which was filmed at slow speed until the units actually coupled.

The Santa Fe's is a collision with a caboose, which was filmed as the camera backed away from the caboose, and is shown in reverse. The scenario takes place on a curve. The train that's being operated at the simulator is pulling into a siding, its forward view limited by a train on the main. The train eases around the curve only to find another train occupying the siding. These collisions test an engineer's observance of Rule 240, and the definition of restricted speed, "A speed that will permit stopping within half the range of vision, but not exceeding 20 miles per hour."

Back at milepost 475 we're in the 6th notch of dynamic braking, descending a 1.42 percent grade between Peach Springs and Truxton at a cool 71 mph, just slightly too fast. The instructor is probably figuring how soon he'll "fire" us. The snow-covered scenery flashes past.

At milepost 479 we have to be down to 25 mph for a sharp curve. After running 70 mph for the last four or five miles, we notch down and kick on the dynamics, then set the air slightly just past Truxton and begin to drop speed. By milepost 477 we're at 57 mph and the speed is falling off quickly. A second air application has us losing 20 mph per minute, as indicated on the speedometer by a secondary display reading "-20".

"That was too much air too soon, I'd have waited another half-mile," the engineer-trainer says, "but you'll be ok."

By milepost 479 we're well under the speed limit, rolling at 18 mph. We kick off the dynamics and notch the units back up as the day ends.

It's a fine mid-summer evening at Fort Madison, Iowa, the day's heat cooling as the sun slowly sinks into the western horizon. A headlight appears to the east, flashing through the gathering gloom. A four-unit lashup of DASH 8-40BWs rumbles by the depot with a long string of TOFC equipment: train 199. The train pauses for about 90 seconds, a Chicago crew stepping off one side while a Kansas City crew climbs up the other. A few seconds later the engineer bales off the air, notches 'em up, and roars out of town.

Ten minutes later the same scenario occurs with another intermodal train, this one powered by two GP60Ms bracketing two GP60Bs and a DASH 8-40BW. A long row of semi-trailers zip past. It must be 198, running right on time. Crew change complete, its flashing end-of-train device vanishes into the night, as steel wheels sing on welded rail, accompanied by crickets and the flutter of mayflys and June bugs dancing under the platform lights.

Five more minutes elapse, and the signal on the TCS siding changes to green. Train #3, the Southwest Chief, is near. A few moments pass and a headlight appears. The train swings into the 10,490-foot siding, and its new GEs chuff to a stop in front of the depot. The passengers begin to

board. In a moment they've exchanged the incandescent glow of the platform lights for the soft fluorescent lights of Superliners, muggy air smelling of lush countryside for sterilized air-conditioned chill. The train departs into the night, three minutes late.

In a few minutes the mist-shrouded landscape is blurring past at 90 mph. A low whoosh to the left interrupts the Southwest Chief's interior hush. It's slowly overtaking 198's piggy-backs, which are rolling west at a slightly slower pace on the south main.

It's a different story outside. The two trains are howling through the darkness, flinging a shower of dust and debris into the night sky. In a few moments 198's units are overtaken. Their diesels are roaring with incredible fury. At last they fall behind, the 198's headlight reflecting for a few minutes on the south main's parallel iron until it too is left behind.

In a few moments the sound of a parallel train builds again. Once again passenger overtakes freight, this time the 199. Once again the headlight beam of the overtaken freight slowly fades into darkness.

Minutes pass, or maybe hours. The train abruptly lurches, but gently. The speed has noticeably lessened, for the Southwest

SD40-2 5028 leads three six-axle units in a westbound charge through Ethel on April 15, 1989. Ethel lies in the midst of a "short mile," a mile with only 5,041.2 feet between the mileposts. This is a common practice when a track realignment reduces mileage (long miles when mileage is increased), as moving every milepost on the railroad and rewriting every piece of paper from timetable on down would be expensive. Use of a signal bridge facing one way and a cantilever facing the other is a common Santa Fe practice in Missouri, done to accommodate the ICC's now-cancelled requirement for field-side signalling. *Jill Oroszi*

Chief has just passed through a pair of #24 crossovers, which are only good for 50 mph. A few minutes later the reason for switching mains becomes apparent. A headlight suddenly appears on the right side, and disappears just as quickly, in a roar of steel passing steel at a combined closure of 160 mph. Undoubtedly its another Santa Fe intermodal train charging through the night to Chicago.

Arrival in Kansas City is seven minutes early, 12:38 a.m. Many freights have either been met or overtaken, all at speed.

On March 18, 1989, GP39-2 3446 leads
a GP30 and an SD40-2 on a transfer run
en route to Norfolk Southern's yard north
of the Missouri River in Kansas City.
The train is eastbound through the
"Gooseneck," in the northwest corner
of the city. The 2245 and 2373 are heading
back to Argentine Yard after delivering
a transfer to UP's ex-MoPac Neff Yard.
They're moving up the "Mop Incline,"
heading towards the Gooseneck, and
Santa Fe Junction. *Keith Wilhite*

On a very muggy August 5, 1985, two
eastbounds wait side by side at the east end
of the Kansas City Terminal, waiting for
the KCT dispatcher to clear them through
Sheffield Interlocking on the northeast
side of Kansas City. In a little over a mile
they'll leave the big city behind for the
fast track to Chicago. *Keith Wilhite*

The Southwest Chief *has regained the three minutes it lost east of Fort Madison plus seven more, all while weaving through a double-direction parade of freights. Though at one level, this has just been a pleasant way to travel from point A to point B, it's also been a fascinating tour of first class railroading at its finest, on Santa Fe's Missouri Main.*

The Santa Fe operates 199.5 mainline miles in Missouri, the "Show Me" state. Santa Fe's Missouri's mileage also includes 20 branchline miles, from the Missouri River bridge at Winthrop north to St. Joseph. The trackage between Winthrop and Rushville is also used by Union Pacific and Burlington Northern. Santa Fe's St. Joseph trackage is now isolated from the Santa Fe system, and is accessed via the BN mainline north from Kansas City.

A small piece of Santa Fe's Missouri mainline is owned by the Kansas City Terminal. Santa Fe uses the KCT for 6.4 miles, between Santa Fe Junction on the Kansas/Missouri state line and a point just east of Armco, on Kansas City's east side.

Santa Fe's Missouri trackage has no mountains, no beaches by the ocean, no deserts and no tunnels, but it does have immaculate, Class 5 CTC-signalled double-track, and a nonstop procession of fast trains.

This portion of the Santa Fe dates to William Barstow Strong's massive expansion of the railroad in the 1880s. Strong became Santa Fe's top man in 1881, and immediately began converting revenue into route-miles.

Strong decided the Santa Fe needed its own line to Chicago. He intentionally chose to ignore local traffic en route, feeling it had already been spoken for by competitors, and that it would degrade from the route's true purpose, which was to connect Kansas City and Chicago in the shortest, flattest, quickest means possible.

Chartered as the Chicago, Santa Fe & California on December 3, 1886, the new road was soon surveyed. Track gangs worked from many points simultaneously. At 6:00 p.m. on December 31, 1887, near Medill, Missouri, the last spike was driven.

The following year, the massive steel bridge over the mighty Missouri River at Sibley was completed, eliminating ferry service. Traffic volume greatly increased after the turn of the century, so the line was double-tracked between 1904 and 1915. The bridge at Sibley was completely rebuilt (while remaining open to traffic) between September 1911 and March 1914 to accommodate heavier trains.

Since the Kansas City-Chicago line was built as an "air line," it had few connections with other railroads. Since it was a relative latecomer, typically it was required to build fly-overs where it met other railroads, which were already occupying ground level. In Missouri, the mainline crossed seven railroads, not counting the KCT diamonds at Santa Fe Junction and Sheffield in Kansas City.

The busiest miles of Santa Fe's trackage in Missouri are the first 16 miles running east from the Kansas/Missouri state line.

The first 6.4 miles, owned by KCT, support several hundred rail movements a day, including Santa Fe, C&NW, Gateway Western, and Soo Line road freights, plus all Amtrak trains serving Kansas City and innumerable transfers. At one time Santa Fe Junction to Sheffield was quadruple track, but the installation of automatic CTC interlockings allowed its recent reduction to double track.

East of Union Station, at what would be Santa Fe milepost 451, the railroad heads northeast across the city on a 1.34 percent ruling grade peaking at Prospect Street. This area between Union Station and Prospect is known to Santa Fe employees as "the ditch," because of its below-grade location.

From Prospect Street, the railroad runs at a slight downgrade to Sheffield, where the KCT crosses UP's ex-MoPac Kansas City-Coffeyville, Kansas, mainline, and then Kansas City Southern's north-south mainline, and lastly an Armco Steel intraplant line at grade. Also, the mainline bridges the Big Blue River.

A dog's breakfast lashup eases through Sugar Creek with a westbound on December 7, 1991 — a GP30, two GP7s, SDFP45 93, and B23-7 6374. They'll pass the Sugar Creek depot in a few seconds. There was once a seven-track yard at Sugar Creek to handle the refinery's business. A maintenance-of-way siding and one track used for loading scrap metal from the disassembled refinery is all that remains.
Kevin EuDaly

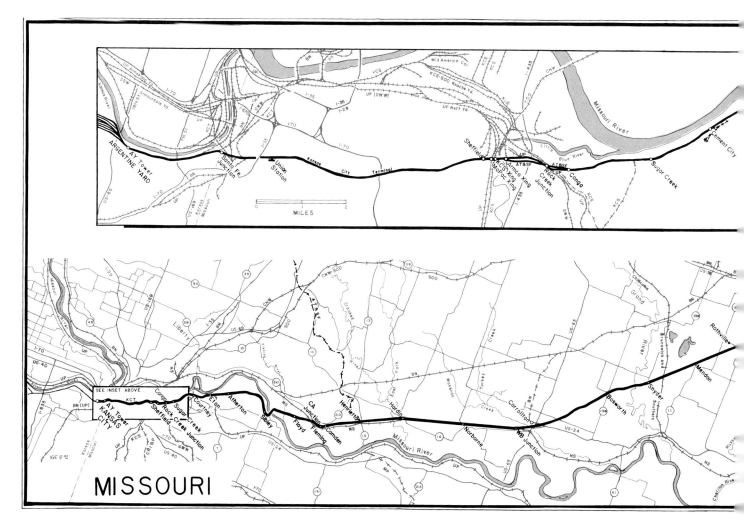

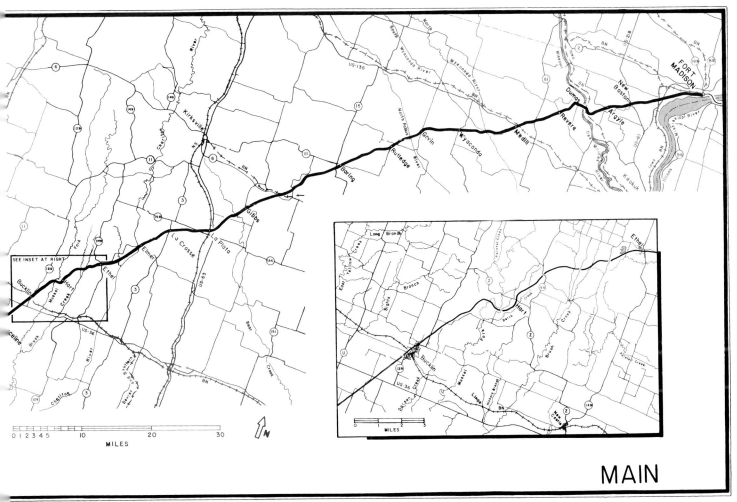

MAIN

During November 1991 GP38 2312 is reliably ticking off miles in its ninth year since remanufacture. The eastbound train it's leading is ascending the river bluffs just west of Sibley during November 1991, and will soon cross Santa Fe's bridge over the Missouri River. The speed limit here is 50 mph, though the engineer will soon be notching down his power to comply with the 30 mph speed limit over the bridge. On the mainline across Missouri left-handed operation is common, as Santa Fe's dispatchers shuffle hot trains around slow trains to avoid a bottleneck at the single-track Sibley Bridge. *Keith Wilhite*

Four GE Super Fleet units roll an early morning pig train across the bridge at Sibley and towards Chicago. Missouri Public Service's Sibley Plant is in the background. At this point the Missouri River is about a quarter-mile wide. The train will make a sharp right hand turn, then speed down the long ramp into the river bottoms at C.A. Junction, seven miles away. *Dave Cohen*

East of Sheffield the Santa Fe climbs up the south bluff of the Missouri River. At Rock Creek Junction it flies over UP's ex-MoPac mainline to St. Louis. This is followed by the UP connection one mile east of Rock Creek at Congo. Rock Creek also has the connection with the Gateway Western mainline to St. Louis.

Congo is accessible only by train or on foot from Rock Creek, or by driving down an often-locked wastewater treatment plant road from Sugar Creek. The tracks at Congo negotiate a five degree, 33 minute curve to get around the bluff east of the double crossovers. These crossovers allow access to or from either the UP low line or the Santa Fe high line. The two routes through Rock Creek are operated as double track, though normally only Santa Fe trains use the high line.

The next eight miles east of Congo are characterized by numerous curves, as the tracks skirt the river bluffs on the south side of the Missouri. Traffic here is doubly busy, as UP's Kansas City-Jefferson City River Subdivision runs joint with the Santa Fe from Congo to Eton.

Four miles west of Bosworth, veteran SDF45 5967 sails west on May 1, 1992, with the Q-CHHO1-29, which began its trip the day before in Chicago. The manifest's speed is limited only by its empty cars, as this is 80-mph trackage and there's plenty of horsepower on the head end. Nevertheless, this crew has been watching hotshots pass them all morning, as the Q-CHHO is one of the slower trains between Fort Madison and Kansas City. The two main tracks rejoin here after a slight separation for the previous one and one-half miles. *Kevin EuDaly*

At Sugar Creek, the hulking remnants of an abandoned oil refinery repose at trackside. The agency serving the refinery, when it was operating, was housed in the Sugar Creek depot on Kentucky Road. Now the depot merely provides shelter for maintenance-of-way tools and supplies.

Just to the east is Cement City, where a large cement plant was once accessed by a switchback. At Courtney a short spur houses maintenance-of-way equipment, and the main crosses Mill Creek.

Two miles east of the Courtney Road crossing at Courtney, the railroad negotiates a sharp, five degree, 53 minute curve, necessary to bend around a bluff and into Eton. The tracks continue to hug the bluffs through an inaccessible area to Eton. At Eton, UP's River Subdivision diverges, dipping south through Lake City, then following the Missouri River to Jefferson City. Crossovers are located on either side of the UP connection, allowing UP westbounds to cross over to Santa Fe's north track.

Fast track prevails from Eton east through Atherton, as here the mainline lies in the Missouri River flood plain. Mile-long tangents are interspersed with short, broad curves. The longest tangent runs for two miles through Atherton.

After crossing the Little Blue River east of Atherton, the mainline climbs up the river bluffs west of Sibley, gaining the elevation it needs to cross the navigable Missouri River on the huge bridge at Sibley. Sibley is also the site of a large Missouri Public Service power plant, which is fed by southern Illinois coal interchanged by the UP to the Santa Fe through Eton at Sugar Creek.

At West Sibley, the railroad necks down to single track and crosses the Missouri River on the 4,057-foot-long Sibley Bridge. This one and one-half mile stretch is the only piece of true single track on the Missouri Mainline. It's also a bottleneck.

A quarter-mile-long, six degree curve at each end of the bridge — the sharpest curves on the Missouri Main — and the bridge itself limit speeds to 30 mph. Both curves are protected by Automatic Train Stop.

On the south bank, the track pops out of the bluffs 100 feet above the river, passes through three 396-foot through-trusses, then the 4,000-foot-long east approach, and after negotiating the six degree curve on the river's north side expands back to double track. A two mile-long fill then carries the railroad 65 feet above the flood plain. The tangent east of the bridge at East Sibley through Floyd to the NS flyover is nearly seven miles long.

After racing down the long straight through Floyd, trains hit a curve west of C.A. Junction, where the Santa Fe crosses over NS's Kansas City-Moberly, Missouri, mainline. Crossovers connect both Santa Fe mains with the parallel NS main at C.A. Junction.

From C.A. Junction to the crossovers at Hardin, 12.8 miles, the north two tracks are Santa Fe's, and the south track is NS's. This section is operated as triple-track, though the NS main has a lower speed limit.

The railroad lies in the flat Missouri River flood plain through Henrietta to Carrollton. From Hardin to the double crossovers at W.B. Junction (just west of Carrollton), the north track is Santa Fe and the south track is NS, providing a joint double-track operation.

At Henrietta, the secondary mainline to St. Joseph formerly diverged to the northwest. This line also continued on to the southeast until the 1930s, to reach North Lexington. The line to St. Joseph was abandoned in several stages in the late 1970s, the final five miles on January 31, 1984. The depot at Henrietta has been used by maintenance-of-way crews since its closure a decade ago.

The 30.5 miles from Camden to Carrollton includes only six curves on the north track, and the entire 7.9 miles from Norborne to W.B. Junction is dead straight. Imaginative photography in this area is a formidable challenge. At W.B. Junction a final set of double crossovers marks the end of NS joint trackage.

After crossing Wakenda Creek and passing the depot at Carrollton, the railroad leaves the flat Missouri River flood plains for the gently rolling countryside of northern Missouri. To leave the valley, the railroad angles northeast up a feeder of Little Wakenda Creek. In keeping with its air line concept, the mainline slashes northeast across the remainder of Missouri with little in the way of interchanges, branches or spurs.

At several locations between Carrollton and Mendon, the two mains separate slightly, providing photographic interest. The first separation is a one-half mile section just east of Carrollton between mileposts 385 and 384. After one-half mile of normal double track, the lines again separate slightly between MP 383.8 and MP 381.1.

After crossing Big Creek at MP 378.5, the tracks separate at MP 378, four miles west of Bosworth. A bridge over the tracks at this location offers a wonderful place to watch Santa Fe's trains sailing across Missouri. The south track is at a slightly higher elevation than the north track on this stretch. The tracks swing back together at MP 376.5, and run side by side into Bosworth.

East of the double crossovers at Bosworth, the tracks separate slightly for three miles and race across the Grand River valley to Rothville, on near-tangent track which include a pair of crossovers at Mendon. Past the Grand River Bridge at MP 370, and following the curve at MP 368.8, there is only one curve (if a 30-minute curve can even be called a curve!) clear to the other side of Rothville, a distance of 14.6 miles.

Climbing out of the Mussel Fork River Valley just east of Hart, GP39-2 3705 and company have the battle almost won as they pass milepost 335 eastbound with train 1-781-08. Another half a mile and the train will crest the top of the 0.8 percent climb it's been on since milepost 337.6. Curves in this area suppress the speed limit to 40 mph. Thanks to the long strings of pigs in tow, that's about all these units can do. *Kevin EuDaly*

The area between Carrollton and Rothville ranges from short small grades of less than one percent, each less than a half-mile in length, to a dead flat stretch between the Grand River and Rothville.

At Rothville, the tracks begin a five mile climb up a 0.8 percent ruling grade into Marceline. Marceline is a classic midwest railroad town, with rows of well-kept brick homes on quiet, tree-lined streets. The yard at Marceline, which was a crew change point for all crews until recently, is situated between the two mains. Crossovers are located on either side of the yard.

East of Marceline the railroad is just a touch more undulating than to the west. At Bucklin, the Santa Fe flies over BN's east-west Galesburg, Illinois-Kansas City mainline. A seldom-used interchange track is located on the northwest side of the crossing.

East of Bucklin the fun begins. The next ten miles are about the prettiest of Santa Fe's Missouri Main. A three and one-half mile, 0.8 percent downgrade puts the railroad into position to cross Mussel Fork. Then it climbs three miles back up on the same gradient to leave the Mussel Fork drainage. The valley is comprised of rolling farms interspersed with woodlands inhabited by deer and wild turkeys. Missouri Road Z crosses the tracks on the east side of the valley at Hart.

Curves predominate until the rails reach Ethel, which has a crossover at both ends of town and a CTC-controlled siding off the south main accessible from both tracks. Two other locations in Missouri share the same set-up, Baring and Medill.

Between Bucklin and Elmer several roads cross the tracks, but otherwise this territory is largely not road accessible. It's also an area where 40 and 45 mph speed restrictions are the norm, due to many three and four degree curves.

High speed track returns east of Ethel, as the terrain flattens out. At Elmer a four mile, 0.83 percent climb begins, Cardy Hill. It's the toughest climb for eastbounds in Missouri, and peaks at Cardy. Undulating terrain resumes through La Plata, which

has double crossovers west of town. It remains much the same through Gorin, which also has double crossovers east of town, and Wyaconda. The final set of crossovers in Missouri are located at Medill, which is also the easternmost CTC siding in Missouri.

From Medill the tracks drop down a three mile-long 0.8 percent grade to the Fox River Bridge, then climb up about three miles of 0.8 percent ruling grade to Revere, and finally drop down four miles of 0.8 percent to the Iowa state line at the Des Moines River Bridge, MP 252. There are many nice scenes in the rolling hills west of the Des Moines River. The mainline crosses the Des Moines River and heads towards Fort Madison on Santa Fe's 20.0 miles of Iowa mainline.

The bulk of Santa Fe's traffic across Missouri is intermodal trains to and from Chicago. The 213 and 952 operate to and from the Conrail connection at Streator, Illinois. The 103 and 301 are most likely the slowest Santa Fe trains between Chicago and Kansas City. The stars are the Q-NYLA/Q-LANY and the 199/991, which race across the state every day. Amtrak's *Southwest Chief* runs across the state eastbound in daylight, but the westbound normally traverses Missouri in darkness.

The schedule included in this article summarizes Missouri's Santa Fe freights. It's important to realize that scheduled times are often dependent on connecting traffic, e.g., S-LACH5 and S-LACH8, which depend on trans-Pacific container traffic, and trains often run early or late. Some of the hotter trains, such as Q-LANY and Q-NYLA, are regularly early, sometimes by two or three hours. The traffic across Missouri tends to be heavier from early morning through early afternoon. The days of operation column has been adjusted to reflect the actual days the trains run across Missouri, not the days the train arrives or departs some far-off terminal.

On the KCT one can see nearly anything that operates into Kansas City, though the Santa Fe is the biggest player. This track hosts the four daily Gateway Western freights to and from St. Louis: 233 arriving Kansas City at 12:00; 268 arriving at 15:00; 322 departing Kansas City at 04:00; and 332 departing at 12:30. These operate on both the KCT and Santa Fe's main from the Kansas state line to Rock Creek Junction. From Rock Creek east they run on Gateway Western, which is former Chicago Missouri & Western, ex-Illinois Central Gulf, ex-Gulf Mobile & Ohio, and originally ex-Chicago & Alton. From Rock Creek Junction to Eton there is additional UP traffic, and Cotton Belt via trackage rights.

The Sibley coal trains are one of the more interesting movements on the Missouri Mainline. These trains load at one of three mines in southern Illinois; Captain, Burning Star #2, or Zeigler #11. UP crews take the trains westbound from the mines through St. Louis to Eton, where they get on joint Santa Fe-UP track, and take the train into Sugar Creek. After cutting off the power (usually four UP units) east of the depot, the UP crew ties down the power to the depot and calls a taxi, for their work day is over.

The Santa Fe is notified, and sends out a replacement crew. The Santa Fe crew takes the power light through Congo, then reverses direction and runs back east, crossing over to the other main and back past the patiently waiting string of "Reddi Kilowatt" Missouri

Public Service cars, pausing to attach an end-of-train device. When cabooses were still in use, two were used on these trains, one on each end.

The power runs east to Eton, crosses over, and backs down on the train. The train is hauled 16 miles east to Sibley, where it enters the plant's balloon track. Unloading takes about eight hours, so an unloading trip is a full crew day. After unloading, the train is left at Sugar Creek for a UP crew, who will reverse the whole procedure.

Missouri Public Service owns only one train set, which makes two to three round trips a week when coal is needed. When sufficient coal is stockpiled, the train lays over at the power plant. According to Roy Runyon, the plant's Fuel Superintendent, Sibley will continue to burn southern Illinois coal through 1992, but by mid-1993 it will probably switch to Powder River Basin coal. Several test burns of western coal have already been completed.

Besides the extra traffic on the Rock Creek to Eton segment, there also is NS traffic between C.A. Junction and W.B. Junction, amounting to five or six trains each way daily. This includes a Triple Crown RoadRailer in each direction. Occasionally the NS and Santa Fe detour on each other's trackage between C.A. Junction and Kansas City because of mishaps or maintenance windows.

The next time you are wandering across the middle of Missouri with a few hours on your hands, forget boring I-70, and head across the state on U.S. Highway 36. Leave 36 at Bucklin, and drive five minutes to Hart. Now you're in position to enjoy high-iron double-track railroading at its finest. Don't forget to pack a lunch, or at least a snack, because when the parade hits, it can be tough to leave.

At Union Station in Kansas City, the engineer on #3 hits his distinctive K5LA horn twice. The train eases out of the station, gathering speed down the hill toward Santa Fe Junction.

Darkness comes and goes as the moon passes in and out of large clouds moving in from the northwest. In a few short moments a rumble is heard. A westbound headlight pierces the darkness, shining off the rails in a shimmering display of scattered light. Distant thunder rolls through the darkness as large drops begin to splatter the concrete platform. Four DASH 8-40BWs rumble slowly by, the rails creaking under their weight.

The engineer on 199, with some help from the dispatcher, has made up lost time. The conductor waves from the cab. He's almost home, for the Missouri Main is behind him.

A clean SD40-2 eases its train off the west end of the Sibley Bridge, and onto the south bank of the river on January 2, 1989. The train is stretched across the bridge's three 396-foot through trusses. The 5039 is from the Santa Fe's first order for SD40-2s, built in October 1977. Remanufactured in September 1988, it's just beginning its second career. *John Hake*

Trains on the Show Me Main

Eastbound Trains
(Departing Kansas City, Arriving Fort Madison)

Train	Days	Dp KC	Ar FM
951	Fri-Tue	00:40	06:15
771	Thur-Mon	01:15	06:10
961	Thur-Mon	04:40	10:00
991	Thur-Mon	04:45	09:25
971	Thur-Tue	04:55	10:05
S-LACH1	Daily	05:30	10:55
S-LACH5	Wednesday	05:30	10:55
791	Mon/Thur/Sat	05:45	10:35
391	Tue/Thur/Sun	07:30	13:30
Amt #41	Daily	07:40	11:10
781	Wed/Fri	07:40	13:00
881	Sun-Mon	08:20	13:15
952	Thur-Tue	09:00	15:40
Q-LANY1	Daily	11:05	15:45
Q-HOCH1	Daily	19:00	01:00
301	Mon-Sat	19:00	05:00
581	Tue-Sat	19:20	01:00
861	Sat-Mon	20:30	03:15
891	Wed-Mon	21:35	02:15
S-LACH8	Thursday	23:30	04:15

Westbound Trains
(Departing Fort Madison, Arriving Kansas City)

Train	Days	Dp FM	Ar KC
185B	Sat-Sun	01:25	06:10
185A	Mon-Fri	02:05	07:00
189	Daily	02:45	07:30
183	Mon-Sat	03:00	07:55
Q-CHHO1	Daily	03:45	11:30
213	Daily	04:00	12:30
S-CHLA1	Tue-Sat	06:05	11:05
169	Tue-Sat	09:10	14:40
194	Tue-Sun	10:10	15:05
188	As Req.	10:30	15:30
168	Wed-Sat	14:45	20:00
Q-NYLA1	Daily	15:10	20:00
197	Tue/Thur/Sun	16:40	21:50
165	Tue-Sat	18:05	22:55
199	Daily	18:30	23:00
103	Mon-Sat	19:00	05:00
Amt #31	Daily	21:05	00:45
198	Daily	21:30	02:15

Three TP&W GP20s roll past the station sign at El Paso, Illinois, with an eastbound on March 11, 1989. El Paso is just under 30 miles east of East Peoria, amidst one of the many stretches of tangent track typical of the TP&W. The railroad is also painfully flat — painful for the power, because TP&W's trains are usually assigned just enough units to grind up its inclines. The TP&W's longest climb is about three miles. *David Fasules*

Three freshly remanufactured, repainted ex-TP&W units sit outside the shops at San Bernardino, California, ready to go to work for their new owner on March 23, 1985. Trailing GP40 2964 was wrecked three years later at Pico Rivera, California. The TP&W was always able to afford better motive power than most railroads its size, thanks to its 50/50 Santa Fe and Pennsylvania Railroad ownership. *Gary Sugg*

The paint scheme chosen for the "new" TP&W is derived from the New York Central's two-tone grey lightning-stripe scheme, as modeled by GP20 2003 on March 4, 1990, in East Peoria, Illinois. Only a handful of the TP&W's units have been repainted to date. *George Horna*

the Hoosier State), adjacent to I-65 between Remington and Wolcott, Indiana. Its capacity, when completed that November, was 34 flat cars. Westbound, the Hoosier Lift was served by train 278 departing at 02:30 for Los Angeles. Eastbound, piggyback service was provided by the 282, scheduled out of Fort Madison, Iowa, at 00:30, and arriving Hoosier Lift at 11:00.

It should be noted that the TP&W's mainline relied on two sections of trackage rights. Rights over terminal road Peoria & Pekin Union were used for about five miles in Peoria, track which included the P&PU's drawbridge over the Illinois River. Rights were granted to the TP&W in the 1960s over the Santa Fe between the TP&W's west end at Lomax, Illinois, and Fort Madison, Iowa, 16 miles, to achieve better operating efficiency for both carriers.

Prior to July 1983, the Santa Fe had a secondary, northern connection with the TP&W, via a branch between Ancona and Pekin, Illinois, which crossed the TP&W at Eureka. The Santa Fe used six miles of TP&W trackage rights between Eureka and Pekin Junction to reach the southern end of the branch. With the TP&W purchase in the offing, the Santa Fe had little need of the branch, and abandoned it on July 7, 1983. The TP&W leased a portion of the branch's south end, between Pekin Junction and Morton, for some time to serve remaining customers. The TP&W wasn't happy with the arrangement due to excessive operating costs, so it obtained trackage rights over the N&W to Morton on November 8, 1983.

The TP&W's trains were renumbered by the Santa Fe on October 1, 1983. The eastbound Effner Local, #24, became the 471, and westbound #25 became the 174. Peoria-Kansas City road freight #121 became 223, and its counterpart, the #122, became Santa Fe 322. Train #21 became 172. The Hoosier Lift trains retained their Santa Fe numbers, 278 westbound and 282 eastbound.

Three years later, in 1986, the Santa Fe had changed its mind about the TP&W, and set about to rid itself of what had turned out to be a marginal, unimportant operation. In June 1986, the TP&W's 28-mile secondary line from La Harpe to Keokuk, Iowa, by now a rather weedy branchline, was sold to the Keokuk Junction Railway.

During November 1987, the Santa Fe announced plans to sell the TP&W to a New Jersey partnership, the TP&W Acquisition Corporation. The sale was soon postponed by the threat of a strike, until a court ruling upheld the rights of railroads to sell branchlines without reaching new labor agreements with involved employees.

On January 31, 1989, the Toledo, Peoria & Western was resurrected. The deal included 19 Santa Fe GP20s, rolling stock, and the Hoosier Lift.

The TP&W Acquisition Corporation began operating the railroad on February 3, 1989. The TP&W was its own railroad again. Though it went through initial growing pains common to many spinoffs, it has since managed to rebuild much of its track, win new coal business, and even repaint a few of its locomotives in its New York Central-derived lightning-stripe scheme.

Toledo, Peoria & Western's 1980s Pre-Merger Roster

Road#	Model	Built	Build#	Disposition	Notes
102	GP7	01/52	15634	To Michigan Northern-1607 12/83	
103	GP7	01/52	15635	To Michigan Northern-1608 12/83	
202	RS-2	05/49	76819	To Octoraro Railway-2 11/83	2
205	RS-2	09/49	77404	To Octoraro Railway-5 11/83	
206	RS-2	12/49	77886	Scrapped mid-1980	3
207	RS-3	12/50	78460	Scrapped 05/83	4
303	SW1500	02/68	33520	To Chrome Crankshaft 12/83, to NASA	5
304	SW1500	02/68	33521	To Clarendon & Pittsford-502 12/83	5
305	SW1500	05/70	36164	To Chrome Crankshaft 12/83, to NASA	6
306	SW1500	05/70	36165	To Chrome Crankshaft 12/83m to NASA	6
400	RS-11	11/58	83008	To Illinois Railway Museum 11/83	7
401	RS-11	11/58	83009	To B&K Engineering 09/83	1,8
402	RS-11	06/59	83444	To KB&S-11/83	9
600	GP18	04/61	26655	To Vermont Railway-801 12/83	
700	GP30	09/63	28534	To Santa Fe-3285 01/16/84	10
800	C-424	09/64	3382-1	To Morristown & Erie-18 12/83	11
801	C-424	09/64	3382-2	To Morristown & Erie-19 12/83	1,12
900	GP35	11/65	31061	To Santa Fe-3462 01/12/84	13
901	GP35	11/65	31062	To Santa Fe-3463 01/25/84	14
902	GP35	11/65	31063	To Santa Fe-3464 01/12/84	15
1000	GP40	05/69	35054	To Santa Fe 01/16/84	16
2001	GP38-2	05/77	766058-1	To Santa Fe-3561 01/16/84	1,17
2002	GP38-2	05/77	766058-2	To Santa Fe-3562 02/10/84	18
2003	GP38-2	05/77	766058-3	To Santa Fe-3563 01/31/84	19
2004	GP38-2	05/77	766058-4	To Santa Fe-3564 01/24/84	20
2005	GP38-2	10/78	776122-1	To Santa Fe-3565 01/24/84	21
2006	GP38-2	10/78	776122-2	To Santa Fe-3566 01/31/84	22
2007	GP38-2	10/78	776122-3	To Santa Fe-3567 02/04/84	23
2008	GP38-2	10/78	776122-4	To Santa Fe-3568 03/28/84	24
2009	GP38-2	10/78	776122-5	To Santa Fe-3569 03/11/84	25
2010	GP38-2	10/78	776122-6	To Santa Fe-3570 01/08/84	1,26
2011	GP38-2	10/78	776122-7	To Santa Fe-3571 01/13/84	2

Notes:

1. Briefly wore Santa Fe-style herald
2. Nose chopped 08/71 and repainted red
3. First unit repainted in red and white scheme
4. Nose chopped 1972
5. Flexicoil trucks, MU connections. Delivered in red and white scheme
6. Flexicoil trucks, no MU connections. Delivered in red and white scheme
7. Repainted red 02/71
8. Wrecked 08/28/64 at U.E. Jct., rebuilt with chopped nose 12/64
9. Converted to snowplow. Sold to Kankakee, Beaverville & Southern
10. Wore TP&W's bicentennial paint scheme. Remanufactured and renumbered 2785:2 by Santa Fe, Cleburne, Texas, 07/03/84
11. Wrecked shortly after delivery and rebuilt in kind by Alco 06/65. Painted red 10/70
12. Wrecked shortly after delivery and replaced by an essentially new C-424 06/65
13. Rode on trucks from trade-in RS-2 200. Remanufactured by Santa Fe as 2961, San Bernardino, 01/23/85, using Blomberg trucks
14. Rode on trucks from trade-in RS-2 201. Remanufactured by Santa Fe 2962, San Bernardino, 10/30/84, using Blomberg trucks
15. Rode on trucks from trade-in RS-2 203. Remanufactured by Santa Fe as 2963, San Bernardino, 12/27/84, using Blomberg trucks
16. Built as EMD-21 "loaner unit," arrived on TP&W 07/19/69, acquired by TP&W 10/10/69. Only modern TP&W unit with dynamic brakes (F3As 100 and 101 also so equipped). Renumbered 1000 10/28/69. Remanufactured as 2964 by Santa Fe (to GP35 specifications), San Bernardino, 08/29/84, classed "GP35." Retired 02/24/88 following 01/22/88 wreck at Pico Rivera, California
17. Renumbered 2370:2 03/24/85
18. Renumbered 2371:2 03/16/85
19. Renumbered 2372:2 04/07/85
20. Renumbered 2373:2 05/03/85
21. Renumbered 2374:2 04/08/85
22. Renumbered 2375:2 05/01/85
23. Renumbered 2376:2 04/06/85
24. Renumbered 2377:2 03/13/85
25. Renumbered 2378:2 04/30/85
26. Renumbered 2379:3 05/13/85
27. Renumbered 2380:3 05/17/85

The Santa Fe doesn't go to Santa Fe anymore. Nor does the Santa Fe even connect Atchison and Topeka now, except rather indirectly. Take a Santa Fe system map of the 1960s, and lay the system map of 1992 over it, and something is immediately apparent: the Santa Fe's branchlines are fading away.

Throughout the 1980s the Santa Fe's mileage was almost perfectly static. So static that the sale to the Keokuk Junction Railway on June 12, 1986, of 33 miles of former TP&W trackage between La Harpe, Illinois, and Keokuk, Iowa, and Hamilton and Warsaw, Illinois, was considered highly newsworthy. Though other large railroads, in particular CSX, NS and Conrail, sold off hundreds of small, unprofitable fragments, the Santa Fe seemed content with its mileage, and with the SFSP merger on the horizon, selling off a few unimportant branchlines wasn't of great import.

In actuality there were a number of abandonments and sales, but most of these were small branch lines with no remaining customers and received little notice. Examples of such are the abandonment of the Prescott Branch between Abra and Prescott, Arizona, on August 16, 1984, following minor washout damage. The Cushing District in central Oklahoma was next. This line, from Camp to Cushing, 25.5 miles, became the Cimarron River Valley Railway on January 1, 1985 (and has since been abandoned). The branches from Pauls Valley to Lindsey and Camp to Fairfax, Oklahoma, were abandoned at the same time, on April 14, 1986.

After the merger failed, the Santa Fe took a renewed interest in streamlining the railroad, and in the past four years it has made up for its lost time by trimming with a vengeance.

In mid-1988, the Santa Fe announced its former Orient Line was for sale. This lengthy branchline in western Oklahoma and Texas was a big part of the never-completed Kansas City, Mexico & Orient, purchased by the Santa Fe in 1928. Thus began the Santa Fe's branchline sale program. In the west, only the UP has been as equally ruthless in eliminating low-density trackage. Coincidentally or not, almost all of the track sold to date by UP has been former Missouri Pacific branchlines in much the same service area as many of the Santa Fe branches that have been sold off.

The Santa Fe then announced it wanted to trim its mileage by one-fourth, and that it preferred sales rather than abandonments. How serious were they? In 1988 the Santa Fe had approximately 12,000 route miles. By early 1993, the Santa Fe will be about a 9,300-mile carrier, losing about 2,700 miles through sale (or pending sale), just shy of the one-fourth goal.

The first major divesture was the TP&W, which was sold to the TP&W Acquisition Corporation on February 3, 1989. This was followed by the sale of the 38-mile Clarkdale Branch between Drake and Clarkdale, Arizona, to the Arizona Central on April 13, 1989. The primary customer on this line is a cement plant, but some tourist business has since been developed.

Thirty miles of western Kansas trackage was sold to the Garden City Northern Railway (a subsidiary of the Garden City Western) in late 1989. This trackage, the west end of the severed Great Bend Subdivision (which looped through central Kansas to the north of the passenger mainline) ran from Garden City to Shallow Water, and originates grain.

The long-dormant Grand Canyon Branch from Williams Junction to Grand Canyon, Arizona, 64 miles, was sold on September 17, 1989, becoming a tourist line, the Grand Canyon Railway. This company ran its first excursion train on September 18, 1989, behind a 2-8-0, and has since become a surprisingly successful operation.

Next went the tiny Tonkawa Spur in Oklahoma to the North Central Oklahoma & Midland Railway, on October 30, 1989.

The 39.2 mile Crosbyton Subdivision and the connected 2.0-mile Snyder Spur in the Texas Panhandle were sold to the Crosbyton Railroad on December 21, 1989. This railroad ran only a few trains, using Santa Fe equipment, before giving up and abandoning its trackage on September 14, 1990.

In 1990, the Santa Fe got down to business. The northernmost 60.1 miles of the Paris Subdivision from Paris to Farmersville, Texas, was sold to Chaparral Railway Company (a Kiamichi subsidiary) on April 6th. This has been a successful operation, in large part due to Kiamichi's experience and because of good on-line traffic.

The 26.9-mile Floydada Subdivision between Floydada Junction (Plainview) and Floydada in the Texas Panhandle went to the Floydada & Plainview on May 7th. This line is still in operation, running several times weekly.

The 65-mile Seagraves Subdivision and the connected 39.8-mile Lehman Subdivision went to the American Railway Company on April 1st, for operation by the Seagraves, Whiteface & Lubbock. The first-named line runs from Lubbock to Seagraves, Texas; the second from Doud to Whiteface, Texas. This line is likewise still operating, relying like the F&P on agricultural customers.

Eight random branches and spurs in Kansas, Texas, and Colorado, all dormant, went to KCT Railway Corporation (the initials standing for Kansas, Colorado & Texas) on May 2, 1990. Owned by Salt Lake City-based A&K Railroad Materials, a used-rail dealer, it's doubtful the KCT has ever run a train, and most of the KCT track has since been pulled up.

The Santa Fe branch in Kansas sold to KCT was a 52.6-mile portion of the Tulsa Subdivision between Iola and Ottawa. It was abandoned later that year.

In Texas, KCT purchased four branches, three of which were abandoned within two months. Those KCT lines abandoned by July were the 9.6 mile Garwood Subdivision between Rayner Junction and Garwood, the

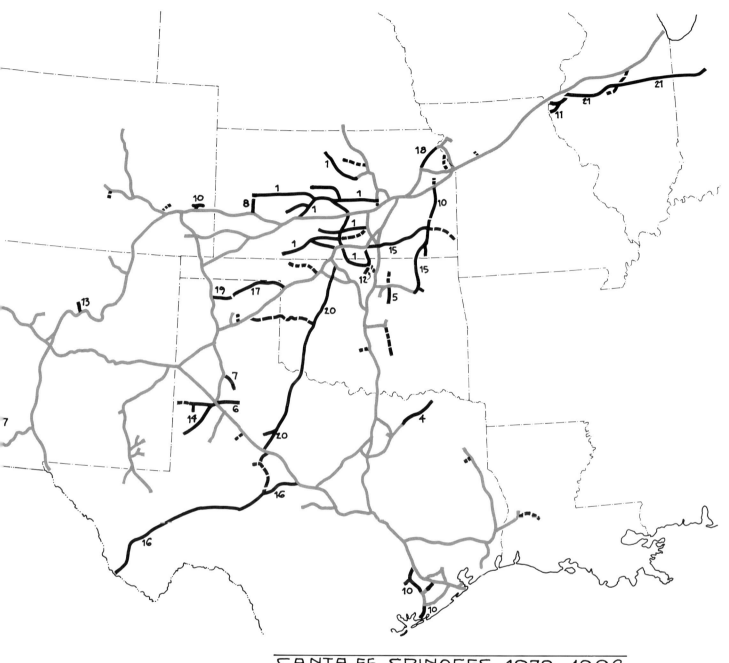

SANTA FE SPINOFFS: 1979-1992

1 AMERICAN RAILWAY
2 ARIZONA & CALIFORNIA
3 ARIZONA CENTRAL
4 CHAPARRAL RAILWAY
5 CIMARRON RIVER VALLEY RAILWAY
6 CROSBYTON RAILROAD
7 FLOYDADA & PLAINVIEW
8 GARDEN CITY NORTHERN RAILWAY
9 GRAND CANYON RAILWAY
10 KCT RAILWAY
11 KEOKUK JUNCTION RAILWAY

12 NORTH CENTRAL OKLAHOMA & MIDLAND
13 SANTA FE SOUTHERN
14 SEAGRAVES, WHITEFACE & LUBBOCK
15 SOUTH KANSAS & OKLAHOMA
16 SOUTH ORIENT RAILROAD
17 SOUTHWESTERN RAILWAY
18 T&P RAILWAY
19 TEXAS-NORTH WESTERN RAILWAY
20 TEXAS & OKLAHOMA RAILROAD
21 TOLEDO, PEORIA & WESTERN

EXISTING LINES 1992
LINES SPUNOFF 1979-1992
LINES ABANDONED 1979-1992

MWH - 8-92

The branch from Lamy to Santa Fe, New Mexico, was sold to the Santa Fe Southern on March 16, 1992. Included was GP7 92, ex-Santa Fe 2075, and caboose 999569, at Santa Fe the day before operations began. Both have been painted into Santa Fe Southern's snappy red and yellow scheme. *Chris Raught*

southernmost 10.4 miles of the Matagorda Subdivision between Wadsworth and Matagorda, Texas, and the middle portion of the Hall Subdivision between New Gulf and Smithers Lake, 25.1 miles. The other Texas trackage was the northernmost portion of the Matagorda Subdivision between Sealy and Wharton, 43.1 miles. This was also subsequently abandoned.

Colorado trackage purchased was the 2.0 mile La Junta Industrial Air Base Spur, the Lamar Industrial Spur from Lamar to Wilson Junction, 6.1 miles, and the Wilson Junction Industrial Spur from Wilson Junction to Wiley, 4.9 miles. Agricultural customers on these lines long ago vanished. Of KCT's track, only the Lamar Industrial Spur is still in place, as the city of Lamar is fighting its abandonment and may purchase the line.

Two widely-separated lines were sold to Southwestern Railway Company on April 14, 1990. One of these was a bundle of copper mine spurs in southwestern New Mexico's Silver City Mining District, the 16.3 mile Santa Rita Subdivision between Whitewater and Santa Rita, plus the Tyrone Spur and the Fierro Industrial Spur. The other line is a seasonal grain-originating line in the Texas Panhandle, the 102.1 mile Shattuck Subdivision from Shattuck, Oklahoma, to Morse, Texas (which is only operated as far as Perryton).

On January 1, 1991, the South Kansas & Oklahoma Railroad, a subsidiary of short-line operator Watco, Inc., took over the westernmost 145.7 miles of the Tulsa Subdivision between Iola, Kansas, and Tulsa, Oklahoma (the remainder of the subdivision north of Iola had previously been sold to KCT and abandoned). It also took over the 123-mile Moline Subdivision from Chanute to Wellington, Kansas, and the 16.9-mile Coffeyville Subdivision from Cherryvale to S.E.K. Crossing, Kansas, just south of Coffeyville. The South Kansas & Oklahoma connects with the Southeast Kansas Railroad, also a Watco operation, at S.E.K. Crossing.

The most important sale since the TP&W sale was on May 1, 1991, when mini-regional Arizona & California Railroad was created from Santa Fe's secondary line from southern California to Phoenix, Arizona. Sold to the A&C were the Cadiz, Parker and Ripley Subdivisions in California and Arizona, 240 miles. Santa Fe guarantees overhead traffic between California and Phoenix to the Arizona & California, plus there's some on-line produce business on the Ripley Subdivision.

On June 25, 1991, 43 miles of the original mainline between Parnell (just west of Atchison) and Topeka, Kansas, were sold to the T&P Railway. Like the KCT, this is an A&K Railroad Materials operation, and since traffic is non-existent it's likely headed for abandonment.

The long-awaited sale of the Orient Line came as no surprise, but the sale was difficult. The original buyer couldn't com-

plete the deal, and there was controversy as counties the Orient Line passes through, plus shippers, worried that a shortline operator wouldn't be able to make a go of the sparsely-trafficked line.

On June 1, 1991, the Texas & Oklahoma Railroad Company began operations on the northern segment of the Orient, between Cherokee, Oklahoma, and Maryneal, Texas, 358.7 miles. This was previously Santa Fe's Altus Subdivision between Cherokee and Altus, Oklahoma, the Hamlin Subdivision between Altus and Hamlin, Texas, and the Sayard Subdivision between Hamlin and Maryneal.

Operation of the Altus Subdivision was contracted to Rio Grande Pacific, an affiliate of Texas shortline Wichita, Tillman & Jackson. Operation of the Hamlin and Sayard Subdivisions was contracted to Texas North Orient Railroad, an American Railroads Corporation subsidiary. Each operator purchased four Santa Fe GP7s, which says everything about the minimal

Freshly repainted in a sharp gray, red and yellow scheme, South Orient GP9 204 rests at Saginaw, Texas, on March 6, 1992. The railroad started up operations with leased Santa Fe power. These were replaced by five ex-Rio Grande GP9s, 5903, 5904, 5922, 5942 and 5941, which became the 200-204, respectively. This extremely long-distance operation runs through some of the most barren desert in North America. *Mark Lynn*

One of Santa Fe's most intriguing spinoffs is the Arizona & California, a sale which indicates the Santa Fe may not merely be interested in selling off weedy branchlines, but also secondary mainlines. Evidence is this westbound A&C train near Grommet, California, on November 16, 1991, heavy with overhead Santa Fe business behind its three GP38s. A&C's green, cream and yellow scheme is one of the best paint schemes around, a refreshing improvement on the awful, ugly schemes which defile far too many regionals and shortlines. *Chris Butts*

traffic density on the Orient, and why the Santa Fe saw no reason to retain it. Texas North Orient has already applied to abandon 77 miles between Cherokee and Thomas, Oklahoma.

The south end of the Orient, Santa Fe's San Angelo Subdivision from San Angelo Junction to the Texas-Mexico border at Presidio, 386.6 miles (including 11.1 miles of trackage rights on SP's Sunset Route), was sold on January 1, 1992, to the South Orient Railroad. The $5.5 million purchase price was paid by the counties the line runs through and several Dallas investors.

Operation of the South Orient has been contracted to a Kiamichi subsidiary. Five ex-Rio Grande GP9s were purchased for operations; like its northern two counterparts, it's a lot of track for very few locomotives, summing up its limited traffic base in one fact. Sale of these lines eliminated almost all remaining branchline trackage in West Texas from Santa Fe's system map.

On March 16, 1992, the Santa Fe Branch, from the mainline junction at Lamy to Santa Fe, New Mexico, 18.1 miles, was sold to the Santa Fe Southern, along with one GP7 and a caboose. The Santa Fe now no longer goes to its namesake city.

Most recently, the Santa Fe announced a sale of over 850 miles of Kansas and Oklahoma trackage to American Railway Corporation, due to close on September 1, 1992. This trackage will gut out almost all Santa Fe branchline trackage from southern and central Kansas, and northern Oklahoma.

The lines to be sold in central Kansas are the 88.4-mile McPherson Subdivision between Marion and Ellinwood, the 120.1-mile Great Bend Subdivision from Great Bend to Scott City, the 98.4-mile Hutchinson Subdivision between Yaggy and Kinsley (except for the easternmost 4.9 miles between Yaggy and Hutchinson), the 46.2-mile Larned Subdivision between Larned and Jetmore, and the 53.4-mile Little River Subdivision between Lyons and Galatia. These lines are all connected. An isolated piece of Kansas trackage included in the deal are the westernmost 80.8 miles of the Osborne Subdivision between Salina and Osborne.

In southern Kansas, the lines sold to American Railway Corp. will be the 161-mile H&S Subdivision between Hutchinson and Wellington, Kansas (which loops into Oklahoma, as far south as Blackwell), the 77.6-mile Wichita Subdivision between Wichita and Pratt, the westernmost 119.6 miles of the Englewood Subdivision between Rago and Englewood, and the 50.6-mile Medicine Lodge Subdivision between Attica and O.B. Junction. These lines are likewise

all connected, and connect with the northern lines at Hutchinson.

The mileage reduction trend will undoubtedly continue. The branchlines in California's Central Valley will probably be the next to go.

Within a few more years the Santa Fe map won't have the ball of yarn in its midsection that made the railway's map distinctive for decades. It will be nothing but trunk lines, connecting Chicago, Kansas City, Dallas-Fort Worth, Houston, Los Angeles and San Francisco. The original mainline via Raton Pass will probably survive, thanks to increased coal business.

A few branches with major industrial customers, like the Carlsbad Subdivision in eastern New Mexico, and a few secondary lines that handle big through trains, like the Boise City Subdivision, are unlikely candidates to leave the Santa Fe system. In other words, if it doesn't have signals or big rail, it won't be Santa Fe for long.

Southwestern Railway acquired six Santa Fe GP7s, 2072, 2163, 2164, 2171, 2182 and 2211, as well as SD45 5316, to handle its business in New Mexico, Oklahoma and Texas. An empty concentrate train is led westbound by 2163 and 2164 at Burro Mountain Junction, New Mexico, on the Tyrone Industrial Spur during November 1990. Most of Southwestern's power has since been repainted in a scheme derived from Santa Fe's war bonnet. *Jim Pallow*

Business Car Fleet

Few railroads are able to assemble a passenger train as attractive as Santa Fe's stainless-steel fleet. Santa Fe's business and excursion cars are maintained in virtually spotless condition. They're used for everything from Director's Specials to one or two car outings for local groups. The Santa Fe's seven business cars are based at Argentine Yard in Kansas City, and are under the supervision of Homer Henry, Director Operating Practices and Manpower Planning. The rest of the fleet is based at Topeka, Kansas.

The history of Santa Fe business cars is an interesting affair. The first two cars for official use were built by Pullman in 1893. Two more came in 1907, and from there the fleet expanded to meet the rising needs of the railroad.

The Santa Fe built many of their own business cars at the railway's coach construction shops, using oak, fine Philippine mahogany, elegant wool rugs and a great deal of polished brass fittings. In the late 1920s, most of Santa Fe's wood business cars were sheathed in steel to extend their useful life.

Two types of cars predominated in Santa Fe's fleet, long cars for ranking officers, and short cars for division superintendents. General managers also had their own cars, in between the short and long cars in both size and quality of interior appointments.

Santa Fe's division superintendents used their cars as both a work place and living quarters while away from home. The superintendent's car was an absolute necessity for his travel to every corner of his territory. Roads were lousy, automobiles unreliable, and the few motels existent were "Motor Courts" more suitable for fisherman than the conduct of company business.

Assignment of business cars to superintendents was no longer necessary once paved highways extended into every corner of the Santa Fe system, and the practice was discontinued in the 1960s. By the 1980s Santa Fe's general managers lost their cars as well. The fleet was consolidated, and unnecessary equipment was eliminated from the roster. Remaining cars were rebuilt for use as system business cars.

"Signing up for business cars within the Santa Fe is much like reserving a meeting room for business purposes," says Santa Fe's Janelle Gossett, who oversees the daily operations of the fleet.

Primary uses for the cars are marketing, holding meetings with clients, and meeting with railroad and government officials. Of course, the directors can't be left out, and Santa Fe's Director's Specials are matched by few railroads and bettered by none.

Each of Santa Fe's cars is decorated with paintings and artwork representative of the railway's Southwestern heritage. Exotic inlaid woods are used for much of the interior finish. The interior of each car is essentially customized, with its own color scheme, furniture and matching upholstery. Much of the furniture tends to be on the

A Director's Special winds slowly down the three percent grade on the west side of Glorieta Pass in New Mexico, under light drizzle on April 21, 1985. The SDFP45s for many years were about the *only* motive power for Santa Fe passenger specials; this one has a trio of the 3,600-hp cowl units. *John Lucas*

A full-length dome provides an excellent view of the countryside. Car 60 is currently the Director's Dome Lounge Car. Fourteen full-domes were built for Santa Fe by Budd (plus six for Great Northern), for the *El Capitan, San Francisco Chief, Kansas Cityan,* and *Chicagoan.* Santa Fe retained just one; it's deadheading back to Argentine Yard on train Q-LANY at Holliday, Kansas, on February 22, 1992. *Kevin EuDaly*

small side, though it's equally stylish. Most chairs are weighted with lead to ensure stability.

Most of the cars contain a plaque with information on the car's history. Interior equipment includes microwaves, refrigerators, televisions and computers. The *William Barstow Strong,* car 89, also has a complete set of grade profiles for consultation during track inspections.

Several Santa Fe trains frequently get the railway's stainless steel on their tail end. Probably the most commonly used trains for carrying Santa Fe's business cars across the system are the Q-LANY/Q-NYLA and the 199/991. Another very common move, though with limited geographic interest, is on train 326, which moves cars based at Topeka between Topeka and Argentine (Kansas City).

Solid business car trains are designated "O" for Officer trains. A similar symbol is "T", used for Track Geometry or Inspection trains.

Santa Fe currently has no plans to either curtail its business car fleet, nor to greatly expand it.

The following roster provides details on cars on the roster during the last 15 to 20 years. The majority of the information comes directly from Santa Fe's business car profile book, maintained with the business cars at Argentine. Fortunately, the Santa Fe has retained most of its business cars records.

In general, the roster is identical to Santa Fe's business car profile book, though a few corrections have been made. Information on the most recent rebuilding of the cars is provided so far as it's known.

The bar area of full-dome 60 is decorated in southwestern Indian designs, as are many of Santa Fe's business car interiors. This April 1986 view reveals the car's original porcelain, crystal and silver have been replaced by the ubiquitous styrofoam cup. *John Huke*

Track Geometry car 89 brings up the rear of a Director's Special, eastbound at Rowe, New Mexico, on April 23, 1985. Rowe is on the passenger main between Las Vegas and Lamy, New Mexico. Westbound coal from the York Canyon Mine rolls over this route, as well as Amtrak's *Southwest Chief* and Denver freights 448 and 844. In 1985 the 89 had not yet been rebuilt into the *William Barstow Strong.* The car's outward appearance remained much the same after rebuilding in 1990. *John Lucas*

Business car 50, the *Santa Fe,* is one of two such business cars built by Budd for Santa Fe in 1957. The CB&Q purchased a similar car, the *Burlington.* These were the only business cars ever built by Budd. Based out of Argentine, the *Santa Fe* frequently brings up the rear of business car specials and passenger excursions. Here, the *Santa Fe* is on a special en route to Abilene, Kansas, to commemorate Dwight D. Eisenhower's 100th birthday on October 14, 1990. The Santa Fe was used on Eisenhower's funeral train in 1969. *Kevin EuDaly*

The only sleepers in Santa Fe's passenger car fleet are six 4-4-2 *Regal*-series sleepers built for the *Super Chief* in 1950. All are based at Topeka, Kansas. These cars are not true stainless-steel cars such as Budd built, but Pullman-built with stainless-steel sheathing over high-tensile steel framing. Car 68, the *Regal Spa,* rolls east toward Chicago on March 31, 1992, on the tail end of Q-LANY1-29 at Hart, Missouri. *Kevin EuDaly*

Santa Fe's Business Car Roster — July 1992

Car #	1st#	2nd#	3rd#	4th#	Builder	Built	Order#	Date Reno.	Length	Width	Eave Height	Extreme Height	Truck Centers	Wheel-base	Weight*	Notes
50	5003				Budd	1957	9664-186	12/89	87'6"	9'10"	13'6"	15'10"	62'0"	73'0"	175,140	1,40,44,45,46
51	5002				Budd	1957	9664-186	05/90	87'6"	9'10"	15'10"	15'10"	62'0"	73'0"	174,100	2,40,44,45,46
52	5001				Pullman	1949	6882	08/88	85'0"	10'0"	13'6"	14'7"	59'6"	68'0"	161,240	3,40,42,45,46
53	5004				Pullman	1949	6835	11/90	85'0"	10'0"	13'6"	15'1"	59'6"	68'0"	152,320	4,40,42,45,46
55	32				Pullman	1924			81'11"	9'10"	14'2"		57'6"	68'6"	184,600	5,40,44,45,46
56	34				Pullman	1923										6,43,45,46
57	35				Pullman	1924										7,43,45,46
58	38				Pullman	1925	4883	07/81	81'11"	9'10"	14'2"		57'6"	68'6"	195,200	8,41,44,45,46
60	506				Budd	1954	9646-129	02/85	85'0"	9'10"	15'6"	15'7"	59'6"	70'6"	184,960	9,41,43,45,47
61	600				Pullman	1950	6851	02/82	85'0"	10'0"	13'6"		59'6"	68'6"	157,860	10,41,42,45,46
62	1348				Pullman	1947	6734	04/82	85'0"	10'0"	13'6"		59'6"	68'6"	130,400	11,41,42,45,46
63					ACF	1950	3358	05/82	85'0"	10'6"	13'6"	14'3"	59'6"	68'6"	150,793	12,18,41,42,45,46,49
64					ACF	1950	3358	05/82	85'0"	10'6"	13'6"	14'3"	59'6"	68'6"	150,793	13,18,41,42,45,46,49
65					ACF	1950	3358	05/82	85'0"	10'6"	13'6"	14'3"	59'6"	68'6"	150,793	14,18,41,42,45,46,50
66					ACF	1950	3358	05/82	85'0"	10'6"	13'6"	14'3"	59'6"	68'6"	150,793	15,18,41,42,45,46,50
67					ACF	1950	3358	05/82	85'0"	10'6"	13'6"	14'3"	59'6"	68'6"	150,793	16,18,41,42,45,46,50
68					ACF	1950	3358	05/82	85'0"	10'6"	13'6"	14'3"	59'6"	68'6"	150,793	17,18,41,42,45,46,50
70	3179	5008			Pullman	1947	6734		85'0"	10'0"	13'6"		59'6"	68'6"	155,000	19,42,45,46
73	30	5009			Pullman	1918			82'0"	9'10"	14'2"		57'6"	68'6"	192,300	20,43,45,48
74	3935				Pullman	1965			73'11"	10'0"		13'6"	48'5"	55'9	184,600	21,42,45,46
75	3906				Pullman	1962	7022		73'11"	10'0"	13'6"		48'5"	55'9	90,960	22,42,45,46,51
76	1346	5010			Pullman	1950	6847		85'0"	10'4"	14'2"		58'6"	67'6"	135,600	23,42,45,48
77	3914				Pullman	1962	7022		73'11"	10'0"	13'6"		48'5"	55'9"	90,960	24,41,42,45,46,51
80	1508	5000			Pullman	1926										25,43,45,46
83	1338	5001	5015		Pullman	1914			77'3"	10'0"	14'3"		54'4"		169,700	26,41,44,45,46
85	39				Pullman	1928	6165	1973	81'11"	9'10"	14'2"	14'8"	57'6"	68'6"	200,480	27,41,43,45,46
86	3922	133	199207		Pullman	1965	Lot 7022		73'11"	10'0"	13'6"		48'5"	55'9"	184,600	28,41,42,45,46
87	2952	3122	1527	5005	Pullman	1930										29,41,45,46
88	3911				Pullman	1964	7010	1979	71'9"	10'0"	13'6"		48'5"	57'5"	119,300	30,40,42,45,46,51
89	1397				Budd	1940	Lot 96902	08/90	79'8"	10'6"	13'6"	15'0"	54'2"	63'2"	124,940	31,40,42,45,46
131	3927				Pullman	1965	Lot 7022		73'11"	10'0"	13'6"		48'5"	55'9"	184,600	32,42,45,46
134	3916				Pullman	1965	Lot 7022		71'9"	10'0"	13'6"		48'5"	55'9"	120,840	33,42,45,46,52
135	3936				Pullman	1965	Lot 7022		73'11"	10'0"	13'6"		48'5"	55'9"	184,600	34,42,45,46,52
138	3931	140			Pullman	1965	Lot 7022	1970	73'11"	10'0"	13'6"		48'5"	55'9"	184,600	35,42,45,46
139	3918				Pullman	1965	Lot 7022	1970	73'11"	10'0"	13'6"		48'5"	55'9"	179,120	36,42,45,46
1869	82	31	54		Pullman	1918	Lot 4530	02/90	81'11"	9'10"	14'2"		57'6"	68'6"	197,880	37,40,43,45,46
205878	130	6	9005	3707	Pullman	1956			63'11"	10'0"	13'6"					38,42,45,46,52
205879	132	3920			Pullman	1965	Lot 7022		71'9"	10'0"	13'6"		48'5"	55'9"	120,840	39,42,45,46

Notes:

1. Business Car *Santa Fe*. Rebuilt December 1989.
2. Business Car *Topeka*. Rebuilt May 1990.
3. Business Car *Atchison* (ex-*Santa Fe*). Rebuilt August 1988.
4. Business Car *John S. Reed* (ex-53, the *Mountainair*, ex-U.S. Steel *Laurel Ridge*. Acquired 1962. Rebuilt November 1990.
5. Business Car. Sold to Conrail 1982.
6. Sold to Caboose Antiques, Nederland, Colorado, 1980.
7. Off roster.
8. Business Car. To be rebuilt.
9. Dome Lounge. Built for *El Capitan* service.
10. Diner *Fred Harvey*. Built for *Super Chief* service. Rebuilt February 1982.
11. Club Lounge. Built for *El Capitan* service. Rebuilt April 1982.
12. Sleeper *Regal Crest*.
13. Sleeper *Regal Hunt*.
14. Sleeper *Regal Lane*.
15. Sleeper *Regal Lark*.
16. Sleeper *Regal Manor*.
17. Sleeper *Regal Spa*.
18. 4-compartment, 4-bedroom, 2-drawing room sleeper built for *Super Chief* service.
19. Locomotive Simulator Car. Former 26-seat Chair/Club 3179. Rebuilt 1969 to 5008. Condemned at Topeka as of May 1992.
20. Classroom/Film Car. Former business car. Off roster.
21. Safety instruction car, converted from baggage 1976. Capacity 70,000 pounds. Off roster.
22. Baggage. Capacity 70,000 pounds. Off roster.
23. Air brake instruction car. Former club-lounge, built for *El Capitan*. Converted 1972. Renumbered 1974 to 76. Off roster.
24. Baggage. Capacity 70,000 pounds.
25. Diesel Instruction Car. Previously Observation Cafe 1508. Converted to Diesel Instruction car 1947. Donated to Smokey Hill Railway & Historical Society, Inc. July 1977.
26. Research and Test Car. Former Buffet Library 1338 *San Juan*. Converted in 1939 to Power Plant Test Car 5001, later became Dynamometer Car 5015. Renumbered 83 in 1973.
27. Track Geometry Car. Former business car, converted in 1973.
28. Baggage. Converted to Steam Heat Car 133. Became weed/spray car 199207, then 86. Currently Track Geometry Support Car.
29. Exhibit Car. Burned at Topeka February 1, 1977, scrapped.
30. Display Car. Former baggage. Converted to display car 1978-1979. Displays removed 1984, later reinstalled.
31. Track Inspection Car *William Barstow Strong*. Rebuilt 1975 as track inspection car. Rebuilt again August 1990.
32. Retired 1982.
33. Retired 1982.
34. Retired 1982.
35. Steam Generator Car. Former baggage. Off roster.
36. Steam Generator Car. Former baggage. Off roster.
37. Business Car *Cyrus K. Holliday*. Previously USRA-82, assigned to Santa Fe during WWI. Renumbered 31 in 1920, became the 54 in 1973. Rebuilt February 1990.
38. Tool car 205878, currently in use.
39. Tool car 205879, currently in use.
40. Based in Kansas City, Kansas, at Argentine Yard.
41. Based in Topeka, Kansas.
42. Equipped with 2-axle trucks.
43. Equipped with 3-axle trucks.
44. Equipped with 2-axle trucks, previously had 3-axle trucks.
45. Equipped with 36" wheels and roller bearings.
46. Equipped with disc brakes.
47. Equipped with rotor type brakes.
48. Equipped with clasp type brakes.
49. ACF order 3358, specification 2871.
50. ACF order 3358, specification 2872.
51. Pullman builder's dates for these cars are 1963.
52. Sold to Metal Processing, Vinton, Texas, March 31, 1987, scrapped.

A. Cars numbered in boldface were in service as of June 1992.

B. Baggage weights are either actual or capacity.

Santa Fe FP45 100 glistens in red and silver in its builder's photo at the EMD plant in La Grange, Illinois, during December 1967. Its steam generator is housed at the rear of the unit, between the radiator/equipment rack area and the back wall. *EMD Photo*

The queens of the Santa Fe fleet are its cowl units. Though this design was shared with other Class I freight railroads, only Santa Fe's are still racking up millions of ton miles.

The quintessential Santa Fe cowl units are the red and silver war bonnet SDFP45s. For Santa Fe, indeed even America, the cowl story goes back to the mid-1960s.

The term "cowl" is generally applied to locomotives with a full-width, non-structural carbody. Though somewhat similar in appearance to the "covered wagons" of the past, such as EMD's carbody F-units and E-units, Alco's FAs and PAs, and various Baldwin and Fairbanks-Morse units, cowls are substantially different. The carbody in carbody units is structural, a box steel truss that spans between the trucks, whereas in cowl units the carbody is merely a removable sheet metal appendage.

Structural carbodies were used on the very first diesel-electric locomotives. This was logical, as diesel-electrics were largely an outgrowth of heavy electric locomotives, which typically used structural carbodies.

Beginning with the GP7 in 1949, EMD wisely eliminated structural carbodies and instead began designing heavy underframes which provided all necessary structural strength. No new EMD designs after that date, except for the F9, E9 and FL9, have relied upon structural carbodies.

The Santa Fe initiated cowl designs when they requested from EMD and GE a modern passenger passenger locomotive with an attractive appearance. Despite much misleading press, this was the only major advantage of the cowl. Minor advantages of the cowl design were reduced wind resistance, ease of making minor repairs en route, and reduced area for ice and snow accumulation during winter.

A substantial disadvantage to the cowl design was poor maintenance accessibility. A prime example is the removal and installation of power assemblies, required whether the entire assembly is being replaced or often if something as minor as a seal has gone bad. EMD power assemblies weigh about 1,000 pounds each. GE power assemblies weigh considerably more.

On hood units, machinists can reach through the doors with a small hoist to maneuver a power assembly into and out of the crankcase. On cowl and carbody units, the machinists must wrestle these unwieldy chunks of iron through the engine room door, down the aisle along the side of the engine, lift them to shoulder height then gently lower them into the crankcase, doing this in a cramped, poorly lit engine-room while avoiding squashing anything and maintaining seal integrity. Once you've watched this time-consuming, sweaty procedure it becomes very clear why most

mechanical departments have lost all enthusiasm for repairing cowl and carbody units.

Of course, on cowl units the entire carbody *can* be lifted off to allow good engineroom access, but this requires disconnecting radiator lines, electrical cables to the dynamic brake grids and lights, unbolting a few thousand bolts, etc. Plus, a travelling crane to pick the cowl up is needed, there has to be plenty of overhead clearance to move it, and an empty shop floor to park it on while repairs are being made. An EMD hood unit, conversely, can generally be repaired at night in a Kansas cornfield by two machinists with a good set of wrenches.

GE's answer to Santa Fe's request for cowl units was the U30CG. Six were ordered. They were delivered in November 1967, and thus have the honor of being the first cowl units produced.

The U30CG's cowl was installed on a standard 67'-3" U30C frame. Mechanical and electrical details were essentially identical between the two models; both relied on GE's 3,000-hp 7FDL-17 powerplant. A steam generator was installed behind the

There are a few external difference between SDFP45s and the FP45s they were rebuilt from. The upper headlight and classification lights have been blanked out, the horn relocated, the number boards modified, the steam lines removed and the access plates in the pilot welded over, and a rooftop air conditioner installed. Paint-wise, the "Santa Fe" lettering is red instead of black, the nose stripes are no longer identical in width, and the shape and placement of the war bonnet stripes are different in most details. That's not much change in 22 years, but inside it's a considerably different story. The 102 is at Barstow, California, on November 11, 1989. *Mark Wayman*

Two years of use has made U30CG 405 a bit bedraggled. The 405, in its original red and silver paint scheme, is at Argentine Yard in Kansas City during November 1969. Its carbody was a severe departure from anything else GE built during the 1960s. Only six of the 3,000-hp beasts were built, all for Santa Fe during November 1967. *Harold K. Vollrath Collection*

U30CGs cab; GE had allowed room for a steam generator on the U30C, so no modification of the frame or equipment layout was required. The U30CGs were delivered as 400-405 in Santa Fe's standard passenger red and silver paint scheme. They were the only U30CGs built.

The U30CG's future was soon marred by their possible contribution to the derailment of the westbound *Grand Canyon* on Edelstein Hill two and a half miles west of Chillicothe, Illinois, on February 9, 1969. It was believed by some that the wreck was due to poor tracking characteristics of the U30CGs at high speeds on curves. The derailment also brought the similar U28CGs under suspicion.

On March 3 and 4, 1969, an attempt was made to duplicate the conditions of the derailment, using FP45s 104 and 106, and U28CGs 359 and 354. Though no conclusive cause for the derailment could be determined, the tests indicated that the stability and tracking dynamics of the U28CGs were not entirely satisfactory at high speeds.

The end result was that Santa Fe's ten U28CGs and six U30CGs were removed from passenger service. The U30CGs were later renumbered 8000-8005, and repainted into Santa Fe's solid blue freight scheme.

By mid-1980 the U30CGs were nearing the time when heavy repairs would be required. Given their high cost of main-

tenance, lack of versatility and uniqueness in the fleet, they were offered for sale along with the U28CGs. Not surprisingly, no buyer stepped forward, so on September 22, 1980, the U30CGs and U28CGs were traded in on new GE power. All were subsequently scrapped.

EMD's response to Santa Fe's request for cowl units was the FP45. Though based on the SD45, using the same 20-645E3 engine and AR10 alternator, an entirely new underframe was required, as the SD45 wasn't long enough to accommodate both a steam generator and a cowl carbody. The 3,600-hp FP45s were 72'-4" long, versus 65'-10" for the SD45.

FP45 production began in December 1967 with Santa Fe's order for nine. Unlike the U30CGs, they weren't a Santa Fe exclusive, as the Milwaukee Road also purchased five. About the only changes required to make the FP45s special for passenger service were their steam generator and steam connections, and high-speed gearing. After Amtrak took over Santa Fe's passenger service, they were converted to freight engines.

Santa Fe's FP45s were originally numbered 100-108, and like the U30CGs were delivered in Santa Fe's red and silver passenger scheme. Unlike the U30CGs, they still exist. They were first renumbered into the 5940 series, then the 5990 series, then

back into the 100 series (but not in order), then back into the 5990 series again (though not all got this renumbering), and most recently into the 90 series. One unit has left Santa Fe, the 5944 (originally the 104). It was wrecked at Toland, Texas, on September 13, 1981, and was subsequently scrapped.

Santa Fe liked its EMD passenger cowls, and ordered a freight version, the F45, for high-speed freight service. Production of this model stretched from June 1968 to May 1971, during which 86 were built. Santa Fe bought 40 of the 3,600-hp units, all of which were delivered in June and July 1968. Not needing a steam generator, they were shorter than the FP45s, measuring in at 67'-5-1/2". None have been removed from Santa Fe's roster. The other 46 F45s were ordered by the Great Northern and Burlington Northern, and of these, only a handful remain existent.

An FP45 in its first freight scheme rests at Chicago on June 23, 1974. Excepting the two versions of the red and silver war bonnet scheme, many feel this is the best paint scheme the F45s and FP45s ever wore. *George Horna*

Twenty of Santa Fe's SDF45s and seven SDFP45s received red and yellow SPSF merger colors. SDF45 5989 lounges in the sun at Barstow, California, on February 16, 1987. *Scott O'Dell*

F45 5903 idles at Tulsa, Oklahoma, on May 20, 1980, wearing Santa Fe's modern blue and yellow colors. The blue and yellow version of the war bonnet has been Santa Fe's standard for about two decades. *George Horna*

The F45s, numbered at delivery as the 1900-1939, wore the standard freight scheme of the time, blue with yellow stripes. They were later renumbered 5900-5939, remanufactured in 1982 and 1983, and now are numbered as the 5950-5989.

In April 1978, Santa Fe chose wreck-damaged FP45 5945 as a prototype for a remanufacturing program at San Bernardino for the 5900-series F45s and FP45s and the 5500-series SD45s. Beginning in September 1978, the 5945 underwent remanufacture, during which it was upgraded as closely as feasible to SD45-2 specifications. The unit was completed in December, but not renumbered.

In April 1980 the 5993 was released as the first remanufactured SDFP45. The 5995 followed in August 1981. In late 1981, Santa Fe decided to remanufacture all of its F45s and FP45s, after evaluating the performance of the rebuilt 5945 and 5993 versus the expense of their remanufacturing.

The first program F45 was released on February 17, 1982, as the 5963, following its remanufacture from the 5913. The final F45 to be rebuilt, the 5917, was released as the 5967 on November 10, 1983. The remaining FP45s were released in 1982, the last one out the 5997 on December 20, 1982. Model designations were changed from FP45 to SDFP45, and F45 to SDF45.

When Amtrak took over passenger service in the U.S., they needed new power at once, as the passenger units Amtrak acquired from the Class I carriers, primarily FP7s and E-units, were worn out and used-up.

One hundred and fifty SDP40Fs were ordered from EMD; they were built between June 1973 and August 1974.

Mechanically and electrically, the SDP40Fs were SD40-2s. Carbody-wise, they were equipped with a cowl derived from the FP45/F45. The SDP40F's frame and trucks were modifications of existing EMD designs. The trucks, though basically EMD's HT-C type, used hollow bolsters. Their center of rotation was also further off-center than standard freight HT-C trucks, which were already off-center by a considerable amount. These seemingly slight changes resulted in different truck spacing, weight distribution, centers of gravity and moments of inertia, which resulted in disaster.

Amtrak intended the SDP40F to be its standard long-haul passenger locomotive, its six-motor trucks and heavy weight making it suitable for heavy-grade mountain districts as well as high-speed runs across the Great Plains.

It was not to be. Almost immediately the SDP40Fs were involved in several major pile-ups which had similar characteristics. In each case the train was running between 40 and 60 mph, and entering a curve of about two degrees. It was found that the trailing truck of the trailing unit, or the first truck of the lead baggage car, had exerted extreme lateral pressure on the outside rail, resulting in the rail overturning and a wreck ensuing. In nearly all cases a minor track defect was found, but in each case the defect was not so large as to be disallowed under FRA Class 4 specifications.

Including Canada, a total of nine railroads could have lashed together five six-axle cowl units. Their presence on an intermodal train has an aesthetic appeal far beyond anything else on rails today. **SDFP45 5997 leads SDF45s 5989, 5960, 5950 and 5986 over California's Cajon Pass on the 883 train, during a publicity shoot on February 19, 1983.** *Santa Fe Railway, Mike Martin*

About ten derailments fit this pattern. The heavy yaw characteristics of the SDP40Fs as they entered curves at high speeds was believed the culprit. Nevertheless, the correlation could not be conclusively proven.

None of the pattern derailments occurred on the Santa Fe, perhaps because most Santa Fe trackage used by Amtrak meets FRA Class 5 standards. Three of the SDP40Fs, 501, 504 and 532, were wrecked on the Santa Fe at Lawrence, Kansas, on the *Southwest Limited* on October 2, 1979, but the cause of this derailment was that the train had entered a 30-mph curve at about 60 mph.

BN had the worst luck with the SDP40Fs. After a wreck at Ralston, Nebraska, on December 16, 1976, BN informed Amtrak it would no longer allow SDP40Fs on BN rails. BN later partially relented, and allowed the SDP40Fs to return so long as they were restricted to 40 mph on curves of two degrees or greater.

Thirty days after the wreck at Ralston, another pattern wreck occurred, this time

"Kodachromed" SDFP45 5998 sparkles in the sun on June 3, 1986, just after receiving a fresh coat of red and yellow merger paint. Seven of Santa Fe's eight existent SDFP45s (one had previously been scrapped) got the merger paint. This one's finish has yet to be marred with squashed bugs and road grime. *Gary Zuters*

on the L&N at Newcastle, Alabama. After this, the FRA instituted BN's 40-mph curve restriction nationwide. The restriction was later removed on Class 5 track, which included most of Amtrak's route-miles on Santa Fe.

It was easier, ultimately, for Amtrak to bail out of the SDP40Fs then it was to continue to fight the derailment problem. Despite their short life the SDP40Fs had already accumulated high mileage, and were coming due for major overhaul. Instead of overhauling the SDP40Fs, and making expensive modifications to their tracking characteristics — which since the cause was still unknown might not have solved the problem — Amtrak began trading them in to EMD for F40PHs. Many of the F40PHs were built using SDP40F components, thus carrying the model designation F40PHR. By the end of 1980 only 37 SDP40Fs remained on Amtrak's roster.

Rather than all the SDP40Fs going to scrap, however, a swap was worked out: Amtrak needed switch engines and work train engines, and the Santa Fe had these for sale. The Santa Fe traded 25 CF7s and 18 SSB1200s (SW7 and SW1200 switchers rebuilt at San Bernardino) to Amtrak for 18 SDP40Fs in September 1984.

Amtrak and Santa Fe also swapped the wheelset/traction motor combos between the SDP40Fs, and the CF7s and SSB1200s. The 57:20 high-speed geared combos from the SDP40Fs were sent to Amtrak in return for the 62:15 freight geared combos from the CF7s and SSB1200s. As the traction motors in all cases were D77s, neither Amtrak nor Santa Fe wound up short.

Since the SDP40Fs weren't in the best of condition, all were sent to San Bernardino for remanufacturing into SDF40-2s. The first rebuilt unit emerging from San Bernardino, on January 31, 1985, was the 5250, formerly Amtrak 643. Over the next five months Santa Fe rebuilt all 18. The major noticeable difference after rebuilding was the addition of a walkway and handrails in front of the nose, a feature not needed on passenger units but essential for freight units.

A problem soon arose with the SD40F-2s: crews felt they were difficult to board during rolling crew changes, due to their vertical front corner ladders instead of the usual steps. In October 1985, the Albuquerque Division issued a bulletin stating that crewmen were no longer required to make rolling crew changes when cowl units were on the point.

The next month, San Bernardino Shops began modifying the SDF40-2s. The nose door was locked to prevent its use by crews, a handrail was welded to block access to the front steps from the walkway, and the top two steps were covered over with sheet metal

to prevent use. These modifications were done during the units' 92-day inspections.

Another directive issued at this time banned all Santa Fe cowl units from running on the point. This was due both to the rolling crew change problem plus the difficulty in looking backwards from cowl units to make train inspections. The first reason held the most weight, so after rolling crew changes were banned, the ban on point service was lifted.

To improve access, the SDF40-2s were again modified. This time, a large chunk was sliced from the front corners of the

SDFP45 105 gets a drink at the west end of the fuel tracks at Barstow, California, on December 22, 1989. Behind it SDFP45s 104, 103, 102, 101, are likewise all being fueled. To the right, a large "Q" (for Quality) sign obscures a rendition of the Santa Fe "Chief," an image that graced the sides of Santa Fe's passenger units for several decades. *Mark Wayman*

In 1988, after winning a 14-month argument with the U.S. Customs Service, Santa Fe borrowed one of Canadian National's SD50Fs for in-service observation of CN's Safety Cab and desk-type control console. Crewmen across the system were polled, and the information used to perfect the design of Santa Fe's Super Fleet GP60Ms. Running east on the 891 train, CN-5456 approaches the Colorado River Bridge at Topock, California, on October 20, 1988. *Mark Wayman*

nose to allow full steps to be applied. This made it substantially easier to climb on and off the SDF40-2s, and they again returned to the point of Santa Fe trains.

It seemed here the story of Santa Fe cowls was over, and they would work the rest of their career in relative obscurity. Then, Santa Fe returned the SDFP45s to the limelight.

This time all it took was a paint scheme. Not just a paint scheme, *The* paint scheme: the red and silver war bonnet.

The war bonnet scheme dates to early 1937, when Leland A. Knickerbocker, an illustrator at General Motors Art and Color, Industrial Design Department, was charged with creating a paint scheme for Santa Fe's first E-units. Aware of the Indian motif used by Santa Fe's *Super Chief*, Knicker-bocker created a scheme using the profile of an Indian head and the trailing feathers of a war bonnet. He designed a bright yellow elliptical herald as well, the first time this style of herald was used by the Santa Fe.

His artwork was dated February 17, 1937, and by May the scheme made its debut on E1A number 2. The red and silver war bonnet went on to become probably the most famous railroad paint scheme of all time. After passenger service left the Santa Fe, however, the scheme was dropped.

While Santa Fe's Vice-President during the mid-1980s, Michael R. Haverty began considering ways to promote the railroad's high-speed freight services. By mid-1988 Haverty's office began exploring new paint schemes for locomotives Santa Fe would

soon be ordering for high-speed service. These locomotives would use a new type of cab, its design based on GMD's North American Cab. The new units were planned for delivery in 1990.

Haverty acquired an HO-scale model of a Santa Fe FP45, which had been lettered by Homer Henry, one of his management team, in a modified red and silver war bonnet scheme. On one side, the model was decaled in the FP45's as-delivered style, which used small, black Roman type to spell out Santa Fe. The other side used Santa Fe's current style, and was done in big red letters. Haverty preferred the big letters, and in early 1989 presented his idea to Santa Fe's board of directors. The proposal was not accepted.

Several months later John Swartz relinquished his position as the railway's president, and Mike Haverty moved into the position on June 1, 1989. By late June he had a pair of SDFP45s in red and silver, this time in 12"-to-the-foot scale. Haverty dubbed the red and silver units "Super Fleet" units, and presented them as the forerunners of Santa Fe's new crack intermodal locomotives.

The Super Fleet GP60Ms, delivered in 1990, were the first new locomotives to wear the red and silver since the FP45s were purchased in December 1967. As for Haverty's model, he placed it on his desk with the black lettering facing in, and the red lettering facing out. When he left the railroad, the model understandably went with him.

A freshly remanufactured ex-Amtrak SDP40F, now an SDF40-2, rests at Hobart Yard in Los Angeles during February 1985. The front porch was added by Santa Fe. The vertical front steps that would cause problems for these units at first are evident as well. This unit was released from the rebuild program at San Bernardino on February 4, 1985. Its trip to Hobart represents the only miles the unit has logged for its new owner since rebuilding. *Santa Fe Railway, Mike Martin*

Amtrak SDP40F 640 rests on shop trucks at Santa Fe's San Bernardino Shops, undergoing its remanufacture into SDF40-2 5256 during early 1985. It was released for service on March 6, 1985. The 18 SDP40Fs were acquired from Amtrak in exchange for 25 CF7s and 18 SSB1200s, adding a new cowl model to the roster and making the Santa Fe the nation's six-axle cowl king, with four different models and an all-time total of 73 units. *Kyle Brehm*

A pair of SDF40-2s work helper duty on the Joint Line at Sedalia, Colorado, on February 28, 1988. It's been a long, strange journey for these units, which were built for Amtrak. Oddly enough, they look just as at-home working coal drags as they did pulling Amtrak's finest. *Chuck Conway*

Cleburne

Capital remanufacturing was pioneered by the Illinois Central in 1968. Since dieselization the IC had relied almost exclusively on GP7s and GP9s. After 15 years of hard service on its Geeps, the IC was faced with the need to either replace them, or commit to a heavy overhaul program.

Among the solutions the IC discarded was new locomotives. First, new locomotives had become expensive, and the IC was not a rich railroad. Second, the IC had dieselized all at once, at a late date, so its fleet was wearing out all at once, requiring wholesale replacement at great cost. Third, the IC was a uniformly flat railroad, so high-horsepower locomotives weren't so necessary. Fourth, much of the IC was a maze of low-density, local service intensive secondaries and branches. The problem wasn't that the IC's Geeps were ill-suited to the railroad, or too small for their tasks. They were just worn out.

Instead of overhauling in kind, the IC decided to remanufacture its Geeps from the rails up. This allowed the inclusion of many maintenance reducing, performance enhancing features developed in the past 15 years, features such as solid-state electronic controls instead of troublesome, complicated relays and air-activated power switches, simplified 26L air brakes instead of the older, convoluted 6BL and 24RL designs.

The remanufactured IC locomotives were recapitalized as new locomotives for financing and tax purposes. This allowed a new depreciation cycle and provided big tax savings over locomotives that had been overhauled in kind.

The only components reused in IC's remanufacturing program were large, heavy, indestructible fabrications and castings which merely needed to be cleaned, repaired and inspected before reuse — components such as the frame, truck castings, the crankcase fabrication, and main generator and traction motor cases.

The IC started its program with five GP7s and six GP9s, changing their model designations to GP8s and GP10s, respectively, to reflect their improved performance after remanufacture. The new units were dubbed Paducah Rebuilds, for the IC shop at Paducah, Kentucky, where they were remanufactured.

Santa Fe's Mechanical Department quickly recognized the IC's solution was a good one. The Santa Fe likewise had a great deal of flat, low-density trackage. The Santa Fe also had a huge fleet of F-units which were outmoded in mainline service — not enough horsepower — yet the F-unit fleet represented a huge stockpile of reusable engines, traction motors, generators and so forth.

The result was the CF7, this model designation standing for "Cleburne F7." A prototype for the program, F7A 262C, was chosen and sent to Santa Fe's Cleburne, Texas, Shops. Here it was stripped of its components and carbody, and seemingly squished through a strange mold, emerging as CF7 2649 in February 1970.

There was no mystery to rebuilding diesel

engines, or wiring new electrical cabinets. What did present a problem on the CF7 program was the frame. The F-unit frame consisted of a trussed carbody integral with the roof and floor.

The carbody also made F-units unsuitable for low-revenue local service. Not only was rearward visibility terrible, but the lack of steps and the long climb to the cab from ground level made them uncomfortable for brakemen, who had to hang from a ladder when switching, instead of standing on a step like they could on a Geep. F-units cost more to maintain than Geeps, too, because of their confined and relatively inaccessible engineroom.

Cleburne got around the frame problem by torching off the carbody flush with the floor, and fabricating two large, long fishbelly girders which were welded to each side of the floor. These girders spanned from end to end, and allowed the existing frame to be reused without modification to its truck bolsters, engine mounts, fuel tank mounts and other appliance mounts. It was central to the success of the CF7 program. The solution wasn't entirely satisfactory, however. Frame droop (particularly in the rear, caused by too many hard couplings) and cracked fishbelly girders have been among the causes for subsequent CF7 scrappings.

The prototype CF7 employed a spare GP9 long hood to save money, and was equipped with dynamic brakes. All subsequent CF7s were equipped with newly-fabricated long hoods. It was recognized that locomotives intended for granger branchlines had little need of expensive to install and maintain dynamic brakes, thus this feature was excluded.

Early CF7s also reused some of the F-unit structural framing in the cab area, recognizable by a cab roof that conformed to original F-unit roof contour and recycled F-unit side windows. This was deemed more trouble than it was worth and later CF7s received entirely new cabs.

The CF7 program was the first remanufacturing program undertaken by the Santa Fe, and 233 of the versatile, reliable units were produced. The third CF7 outshopped, the 2647 (they were numbered downwards from 2649), sits at El Paso, Texas, on November 1, 1979. It's a good representative of the first CF7s, with the rounded roof retained from its F-unit parent. As built the 2647 had F-unit cab side windows, which were later replaced. The girder along the frame rail was added for structural strength. *George Horna*

Inside, the CF7s featured modern electrical cabinets, 26L brakes, and many more maintenance-reducing features. The 16-567BC engines, D12B-D14 generators, auxiliary generators, air compressors, and many other components from their F-unit parents were rebuilt in kind. Old D27 and D37 traction motors were rewired to modern D77 specifications by Santa Fe's San Bernardino Shops.

The CF7 program took eight years to be complete and numbered 233 units, 2417-2649. Many more F-units sacrificed their mechanical and electrical components for the program than is indicated by the number of CF7s created. If anyone doubts the worth of the program, just count the number of CF7s now working for dozens of regional and shortline railroads, and industrial switching companies.

During the first year of CF7 production, another experiment was tried at Cleburne. Baldwin VO1000 2200 was rebuilt into a model the Santa Fe lists as "Switcher" in its locomotive folio. The Switcher scarcely resembles its lineage.

The Switcher contains an EMD 16-567BC engine, trucks from an F7, and a GP7 long hood. Mechanically it's equivalent to a CF7, and like the CF7 it's rated at 1,500 horsepower. Now numbered 1460, it was the only Baldwin remanufactured by the Santa Fe. The Switcher is still on the roster, and has been working as the Topeka shop switcher of late.

The "BC" engine designation, it should be noted, refers to a upgrade of EMD's B design crankcase to partial C crankcase characteristics. EMD crankcase design progressed from the B model in the F7/GP7s, to the C model in the GP9/F9, the D model in GP20s through GP35s, E model in the 40 and 40-2 series locomotives, F in the 50-series locomotives, and the current G model in the 60-series locomotives.

Both 567 and 645 power assemblies (the number referring to the displacement in cubic inches of the power assembly) can be slipped into B, C, D and E crankcases, as both types have the same outside diameter. A common upgrade to older B, BC and C model crankcases is the installation of 645 power assemblies.

As an example, B&LE's F7s have 16-645BC engines, though they're still rated at 1,500 horsepower because their cooling and electrical systems can only handle 1,500 hp, and the existing crankshaft can't handle the longer throws of deep-stroke 645 assemblies. It's misleading to refer to these F-units as having "645 engines." It's better to say that they have "BC engines," which creates no confusion as to their rated horsepower.

The B engine was afflicted with water leaks, particularly at the lower liner seals, which after time began allowing water to leak from the liner jacket into the lube oil, which will eventually damage or ruin an engine. The root cause was expansion and contraction of the liners and the crankcase as the engine heated up and cooled down. (This is also one reason why diesel engines are left idling even in warm weather.)

In the mid-1950s EMD developed a BC upgrade for the B engine, which reused the B head and coupled it to a C liner. It also involved installation of water jumpers to route water into the C liners, but all in all it was an inexpensive upgrade.

BC upgrades were performed by many railroads. The Santa Fe performed it on its B engines either before or during the remanufacturing programs. The Santa Fe could have gone on to upgrade its BC and C engines with 645 power assemblies, but didn't feel the additional expense was justified. New 16-645E engines, which would have allowed an increase to 2,000 hp, were also deemed too expensive — at the time they were running about $150,000 apiece.

At the start of Santa Fe's remanufacturing programs, Cleburne was chosen to handle the work. By 1973 Cleburne was also remanufacturing Santa Fe's sizeable fleet of GP7s, and later the GP9s as well. Railfans have termed these GP7Us and GP9Us — U for Upgrade — but the the Santa Fe has never employed this "U" designation on any of its remanufactured units.

Cleburne went on in the next fifteen years to remanufacture 243 GP7s, 56 GP9s, 72 GP30s, 77 GP35s, 59 GP38s, 70 SF30Cs, 50 GP39-2s and one SF30B. Cleburne also built 35 slugs from various types of locomotives, and remanufactured three CRSD20s

from Alco RSD-15s. Except for the CF7s, the CRSD20s and the Switcher 1460, the other units were all remanufactured with little external change, making them difficult to distinguish from their as-built condition.

Some notes on the GP7 and GP9 programs. The first group of GP7s remanufactured, 2000-2004, 2050-2067 and 1300-1311, have four-stack manifolds and chopped noses, but retain their original cabs. Later remanufactured GP7s and GP9s have "Topeka Cabs," an improved cab fabricated at Santa Fe's Topeka Shops. The angular design also allowed for the convenient installation of rooftop air conditioners. GP7s 2005-2027, 2068-2243 and 1312-1329, and GP9s 2244-2299, are equipped with Topeka Cabs. The dynamic brakes were removed from all remanufactured GP7s and GP9s.

The point at which remanufacturing is performed is based on mileage, maintenance expenditures and failure rate. Most of the locomotives the Santa Fe has chosen for remanufacture have accumulated some two to three million miles. Once the locomotive enters the shop, the process is essentially identical no matter what the type.

First, the locomotive is thoroughly washed, in particular underneath the frame and in the engineroom. All fluids are drained, and miscellaneous access panels and engine handhole covers are removed. The trucks, wheelsets and traction motors are dropped out, separated, and each component sent to the shop that will rebuild it. In Santa Fe's case, this might mean that trucks all went to one shop, and traction motors to another. Wheelsets were reused if they still had remaining life, or replaced if not. Axles and gears were reprofiled and machined as required.

The locomotive is moved about on shop trucks for most of the remaining remanufacturing process. The long hood is removed and stripped, then sent elsewhere in the shop for sandblasting, any necessary repairs and modifications (such as the blanking of the dynamic brake grids) and painting with primer. The fuel tanks and air reservoirs are removed for cleaning, inspection, and repainting.

The main and auxiliary generators, and the engine are removed and dispatched to the shop that will handle their rebuilding

Radiators, the air compressor, the equipment rack and the high voltage cabinet are removed, and all wiring and cabling stripped out.

Once the locomotive is reduced to a frame, the remaining steel is sandblasted to remove loose paint and rust, then painted. Air brake piping, high-voltage cables and wiring go in first, then the electrical cabinet is installed and filled with its components and wiring. Much of the electrical cabinet is assembled using prefabricated wiring looms. The brake valves are installed under the cab and piped. The air reservoirs and fuel tank are reinstalled.

Generally the engine is stripped down to the empty crankcase. The crankcase is hot-tanked (soaked in hot cleaning solvent), repainted, and line-bored to return it to like-new tolerances. A new or remachined crankshaft is installed, using new bearings. New power assemblies are installed, along with remachined or new camshafts and gear train. The blowers or turbocharger, as the case may be, are rebuilt, usually by an outside contractor, and reinstalled.

The heavy rotating electrical equipment is either overhauled or remanufactured, as required. Generally main generator windings are sound and don't require replacement. The main generator is hot-tanked, reinsulated, and new bearings, commutators and brushes (on DC main generators) are installed. New diodes are installed on AC main generators if required. The air compressor is completely stripped down and its moving parts are replaced.

The rebuilt engine, generators and air compressor are installed on the frame and carefully aligned, followed by the equipment rack and miscellaneous engineroom components. New dynamic brake grids (if applicable) and new or rebuilt radiators are installed in the long hood, along with new or rebuilt cooling fans, and the long hood is reinstalled on the frame. The wiring and plumbing are hooked up to connect the engine with the radiators and equipment rack, and the cooling fans with the AC power supply system. Lighting is hooked up.

Up front, a rebuilt or new control stand has been installed. The air conditioner is serviced, or added in the case of older units. New seats and toilet are installed. FRA-approved cab window glazing is installed.

SF30C 9541 lays over at La Junta, Colorado, on October 22, 1991. The SF30C program was Cleburne's first major remanufacturing program focused on modern six-axle power. So far this has been the only railroad-run remanufacturing program in the U.S. to tackle big GE power.
Bruce Barrett

The trucks by now have been rebushed and rebuilt, and the rebuilt traction motors are installed using new wheelsets and rebuilt bearings. Often, the Santa Fe modified the brake rigging on remanufactured locomotives, converting double-clasp brakes to single-clasp "Tarrytown" brakes.

Once the locomotive is retrucked, it makes a trip to the paint booth. After painting and decaling, lubricants, fuel and water are added. The locomotive is fired up and its engine functions carefully checked. If all goes well, the locomotive is sent to the test cell for load-testing at full horsepower, often for 24 hours. Assuming no defects are discovered, the locomotive is released for a short test tour and finally to the operating department.

Cleburne was assigned the remanufacturing of U36Cs in 1985, the only large rebuilding program of General Electric locomotives yet performed by a railroad to date. It was also the only major program at Cleburne involving six-axle power.

The first U36C, 8721, was remanufactured and released during April 1985 as the 9500. To assure engine longevity, its horsepower rating was decreased from 3,600 to 3,000. The 9500 was designated an SF30C, for "Santa Fe 3,000 horsepower C-C."

Improvements made in the SF30C program included partial DASH-8 electrical equipment, and GE's Sentry wheelslip system. The electrical equipment was relocated from its original cramped, difficult to access space under the cab into the space behind the cab that GE had provided for a steam generators.

A Dash-7 type tilted oil cooler was added, permitting complete draining of coolant during cold-weather shutdown and eliminating potential freeze damage to the oil cooler. This feature is responsible for the

bulge immediately forward of the radiators at the rear of the SF30Cs. The cab and short hood were heavily revised as well.

Before the Santa Fe committed to the SF30C program, the 9500 was exhaustively performance tested, its maintenance costs and difficulties monitored, and its remanufacturing procedure analyzed for cost and inefficiencies. The information obtained from these studies was carefully number-crunched to determine if the program was economically justifiable.

This was typical for all of Santa Fe's major remanufacturing programs. The single-unit rebuilds were single-unit because they failed in one or more ways — either their performance was disappointing, the remanufacturing cost too high, or a combination of these and other reasons.

The SF30C program was launched full-scale five months later. It was projected that all 98 remaining U36Cs would become SF30Cs, though after 70 were completed the program was cancelled. About the only outward difference between the 9500 and subsequent SF30Cs was class lights on the 9500. In late 1985 the FRA dropped this requirement for locomotives.

While the SF30C program was ongoing, one group of GP39-2s came due for remanufacture. These were also done at Cleburne. The 3400 class GP39-2s (3400-3449) were remanufactured from 50 3617 class GP39-2s between August 1986 and January 1988. The 3648 had previously been destroyed. The 3640 had recently undergone heavy wreck repairs and didn't require remanufacturing. It turned out that these were the last locomotives remanufactured by Cleburne.

In September 1987, Cleburne turned out an interesting one-of-a-kind unit, the 7200. Originally U23B 6332, the 7200 came out of Cleburne as an SF30B, upgraded from

The SF30Cs have been entrusted with mainline road service, and many times they even draw hot intermodal trains. An example is five of the remanufactured units on the 1-881-30 on October 30, 1986, approaching Sullivan's Curve on Cajon Pass in perfect front/front/front/back/back formation. *Santa Fe Railway, Mike Martin*

2,300 hp to 3,000 hp.

Extensively modified, the 7200 had a big 4,000 gallon fuel tank for long-haul service that had been squeezed into the available space, a modified long hood to accommodate the enlarged cooling system that was required, and inside it was somewhat rearranged as well. The 7200 was the prototype for a program that would rebuild 50 aging U23Bs into high-horse road power. However, it was decided the program was too costly, more so because the 7200 was not successful as a 3,000-hp locomotive. The 7200 was renumbered 6419 and derated to 2,300 horsepower.

With the loss of this SF30B program, Cleburne was out of work. The Santa Fe decided it had at least one too many shops, so Cleburne was closed at the end of 1987. The shops were sold to a private firm, Cleburne Railway Shops Inc., which turned out a few repair and repainting jobs before going bankrupt in early 1992.

Santa Fe's shop restructuring sent class overhauls to San Bernardino, GE work to Argentine, and wreck repairs to Topeka. The Santa Fe forces at Cleburne had remanufactured just under 900 units in nearly 18 years. All but a few of Cleburne's remanufactured units are still in service today. The Cleburne reputation for quality is a legacy that will continue for many years to come.

In April 1985, after completing the remanufacture of 59 GP38s, Cleburne started work on the SF30C program. When this program was wrapping up one group of Santa Fe's GP39-2s was remanufactured. Fifty units from the 3617 class became the 3400 class between August 1986 and January 1988. The 3443 was shown at Lubbock, Texas, on New Year's Day 1990. *Marshall Higgins*

The 7200 was later renumbered 6419. Not a success in mainline service, the unit has been banished to locals. On December 18, 1990, a faded 6419 was assigned to local L-K0411-18 at Wellington, Kansas. No more four-axle GE remanufacturing is planned for the future, nor any other Santa Fe remanufacturing programs for that matter. *Keel Middleton*

San Bernardino

Santa Fe's San Bernardino, California, Shops took on its first remanufacturing work in January 1973, the SD26 program. The Santa Fe had a sizeable fleet of SD24s, 80 units, which by then were high-mileage units. Giving impetus for the program was the SD24's design. It wasn't one of EMD's better ideas. This model was chronically afflicted with exciting, ozone-producing failures in its high-voltage and transition circuitry.

Among changes to the SD24s, other than an entirely revised electrical system, was the upgrade of their original 16-567D3 engines to 16-645D3 engines, which increased horsepower from 2,400 to 2,600. The SD24 was built before central filtered air supply systems became standard, so a central air intake behind the cab was installed along with the necessary traction motor blower ducts. To accommodate the central air system's inertial blower the four rooftop air reservoirs were relocated further back on the long hood. Air conditioners were also installed.

The program required five years to complete. It also began a trend: six-axle EMD power would be remanufactured at San Bernardino, and non-EMD power would be remanufactured at the Cleburne Shops. Four-axle EMD power was remanufactured at both shops, San Bernardino being responsible for 29 SSB1200s, 75 GP20s, eight GP30s and 73 GP35s.

The success of the SD26 program launched San Bernardino into its next program. The Santa Fe had purchased most of its switchers very early, and they were all due for replacement or remanufacture. San Bernardino thus took on an assortment of

TR4s, SW9s, SW1200s and NW2s, which were rebuilt into 29 1,200-hp switchers of similar specifications between January 1974 and December 1979. The switchers were dubbed SSB1200s, for "Switcher, San Bernardino, 1,200-horsepower." Despite their fine performance, the Santa Fe soon decided it didn't need small switchers any more, so all were off the roster by May 1985, most going to Amtrak in trade for 18 SDP40Fs.

In addition to the SD26s, SSB1200s, GP20s and GP35s, in the 1970s and 1980s San Bernardino remanufactured eight FP45s (as SDFP45s), 20 SD39s, 19 SD40s (the 5011 had been wrecked), the aforementioned 18 ex-Amtrak SDP40Fs (into SDF40-2s), 117 SD45s, three SD45s (into SD45Bs), and 40 F45s (into SDF45s). Changes made on the SDF40-2s included installation of a snowplow pilot, front walkway, air conditioning, 20,000 pounds of concrete ballast in the boiler space, and handrails on both ends. Fuel capacity was boosted to 4,000 gallons by the simple expedient of removing the divider that had previously separated the fuel portion of the tank from the water (for the steam generator) portion.

San Bernardino also handled Santa Fe's brief experiments with repowering. Four SD45s, 5541, 5515, 5530 and 5551, were repowered in 1980, in conjunction with

Morrison-Knudsen, with Sulzer 16-ASV25/30 engines, and renumbered 5496-5499. This experiment lasted for only five years. The Sulzers weren't judged to be any improvement over EMD engines, so in February 1985 the four Sulzer units went back into the shop for reinstallation of their SD45-standard EMD 20-645E3 engines. They were then renumbered as 5405-5408.

The other experimental repowering was SD45-2 5855, which received a 12-cylinder, 4,200-hp Caterpillar 3612-model prime mover when remanufactured in July 1987. Though the unit is still powered by Caterpillar, perhaps the most obvious answer to the success (or lack of success) of this program it that it hasn't been duplicated.

San Bernardino and Cleburne both built slugs. San Bernardino's seven were designed for hump service. These slugs are somewhat unusual because their fuel tanks are indeed fuel tanks, and supply fuel to the hump locomotives they are mated to.

In the late 1980s, San Bernardino remanufactured the railway's 20 SD39s, and renumbered them into the 1556 class. The SD39s, built as road engines, were remanufactured as slug mothers for heavy hump, flat switch and transfer service.

When remanufacturing a class of locomotives, the Santa Fe often renumbers them, but this is not always the case. For

San Bernardino kicked off its venture into remanufacturing in January 1973 with the SD24s, which were rebuilt into 2,625-hp SD26s. The 4639 is at Barstow, California, the day after Christmas 1982. The SD26s were sentenced to a life of hard service in coal train and heavy manifest service. All have left the roster. *Gary Sugg*

Another San Bernardino experiment was the installation of a 3612 Caterpillar engine in one of the SD45-2s in for remanufacturing at the time. Called the SD-Cat, the recipient was the 5855, shown on August 2, 1991 at Topeka, Kansas. Externally there is little external difference between the SD-Cat and its SD45-2 brethren, except in the radiator section. *Thomas Chenoweth*

example, the 5000 class SD40s were remanufactured between November 1980 and December 1981, but retained their 5000 class number series.

Later in the 1980s San Bernardino remanufactured eight SD45-2s into SD45-2Bs by simply removing their cabs and noses and extending the long hood. The B-units were completed between September 1987 and January 1988.

Eliminating the cab allowed the dynamic brakes to be moved away from the cramped, hot engine room and into the empty, cooler space where the short-hood had once been. San Bernardino shop crews soon nicknamed them "hammerheads" for their distinctive appearance. This change was made after the first SD45-2B, the 5510, had been completed with its dynamic brakes in the usual location above the prime mover.

The last San Bernardino remanufactured products were 69 SD45-2s, which emerged as 5800-class units between February 1986 and March 1988, and 38 SD40-2s, 5020-5057, remanufactured between April and December 1988. The last unit remanufactured to date by the Santa Fe was SD40-2 5023, released from San Bernardino with the same number on December 28, 1988.

It's been reported that Santa Fe's remanufacturing programs were restarted with SD40-2s 5072 and 5213, but these were Class III overhauls, not a remanufacturing. A number of other SD40-2s, slugs and SDFP45s have also been reported as being "recapitalized," but again these were only overhauls, not a remanufacturing.

The Santa Fe plans to close San Bernardino Shops in early 1993. To take its place, the Topeka Shops will be expanded, and

The red and yellow SD45-2 remanufactured units went up through 7229. When the merger was denied, they were quickly renumbered into the 5800 series, though all but one retained their red and yellow paint for a while. The 5827 displays the Kodachrome paint scheme on February 16, 1987, at Barstow, California. *Scott O'Dell*

While the SD45-2s were being remanufactured, another interesting development was the remanufacture of eight SD45-2s into SD45-2B cabless units. The first unit, 5510, had its dynamic brake grids in the standard location over the engineroom, the rest had the dynamics over what had been the short hood. Just-completed SD45-2B 5512 displays the latter "hammerhead" arrangement at San Bernardino. *Santa Fe Railway*

One of San Bernardino's more ambitious programs was the installation of Sulzer engines in four SD45s, 5496-5499. The 5498 proudly displays a "Sulzer Powered" stencil on its short hood at Barstow, California, on January 31, 1982. Though a precision, well-conceived engine, the Sulzers couldn't hack the rigors of heavy-duty American railroading, and soon the Santa Fe was putting 20-645E3s back into the 5498's engineroom. *Thomas Chenoweth*

become Santa Fe's system locomotive and car shops. It's expected that Topeka will be handling all major locomotive repair by November 1, 1992.

In total, San Bernardino Shops remanufactured just over 600 units. Adding this to Cleburne's production gives a total of over 1,500 units remanufactured by Santa Fe forces in less than 20 years, approximately equal to the number of units in Santa Fe service today. There is no doubt that San Bernardino's and Cleburne's remanufacturing programs were integral to the success of the Santa Fe in the 1970s and 1980s. The roster will reflect that for at least another decade.

After turning out SD26s, SSB1200s, GP20s, GP35s, SD40s, SDFP45s, SD45s, SD45Bs, and SDF40-2s, San Bernardino quickly chewed through the SD39s. Twenty SD39s were remanufactured between October 1985 and February 1986. The first SD39 remanufactured, 1557, is at Hobart Yard in Los Angeles in late October 1985. The numbers chosen for these units, in the 1556 class, was part of the proposed SPSF merger scheme, and though the merger was killed, the number series was **not.** *Santa Fe Railway, Mike Martin*

New GP60 4007 waits for its first revenue trip in Chicago on June 5, 1988. The units in this order were the first on the Santa Fe with EMD's 710G prime mover, rated at 3,800 horsepower. *George Horna*

Train 1-148-04 rolls through McCook, Illinois, with three new GP60s on their maiden trip on June 4, 1988. These units were built at the GMDD plant in London, Ontario, a first for Santa Fe, and featured a new truck snubbing system to relieve hunting problems on previous versions of EMD's Blomberg truck. *David Fasules*

Santa Fe got away with very little in the way of new locomotive purchases in the early to mid-1980s. The last three orders for General Electric units were for 14 C30-7s, 8153-8166, in January 1983, three B39-8s, 7400-7402, in 1984, and 14 B23-7s, 6405-6418, in December 1984.

On the General Motors side a second GP50 order, for 15 units, 3840-3854, arrived in April 1985. At the time the railway was in the midst of its big rebuilding programs at its two major shops, Cleburne, Texas, and San Bernardino, California. The rebuilding programs were putting new life into old war horses, and as traffic levels were stable additional new units weren't needed.

By 1988 the Santa Fe had disposed of enough old power to again require new

units. GP60s were ordered from EMD and DASH 8-40Bs from GE. Both were new models for the Santa Fe; the two classes were delivered at the same time, the first new units in over three years.

EMD had produced three prototype GP60s prior to the Santa Fe order, which made many demonstration trips over the Santa Fe mainline to test adhesion, reliability, and fuel consumption in April 1986. They featured aerodynamically-improved cabs and pilots, but this feature was not of sufficient worth to justify its cost and has never been repeated.

During October and November 1986, Santa Fe again tested the GP60s, this time done on Raton Pass. Satisfied, the Santa Fe placed an initial order for 20 GP60s.

Numbered 4000-4019, they began arriving in May 1988.

The GP60s were the first Santa Fe units with GM's new 710G engine. The 16-cylinder version of this engine in the GP60 produced a four-axle unit with a whopping 3,800 horsepower. Though visually identical to the GP50s of three years prior, inside the GP60 is much different. The 710G engine introduced a larger 710-cubic-inch cylinder displacement, using the same diameter cylinders as the 645 but with a longer stroke. The entire crankcase was redesigned, both to accommodate the longer stroke and also to solve structural deficiencies some railroads had felt were present in the predecessor 645F design.

Electrically, the GP60 was highly evolved

The immediate predecessor to GE's DASH-8 line were the B39-8s, of which Santa Fe bought three prototype units. Numbered 7400-7402, these three units were rated at 3,900 horsepower, the highest horsepower per axle on Santa Fe at the time. The 7400 rests at Topeka, Kansas, on May 26, 1990, waiting its next call to duty. *Thomas Chenoweth*

from the GP50. The GP60 is microprocessor-controlled, using "read-only" software that can be (and is) frequently modified to suit each railroad's operating characteristics, almost trip-by-trip. (It's probably only a matter of a few more years before locomotive performance is monitored continuously and the commands entered to change operating characteristics every second.)

The trucks were redesigned, using a new snubbing system designed to prevent hunting, a term referring to the uncontrolled swivel of trucks at speed, which results in excessive lateral forces on the rail. This truck had been tested on the GP60 demos, 5, 6, and 7, and Santa Fe GP50 3817. The new GP60s were set up in Corwith, and allowed to work their way to Kansas City, where final details such as flange lubricators were added. They were built with 75 mph, 69:18 gearing.

At the same time the new GEs were also arriving. These were 20 DASH 8-40Bs, 7410-7429, delivered in June 1988.

GE had been inching up its B-B horsepower as well. The first of GE's DASH-8 line was an experimental unit, GE-606, which was built in October 1982 as a B36-8, and initially rated at 3,600 horsepower. This unit introduced the microprocessor control on GEs. It was later uprated to 3,800 horsepower.

The B36-8 was never listed in GE's catalog, but was superseded by the 3,900-hp B39-8. GE agreed to supply three prototype B39-8s to the Santa Fe, the 7400-7402, as Santa Fe wanted to take a long, hard look at the new GE design, after its mixed experience with its B36-7s. The prototype units had numerous differences from production B39-8s, including carbody differences.

The trio tested on numerous railroads, and Santa Fe did not get all three until the 7401 arrived at Corwith on January 3, 1985. (The 7401 was incorrectly numbered 7402 by GE at Erie. The error was caught before the unit departed Erie, however.)

The B39-8s at first traveled extensively for testing. In September 1985, the Santa Fe swapped them to Conrail for a few weeks in trade for three Conrail C32-8s, 6617-6619.

The Santa Fe's tests of the B39-8s showed they offered significant fuel savings in high-speed service over 3,000-hp, six-axle units. The 7400 and 7401 were also equipped with RCE equipment for testing in that capacity.

Though the B39-8s weren't perfect, the Santa Fe recognized the potential of GE's DASH-8 series, and agreed to purchase 20 DASH 8-40Bs in 1988. When purchased, the 4,000 horsepower DASH 8-40Bs were the highest horsepower units yet owned by the Santa Fe.

Among other improvements in the DASH 8-40B over the B39-8s was a modified truck design, which used rearranged shock absorbers on their floating bolster trucks. The new truck has four hydraulic shocks mounted between the truck frame and both

ends of each axle, rather than the previous design's two vertical spring snubbers mounted between the truck frame and journal box on diagonally-opposite axle ends. To accommodate this the brake cylinder was mounted further outboard, requiring a lengthened brake rod. The result was greatly improved ride quality, always a sore point with earlier GE models.

The GP60s and DASH 8-40Bs were assigned to high-priority intermodal service, often in pure sets, and after the dust settled, the Santa Fe decided to order more of both models. In April 1989, another batch of 20 DASH 8-40Bs arrived, 7430-7449, and in July and August 1989 another 20 GP60s arrived, 4020-4039.

GE's DASH 8-40B put a unit on the rails with 1,000 horsepower per axle. The Santa Fe ordered 20 of the beasts in early 1988, concurrent with the order for its first 20 GP60s. The GEs were delivered in June 1988, and immediately went into high-priority intermodal service. The 7413 leads the 1-875-27 train eastbound east of Flagstaff, Arizona, on October 28, 1989. The volcanic San Francisco Peaks, as central to Navajo religion as they are to the northern Arizona landscape, are in the background. *Mark Wayman*

Santa Fe's next move was to look at improved cab designs. The Santa Fe was one of the first American railroads to seriously re-evaluate the cab environment, as well as address how existing cabs responded to the technological advances of the last several decades.

Research began with a visit to Canada to study Canadian National's SD50Fs. CN's cab design has substantially more structural strength than standard cabs, extra sound insulation, improved visibility, and desktop control consoles. One of CN's SD50Fs was borrowed by the Santa Fe for tests and evaluation. Santa Fe engineers that saw it were asked to fill out a questionnaire on the CN cab design.

Initially, the Santa Fe planned on acquiring cowl-carbody GP60s to cut wind drag. The Santa Fe wanted cowl units in both A and B-unit versions, much like the F-units of old. When the numbers were added up, however, the cowl's weight was more than could be accommodated with allowed axle loadings. Twenty years ago, the cowl wouldn't have been a problem, but in the interim fuel tanks had grown in size to minimize fuel stops on long-haul runs.

Six-axle cowl units were not in the railroad's plans. The Santa Fe wanted get-up-and-go units with maximum possible acceleration between 40 and 70 mph. So the full-cowl carbody GP60 remained a dream.

Santa Fe's motive power team started with the basic idea that they needed high-horsepower, high-adhesion, high-speed four-axle hot-rods to power their ever growing intermodal fleet. A critical factor was the ability of locomotives to travel long distances at sustained high speeds between fuel stops.

Tests had shown that a GP60 at full throttle consumed approximately 162 gallons per hour, and an SD40-2 consumed 198 gallons under the same conditions. The SD's extra two traction motors also required the expected amount of additional maintenance, as did the larger, heavier truck, and wheelsets on three-axle trucks wear considerably faster than wheelsets on two-axle trucks. Since advanced adhesion systems had made high-horsepower four-axle units viable even in heavy-grade territory, the decision was made: four-axle units it would be.

Based on the tests with the SD50F, a mock-up cab was built in San Bernardino, as well as one at EMD. The cab design was refined, Santa Fe's design team working both with GE and EMD, and dubbed the "safety cab."

The GP60Ms were the first units with Santa Fe's new cab design (reflected by the "M" in the model designation), the 100 and 101 arriving on May 17, 1990. They were ordered in Santa Fe's red and silver Super Fleet paint scheme, and were the first

Geeps to wear Santa Fe's red and silver, ever. (It had been used on E-units, F-units, PAs, Erie-Builts, DL-109s, U28CGs, U30CGs, and FP45s — twice — but never on a Geep.)

From May through September, Santa Fe received 63 GP60Ms. Similar to the GP60 but with improvements, they employ a 16-710G3A engine, likewise have high-speed 69:18 gearing, and weigh 282,000 pounds — very heavy for a four-axle unit. Their first revenue run was on the Q-NYLA1-20 of May 20, 1990, with the 100 and 101 spliced by two SDFP45s.

One of the last GP60Ms to arrive was the 104, as it was retained by EMD for testing. One unit of this group was also used to advertise Maersk, a container shipping line. GP60M 146 was delivered in primer and shipped to Topeka for a coat of Maersk powder blue and silver. It was placed on Maersk double-stacks and spent most of August 13, 1990, on Cajon Pass, for photography. After the shoot, it went back to Topeka for its first coat of red and silver. By September 25th, all 63 new GP60Ms were in service.

GP60M 146 was shipped to Topeka, Kansas, in primer, for decoration in a modification of Santa Fe's Super Fleet design, which used Maersk blue and silver colors, and black lettering. The Maersk publicity train is at Martinez Spur, California, just east of Cajon Summit, during a publicity shoot on August 13, 1990. *Joe Shine*

The other end of the Maersk publicity train had GP60M 144, in "normal" Santa Fe red and silver. The 2912 leads an eastbound train around the publicity train at Devore, California, on August 13, 1990. *Joe Shine*

In between its two orders for DASH 8-40BWs, Santa Fe slipped in an order for 23 GP60Bs. This October 24, 1991, A-B-B-B lashup brings memories of F-units to mind. There's something that's inherently right about B-units. *Eric Blasko*

Slightly grimy DASH 8-40BW 554 is on the point of the 199 at Rheem, California, approaching the yard at Richmond on February 22, 1992. A few days before, the unit was shivering in Chicago's icy winter, and now it's rolling through new grass and spring flowers. *Brian Jennison*

DASH 8-40BW 521 leads two other new DASH 8-40BWs on the 1-893-31 train, eastbound on Cajon Pass on October 31, 1990. The three GEs put out a combined 12,000 horsepower, equivalent to four SD40-2s, or eight F7s. *Joe Blackwell*

A trio of spotless new Dash 8-40BWs glisten at Argentine Yard on March 14, 1992. These are from Santa Fe's second order for Dash 8-40BWs, which arrived from February through April 1992.
Lon Coone

While the new Super Fleet GP60Ms were still breaking in, 60 new Super Fleet GEs, which sported Erie's version of the safety cab, began to arrive. The "W" in their DASH 8-40BW model designation reflects this modification. At first, these units were to be in the 300 series. This was changed and they came in the 500 series. Though some railroads and railfans refer to GE's DASH-8 series such as DASH 8-40BWs as B40-8Ws, the Santa Fe does not. As far as the Santa Fe is concerned, they're DASH 8-40BWs, just like it says on the builder's plates.

Like the earlier DASH 8-40Bs, the DASH 8-40BWs are 4,000-hp machines with 81:22 gearing, and are even heavier than the GP60Ms, at 289,000 pounds. The first two, 503 and 505, arrived on October 12, 1990, and left Chicago on 1-198-12 for Los Angeles.

Since application of Super Fleet red and silver is complex and time consuming, the units were built at GE faster than they could be painted. Santa Fe agreed to paint 12 of the new units, which were shipped to Topeka in primer for final painting by Santa Fe.

The GEs were still arriving when disaster struck the Santa Fe at 4:10 a.m. on November 7, 1990. Two freights collided head-on at Corona, California.

The westbound 818 train with five units and 92 cars had taken the siding at Corona to allow the 891 train (with three of the four-month-old GP60Ms up front) to pass. The investigation revealed that the 818 eased down the siding at seven to eight mph, failed to stop at the west end, and continued out the end of the siding in the face of the oncoming 891, which was moving at 25 to 30 mph.

Tragically, all three crewman on the 818, who were riding lead unit SD45 5363, were killed. On the 891, lead GP60M 137 rolled off the south side of the tracks, the second unit, 148, jackknifed the other way, rolling off to the north. The third unit, 152, remained on the right-of-way and plowed into the 818's units. A brakeman riding the 148 was killed by an ensuing fuel-fed fire.

Amazingly, both the conductor and engineer aboard the 137 survived, evidence that there is virtue to the safety cab. At the time, Mike Martin, Santa Fe's Manager of Public Relations in San Bernardino, said that the units had been designed to protect crewmen, and that there were probably two men still living as a result.

Santa Fe's next locomotive order was placed with EMD, and it caused a lot of eyebrows to raise: it requested 23 GP60Bs, the first B-units built by General Motors since Union Pacific's DD35s of 1964. Once again A-B-B-A sets were a Santa Fe trademark.

The GP60Bs arrived during July and August 1991, in red and silver, but without a war bonnet. Internally and externally,

there is little difference between the GP60Bs and the GP60Ms, other than the obvious, no cab. The GP60Bs are a little lighter, at 273,400 pounds instead of the GP60M's 282,000 pounds. Like on Santa Fe's SD45-2Bs, the dynamic brake blister is moved forward, out of the engineroom.

The first GP60M/GP60B A-B-B-A set ran on 1-198-26 of July 26, 1991, leaving Corwith at 4:30 p.m.

In late 1991, the Santa Fe chose GE over EMD for 90 new units: 23 more DASH 8-40BWs, 560-582; and 67 DASH 8-40CWs.

Deliveries of the DASH 8-40BWs began in March 1992; the first, the 561, arrived on the property on March 2nd. Odd-numbered units from the order were built first, followed by the even-numbered units, because the even-numbered units are

When GE's paint shop lagged behind locomotive production, primarily due to the complexity of the red and silver paint scheme, the Santa Fe agreed to paint 12 DASH 8-40BWs for GE. One of these was the 530, at Argentine Yard en route to Topeka for its dress attire on October 6, 1990. *Lon Coone*

equipped with event recorders and the odd-numbered units are not. This order was set up for service at Argentine Yard in Kansas City rather than Corwith Yard in Chicago, the first time Corwith hasn't had this honor in recent years.

The 67 DASH 8-40CWs were the first six-axle units built for Santa Fe since the 14 C30-7s of January 1983, nine years prior. These units were also equipped with a safety cab, similar to the cab used on the DASH 8-40BWs.

The first 34 of the DASH 8-40CWs were built in April and May 1992; the rest of the order was scheduled for October and November 1992 delivery. The even-numbered units came first, with 800, 802 and 804 arriving on the property on April 13, 1992, via the 213 train from the Conrail connection at Streator. Their maiden run after set-up was on the S-CHLA1-15, of April 15th, beginning a new era of Santa Fe six-axle motive power photography.

The DASH 8-40CWs are intended to replace aging SD45s and SDF45s, which are nearing the end of their economic life after their remanufacture 10 to 12 years ago. These 20-cylinder locomotives are also too fuel-hungry and expensive to maintain, especially when compared to the vastly more fuel-efficient locomotives of today.

The DASH 8-40CW's first assignments have been double-stack trains, grain trains, and coal trains. When the rest of the DASH 8-40CWs arrive, look for Santa Fe's 20-cylindered dinosaurs to begin fading into history.

Nearly any paint scheme looks great right out of the paint shop, but the Santa Fe's is one of the all-time greatest. Glistening DASH 8-40CW 826 has just arrived in Kansas City for set-up from Conrail's Streator connection. *Kevin EuDaly*

The DASH 8-40CWs are the first new six-axle power for Santa Fe since an order of 14 C30-7s that arrived nine years ago. Santa Fe's first three, 800, 802, and 804, lurk in a sea of blue and yellow at Argentine Yard on April 14, 1992, prior to their first revenue assignment. *Kevin EuDaly*

GP40X 3803 and a pair of SD40-2s lead the 195 train through verdant Mill Creek Valley west of Holliday, Kansas, on October 17, 1987. This was a Chicago to Houston TOFC and auto parts train that also protected UPS traffic for Fort Worth and Houston. It ran with 2.9 HPT and 3,800 tons maximum. If this is a full-tonnage train, the 9,500 hp in the lashup makes it slightly below target, at 2.5 HPT. The 195 was deleted from the schedule last year.
Warren Sunkel

The following roster lists the locomotives on Santa Fe's roster, per Santa Fe's on-line computer file as of May 14, 1992. The roster is listed according to Santa Fe classes.

Several classes of locomotives listed on the Santa Fe computer file are no longer on the property, such as the B36-7s and many of the C30-7s. These are shown on the roster as the financial account for these units has not yet been closed out. The Santa Fe does not "officially" retire a locomotive until the accounting books are closed on that unit. Note 104 applies to these units.

The data in the heading of each class contains Santa Fe's model designation for that type. This may or may not be the same

as the manufacturer's model designation, such as with SDFP45s and SF30Cs. Model designation is followed by the Santa Fe class, the rated traction horsepower, and the number of units currently rostered in that class.

The second line lists engine type, tractive effort at the specified minimum continuous speed, and finally the nominal weight of the locomotive. (Minimum continuous speed is the speed at which full horsepower can be used for long periods without damage to the traction motors.) Additional information in the notes gives the type of trucks, gear ratio, axle bearings, size of fuel tank, type of dynamic brakes, Santa Fe remanufacturing information, and other information.

In the roster, the current road number is followed by previous numbers, if applicable, beginning with the original number a locomotive wore, then through each successive renumbering from left to right.

Following the road numbers are the month and year the locomotive was produced by its manufacturer, followed by the date remanufactured by the Santa Fe (if any). A remanufacturing date appears only when the locomotive has been remanufactured, not merely overhauled as designated by the Santa Fe. The builder's number is next, followed by specific notes for each

locomotive.

A colon after a road number indicates other Santa Fe units have worn that particular number. For example, GP60 4000:2 is the second Santa Fe 4000.

As a general note, all Santa Fe locomotives with cabs are air-conditioned, and all units have 40" wheels unless specified by note 1.

Your comments and corrections are welcomed, so that subsequent detailed rosters can be corrected and improved.

Roster Notes:

1. 42" wheels
2. Blomberg trucks, elliptical springs.
3. Blomberg trucks, rubber pads.
4. Blomberg trucks, low-profile elliptical springs.
5. Flexicoil trucks.
6. HT-C trucks.
7. Remanufactured equalizer-type trucks.
8. Equalizer-type trucks.
9. Floating bolster trucks.
10. GSC or Adirondack trucks.
11. 83:20 gearing (4.15:1 ratio).
12. 62:15 gearing (4.13:1 ratio).
13. 70:17 gearing (4.12:1 ratio).
14. 74:18 gearing (4.11:1 ratio).

15. 69:18 gearing (3.83:1 ratio).
16. 81:22 gearing (3.68:1 ratio).
17. 65:18 gearing (3.61:1 ratio).
18. 60:17 gearing (3.53:1 ratio).
19. Hyatt bearings.
20. Timken bearings.
21. 700 gallon fuel tank.
22. 1,200 gallon fuel tank.
23. 1,600 gallon fuel tank.
24. 2,350 gallon fuel tank.
25. 2,500 gallon fuel tank.
26. 2,600 gallon fuel tank.
27. 2,900 gallon fuel tank.
28. 3,000 gallon fuel tank.
29. 3,050 gallon fuel tank.
30. 3,200 gallon fuel tank.
31. 3,250 gallon fuel tank.
32. 3,500 gallon fuel tank.
33. 3,900 gallon fuel tank.
34. 4,000 gallon fuel tank.
35. 5,000 gallon fuel tank.
36. Extended-range tapered dynamic brakes, maximum effectiveness @ 31.0 mph.
37. Extended-range flat 3-speed dynamic brakes, maximum effectiveness @ 28.0 mph.
38. Extended-range tapered dynamic brakes, maximum effectiveness @ 28.0 mph.
39. Extended-range DR1 2-speed flat dynamic brakes, maximum effectiveness @ 8.0 mph.
40. Extended-range flat dynamic brakes, maximum effectiveness @ 28.0 mph.
41. Extended-range flat dynamic brakes, maximum effectiveness @ 27.0 mph.
42. Extended-range flat dynamic brakes, maximum effectiveness @ 25.0 mph.
43. Extended-range flat dynamic brakes, maximum effectiveness @ 24.3 mph.
44. Extended-range tapered dynamic brakes, maximum effectiveness @ 24.0 mph.
45. Extended-range flat dynamic brakes, maximum effectiveness @ 24.0 mph.
46. Extended-range flat 2-speed dynamic brakes, maximum effectiveness @ 24.0 mph.
47. Tapered dynamic brakes, maximum effectiveness @ 24.0 mph.
48. Extended-range flat dynamic brakes, maximum effectiveness @ 22.5 mph.
49. Extended-range tapered dynamic brakes, maximum effectiveness @ 22.0 mph.
50. Extended-range dynamic brakes, maximum effectiveness @ 22.0 mph.
51. Extended-range flat dynamic brakes, maximum effectiveness @ 21.0 mph.
52. Tapered dynamic brakes, maximum effectiveness @ 21.0 mph.
53. Extended-range flat dynamic brakes, maximum effectiveness @ 19.0 mph.
54. 5.5 mph minimum continuous speed.
55. 4.0 mph minimum continuous speed.
56. 3.5 mph minimum continuous speed.
57. Built as FP45, remanufactured as SDFP45 by Santa Fe, San Bernardino.
58. Built as GP9, remanufactured as slug by Santa Fe, Cleburne.
59. Built as GP7, remanufactured as slug by Santa Fe, Cleburne.
60. Built as GP20, remanufactured as slug by Santa Fe, Cleburne.
61. Built as GP9B, remanufactured as slug by Santa Fe, Cleburne.
62. Built as F7B, remanufactured as slug by Santa Fe, Cleburne.
63. Built as SD24B, remanufactured as slug by Santa Fe, Cleburne.

64. Built as SD39, remanufactured as slug by Santa Fe, San Bernardino.
65. Built as SD40, remanufactured as slug by Santa Fe, San Bernardino.
66. Built as SD40-2, remanufactured as slug by Santa Fe, San Bernardino.
67. Built as U33C, remanufactured by Santa Fe, San Bernardino.
68. Built as SD45, remanufactured as slug by Santa Fe, San Bernardino.
69. Built as VO1000, remanufactured as "Switcher" by Santa Fe, Cleburne.
70. Built as GP7B, remanufactured as GP9 by Santa Fe, Cleburne.
71. Built as SDP40F, remanufactured as SDF40-2 by Santa Fe, San Bernardino.
72. Built as SD45, remanufactured as SD45B by Santa Fe, San Bernardino.
73. Built as SD45-2, remanufactured as SD45-2B by Santa Fe, San Bernardino.
74. Built as F45, remanufactured as SDF45 by Santa Fe, San Bernardino.
75. Built as U23B, remanufactured as 3,000 hp SF30B by Santa Fe, Cleburne, later derated to 2,300 hp.
76. Built as U36C, remanufactured as SF30C by Santa Fe, Cleburne.
77. Remanufactured in kind by Santa Fe, San Bernardino.
78. Remanufactured in kind by Santa Fe, Cleburne.
79. 540-559 are rated at 3,800 hp.
80. Upgraded to 3,000 hp by Santa Fe, San Bernardino, later derated to 2,300 hp.
81. Sulzer 16-ASV25/30 engines installed 1980/1981 by Morrison-Knudsen, Boise, Idaho. Replaced with EMD 20-645E3 engines during January and February 1985, by Santa Fe, San Bernardino.
82. Equipped with 20-645E3B engine.
83. Equipped with Caterpillar 3612 engine by Santa Fe, San Bernardino.
84. 8092-8098 equipped with 7FDL-16A6G8 engines.
85. 6405-6418 equipped with 7FDL-12F30UX engines and weigh 266,000 lbs.
86. Weight 362,000 lbs.
87. 8020-8057 weigh 392,500 lbs.
88. 6374-6389 weigh 271,000 lbs.
89. 5502:2 has 82,100 lbs T.E. @ 11.3 mph.
90. Originally equipped with 83:20 gear ratio and rated at 61,000 lbs T.E.
91. Originally equipped with 83:20 gear ratio and rated at 91,500 lbs T.E.

A spotless GP30, 2755, leads the 337 train out the west end of Abo Canyon on June 26, 1990. GP30s in operating condition are getting rare in the 1990s, and no railroad rosters anywhere near the 78 GP30s still on the Santa Fe roster in 1992. Santa Fe's original fleet of 85 GP30s was the third largest, behind UP's 112 (plus 40 GP30Bs) and Southern's 121. UP's GP30s are long gone and the last of Norfolk Southern's GP30s were retired in August 1991. One can hope that the Santa Fe will be a stronghold for GP30s for many more years. *John Lucas*

92. Mother units are 1310 Class GP7s.
93. Mother units are 1556 Class SD39s.
94. Equipped as slug mothers.
95. Equipped with Pacesetter hump controls.
96. Originally equipped as Locotrol lead unit, equipment subsequently removed.
97. Originally equipped as Locotrol remote unit, equipment subsequently removed.
98. Equipped as Radio Control Lead Unit (RCE).
99. Equipped as Radio Control Receiver Unit (RCR).
100. Equipped with 116" (snoot) nose.
101. Former TP&W units, dynamic brakes added by Santa Fe.
102. Delivered in primer and painted in Topeka for Maersk publicity purposes. Painted in Santa Fe colors on August 16th, 1991.
103. Equipped with radial truck (front only) for tests during early 1986.
104. Currently not in active fleet, leased back to General Electric or pending retirement.
105. Placed up for bid as of June 24, 1992, serviceable.
106. Placed up for bid as of June 24, 1992, unserviceable.

Roster Sources: Kevin EuDaly, Lon EuDaly, Mark Hemphill, John Hake, Steve Priest, Ken Ardinger, CTC Board *and* Extra 2200 South. *Additionally, information was provided by Santa Fe employees Ernie Ball, Bob Burnett, Bob Lee, John Nixon, Wayne Tomasewski and Rich Wessler.*

SDFP45	90 Class			3,600 hp			8 units		
20-645E3 engine		82,100 lbs T.E. @ 11.3 mph			399,000 lbs				

Road#	1st#	2nd#	3rd#	4th#	5th#	Built	Rebuilt	Build#	Notes
90	100:2	5940	5990	100:3	5990	12/67	09/82	33189	5,12,19,34,36,57
91	101:3	5941	5991	104:5	5991	12/67	10/82	33190	5,12,19,35,36,57
92	102:2	5942	5992	101:6		12/67	10/82	33191	5,12,19,35,36,57
93	103:2	5943	5993	106:5	5993	12/67	04/80	33192	5,12,19,35,36,57
95	105:2	5945	5995	107:5	5995	12/67	08/81	33194	5,12,19,35,36,57
96	106:2	5946	5996	103:5		12/67	01/82	33195	5,12,19,35,36,57
97	107:2	5947	5997	105:5	5997	12/67	12/82	33196	5,12,19,35,36,57
98	108:2	5948	5998	102:5	5998	12/67	08/82	33197	5,12,19,35,36,57

91, Pueblo, Colorado, August 8, 1991. *Bruce Barrett*

114, Chicago, Illinois, June 9, 1991. *George Horna*

146, Topeka, Kansas, August 2, 1990. *Dan Munson*

GP60M	100 Class	3,800 hp	61 units
16-710G3A engine		62,070 lbs T.E. @ 10.5 mph	282,000 lbs

Road#	Built	Build#	Notes
100:4	05/90	886063-1	3,15,20,30,43
101:7	05/90	886063-2	3,15,20,30,43
102:6	05/90	886063-3	3,15,20,30,43
103:6	05/90	886063-4	3,15,20,30,43
104:6	07/90	886063-5	3,15,20,30,43
105:6	05/90	886063-6	3,15,20,30,43
106:6	05/90	886063-7	3,15,20,30,43
107:6	05/90	886063-8	3,15,20,30,43
108:5	05/90	886063-9	3,15,20,30,43
109:4	05/90	886063-10	3,15,20,30,43
110:3	05/90	886063-11	3,15,20,30,43
111:3	06/90	886063-12	3,15,20,30,43
112:3	06/90	886063-13	3,15,20,30,43
113:3	06/90	886063-14	3,15,20,30,43
114:3	06/90	886063-15	3,15,20,30,43
115:3	06/90	886063-16	3,15,20,30,43
116:3	06/90	886063-17	3,15,20,30,43
117:3	06/90	886063-18	3,15,20,30,43
118:3	08/90	886063-19	3,15,20,30,43
119:3	06/90	886063-20	3,15,20,30,43
120:3	06/90	886063-21	3,15,20,30,43
121:3	06/90	886063-22	3,15,20,30,43
122:2	06/90	886063-23	3,15,20,30,43
123:3	06/90	886063-24	3,15,20,30,43
124:3	06/90	886063-25	3,15,20,30,43
125:3	06/90	886063-26	3,15,20,30,43
126:3	06/90	886063-27	3,15,20,30,43
127:3	06/90	886063-28	3,15,20,30,43
128:3	06/90	886063-29	3,15,20,30,43
129:3	06/90	886063-30	3,15,20,30,43
130:2	06/90	886063-31	3,15,20,30,43
131:2	06/90	886063-32	3,15,20,30,43
132:2	06/90	886063-33	3,15,20,30,43
133:2	07/90	886063-34	3,15,20,30,43
134:2	07/90	886063-35	3,15,20,30,43
135:2	07/90	886063-36	3,15,20,30,43
136:2	07/90	886063-37	3,15,20,30,43
137:2	07/90	886063-38	3,15,20,30,43
138:2	07/90	886063-39	3,15,20,30,43
139:2	07/90	886063-40	3,15,20,30,43
140:4	07/90	886063-41	3,15,20,30,43
141:4	07/90	886063-42	3,15,20,30,43
142:4	07/90	886063-43	3,15,20,30,43
143:4	07/90	886063-44	3,15,20,30,43
144:4	07/90	886063-45	3,15,20,30,43
145:4	07/90	886063-46	3,15,20,30,43
146:4	07/90	886063-47	3,15,20,30,43,102
147:2	07/90	886063-48	3,15,20,30,43
149:2	07/90	886063-50	3,15,20,30,43
150:2	08/90	886063-51	3,15,20,30,43
151:2	08/90	886063-52	3,15,20,30,43
153:2	08/90	886063-54	3,15,20,30,43
154:2	08/90	886063-55	3,15,20,30,43
155:2	08/90	886063-56	3,15,20,30,43
156:2	08/90	886063-57	3,15,20,30,43
157:2	08/90	886063-58	3,15,20,30,43
158:2	09/90	886063-59	3,15,20,30,43
159:2	09/90	886063-60	3,15,20,30,43
160:2	09/90	886063-61	3,15,20,30,43
161:2	09/90	886063-62	3,15,20,30,43
162:2	09/90	886063-63	3,15,20,30,43

GP60B	325 Class	3,800 hp	23 units
16-710G3A engine	62,070 lbs T.E. @ 10.5 mph		273,400 lbs

Road#	Built	Build#	Notes
325	07/91	906143-1	2,15,20,30,43
326	07/91	906143-2	2,15,20,30,43
327	07/91	906143-3	2,15,20,30,43
328	07/91	906143-4	2,15,20,30,43
329	07/91	906143-5	2,15,20,30,43
330	07/91	906143-6	2,15,20,30,43
331	07/91	906143-7	2,15,20,30,43
332	07/91	906143-8	2,15,20,30,43
333	07/91	906143-9	2,15,20,30,43
334	07/91	906143-10	2,15,20,30,43
335	07/91	906143-11	2,15,20,30,43
336	07/91	906143-12	2,15,20,30,43
337	07/91	906143-13	2,15,20,30,43
338	07/91	906143-14	2,15,20,30,43
339	07/91	906143-15	2,15,20,30,43
340	07/91	906143-16	2,15,20,30,43
341	08/91	906143-17	2,15,20,30,43
342	08/91	906143-18	2,15,20,30,43
343	08/91	906143-19	2,15,20,30,43
344	08/91	906143-20	2,15,20,30,43
345	08/91	906143-21	2,15,20,30,43
346	08/91	906143-22	2,15,20,30,43
347	08/91	906143-23	2,15,20,30,43

332, Chicago, Illinois, July 27, 1991. *George Horna*

506, Chicago, Illinois, June 17, 1991. *George Horna*

558, Chriesman, Texas, April 7, 1991. *Rick Bartoskewitz*

DASH 8-40BW	500 Class	4,000 hp*	60 units
7FDL-16 engine	56,500 lbs T.E. @ 21 mph		289,000 lbs

Road#	Built	Build#	Notes
500:2	10/90	46404	1,9,16,20,31,50
501:2	10/90	46405	1,9,16,20,31,50
502:2	10/90	46406	1,9,16,20,31,50
503:2	10/90	46407	1,9,16,20,31,50
504:2	10/90	46408	1,9,16,20,31,50
505:2	10/90	46409	1,9,16,20,31,50
506:2	10/90	46410	1,9,16,20,31,50
507:2	10/90	46411	1,9,16,20,31,50
508:2	10/90	46412	1,9,16,20,31,50
509:2	10/90	46413	1,9,16,20,31,50
510:2	10/90	46414	1,9,16,20,31,50
511:2	10/90	46415	1,9,16,20,31,50
512:2	10/90	46416	1,9,16,20,31,50
513:2	10/90	46417	1,9,16,20,31,50
514:2	10/90	46418	1,9,16,20,31,50
515:2	10/90	46419	1,9,16,20,31,50
516:2	10/90	46420	1,9,16,20,31,50
517:2	10/90	46421	1,9,16,20,31,50
518:2	10/90	46422	1,9,16,20,31,50
519:2	10/90	46423	1,9,16,20,31,50
520:2	10/90	46424	1,9,16,20,31,50
521:2	10/90	46425	1,9,16,20,31,50
522:2	10/90	46426	1,9,16,20,31,50
523:2	10/90	46427	1,9,16,20,31,50
524:2	10/90	46428	1,9,16,20,31,50
525:3	10/90	46429	1,9,16,20,31,50
526:3	10/90	46430	1,9,16,20,31,50
527:3	10/90	46431	1,9,16,20,31,50
528:3	10/90	46432	1,9,16,20,31,50
529:3	10/90	46433	1,9,16,20,31,50
530:3	10/90	46434	1,9,16,20,31,50
531:3	10/90	46435	1,9,16,20,31,50
532:3	10/90	46436	1,9,16,20,31,50
533:3	10/90	46437	1,9,16,20,31,50
534:2	10/90	46438	1,9,16,20,31,50
535:2	10/90	46439	1,9,16,20,31,50
536:2	10/90	46440	1,9,16,20,31,50
537:2	10/90	46441	1,9,16,20,31,50
538:2	10/90	46442	1,9,16,20,31,50
539:2	10/90	46443	1,9,16,20,31,50
540:2	10/90	46444	1,9,16,20,31,50,79
541:2	10/90	46445	1,9,16,20,31,50,79
542:2	10/90	46446	1,9,16,20,31,50,79
543:2	10/90	46447	1,9,16,20,31,50,79
544:2	10/90	46448	1,9,16,20,31,50,79
545:2	10/90	46449	1,9,16,20,31,50,79
546:2	10/90	46450	1,9,16,20,31,50,79

DASH 8-40BW	500 Class		Continued

Road#	Built	Build#	Notes
547:2	10/90	46451	1,9,16,20,31,50,79
548:2	10/90	46452	1,9,16,20,31,50,79
549:2	10/90	46453	1,9,16,20,31,50,79
550:2	10/90	46454	1,9,16,20,31,50,79
551:2	10/90	46455	1,9,16,20,31,50,79
552:2	11/90	46456	1,9,16,20,31,50,79
553:2	11/90	46457	1,9,16,20,31,50,79
554:2	11/90	46458	1,9,16,20,31,50,79
555:2	10/90	46459	1,9,16,20,31,50,79
556:2	11/90	46460	1,9,16,20,31,50,79
557:2	11/90	46461	1,9,16,20,31,50,79
558:2	11/90	46462	1,9,16,20,31,50,79
559:2	11/90	46463	1,9,16,20,31,50,79

569, Kansas City, Kansas, March 14, 1992. *Lon Coone*

826, Kansas City, Kansas, May 1, 1992. *Kevin EuDaly*

1102, Amarillo, Texas, March 28, 1992. *George Horna*

DASH 8-40BW	560 Class	3,800 hp	23 units
7FDL-16 engine		69,200 lbs T.E. @ 21 mph	289,000 lbs

Road#	Built	Build#	Notes
560:2	03/92	46906	1,9,16,20,31,50
561:2	02/92	46907	1,9,16,20,31,50
562:2	03/92	46908	1,9,16,20,31,50
563:2	03/92	46909	1,9,16,20,31,50
564:2	03/92	46910	1,9,16,20,31,50
565	03/92	46911	1,9,16,20,31,50
566	03/92	46912	1,9,16,20,31,50
567	03/92	46913	1,9,16,20,31,50
568	03/92	46914	1,9,16,20,31,50
569	03/92	46915	1,9,16,20,31,50
570	03/92	46916	1,9,16,20,31,50
571	03/92	46917	1,9,16,20,31,50
572	03/92	46918	1,9,16,20,31,50
573	03/92	46919	1,9,16,20,31,50
574	03/92	46920	1,9,16,20,31,50
575	03/92	46921	1,9,16,20,31,50
576	03/92	46922	1,9,16,20,31,50
577	03/92	46923	1,9,16,20,31,50
578	04/92	46924	1,9,16,20,31,50
579	03/92	46925	1,9,16,20,31,50
580	04/92	46926	1,9,16,20,31,50
581	03/92	46927	1,9,16,20,31,50
582	04/92	46928	1,9,16,20,31,50

DASH 8-40CW	800 Class	3,800 hp	34 units
7FDL-16 engine		108,600 lbs T.E. @ 11.0 mph	394,200 lbs

Road#	Built	Build#	Notes
800:2	04/92	46929	1,10,11,20,35,50
802:2	04/92	46931	1,10,11,20,35,50
804:2	04/92	46933	1,10,11,20,35,50
806:2	04/92	46935	1,10,11,20,35,50
808:2	04/92	46937	1,10,11,20,35,50
810:2	04/92	46939	1,10,11,20,35,50
812:2	04/92	46941	1,10,11,20,35,50
814:2	04/92	46943	1,10,11,20,35,50
816:2	04/92	46945	1,10,11,20,35,50
818:2	04/92	46947	1,10,11,20,35,50
820:2	04/92	46949	1,10,11,20,35,50
822:2	04/92	46951	1,10,11,20,35,50
824:2	04/92	46953	1,10,11,20,35,50
826:2	04/92	46955	1,10,11,20,35,50
828:2	04/92	46957	1,10,11,20,35,50
830:2	04/92	46959	1,10,11,20,35,50
832:2	04/92	46961	1,10,11,20,35,50
834:2	04/92	46963	1,10,11,20,35,50
836:2	04/92	46965	1,10,11,20,35,50
838:2	04/92	46967	1,10,11,20,35,50
840:2	04/92	46969	1,10,11,20,35,50
842:2	04/92	46971	1,10,11,20,35,50
844:2	04/92	46973	1,10,11,20,35,50
846:2	04/92	46975	1,10,11,20,35,50
848:2	04/92	46977	1,10,11,20,35,50
850	04/92	46979	1,10,11,20,35,50
852	05/92	46981	1,10,11,20,35,50
854	05/92	46983	1,10,11,20,35,50
856	05/92	46985	1,10,11,20,35,50
858	05/92	46987	1,10,11,20,35,50
860	05/92	46989	1,10,11,20,35,50
862	05/92	46991	1,10,11,20,35,50
864	05/92	46993	1,10,11,20,35,50
866	05/92	46995	1,10,11,20,35,50

Slug		1101 Class		9 units				
249,000 lbs								

Road#	1st#	2nd#	3rd#	4th#	5th#	Built	Rebuilt	Build#	Notes
1101:2	UP-243	ATSF-101:5				01/54	06/81	19129	2,12,19,54,58,9:
1102:2	UP-255	ATSF-102:4				08/54	07/81	19780	2,12,19,54,58,9:
1103:2	UP-267	ATSF-103:4				08/54	09/81	19864	2,12,19,54,58,9:
1104:2	UP-314	ATSF-104:4				07/57	02/82	23670	2,12,19,54,58,9:
1105:2	UP-345	ATSF-105:4				09/57	02/83	23701	2,12,19,54,58,9:
1106:2	NYC-5653	PC-5653	CR-5653	ATSF-106:4		09/51	03/83	14215	2,12,19,54,59,9:
1107:2	PRR-8550	PC-5850:1	PC-5884:2	CR-5884	ATSF-107:4	09/53	06/83	18665	2,12,19,54,59,9:
1108:2	DL&W-970	EL-1409	CR-5929	ATSF-108:4		02/53	08/83	17894	2,12,19,54,59,9:
1109:2	1111	3111:1	3011:2	109:3		06/60	10/83	25584	2,12,19,54,60,9:

Slug — 1115 Class — 8 units

249,000 lbs

Road#	1st#	2nd#	3rd#	Built	Rebuilt	Build#	Notes
1115:2	2063	2707:2	115:2	01/52	10/81	15807	2,12,19,54,59,92
1116:2	UP-145	ATSF-116:2		02/54	09/80	19146	2,12,19,54,60,92
1117:2	UP-143B	ATSF-117:2		02/54	07/80	19219	2,12,19,54,61,92
1118:2	UP-116	ATSF-118:2		08/53	06/80	18575	2,12,19,54,59,92
1119:2	2650	119:2		10/50	04/80	12196	2,12,19,54,59,92
1123:2	272B	123:2		11/53	10/78	18942	2,12,19,54,62,92
1124:2	UP-134B	ATSF-124:2		02/54	03/80	19210	2,12,19,54,61,92
1125:2	UP-158B	ATSF-125:2		02/54	01/80	19234	2,12,19,54,61,92

Slug — 1126 Class — 4 units

387,440 lbs

Road#	1st#	2nd#	Built	Rebuilt	Build#	Notes
1126:2	UP-437B	ATSF-126:2	09/59	05/81	25426	5,12,19,55,63,93
1127:2	UP-401B	ATSF-127:2	06/59	10/80	25389	5,12,19,55,63,93
1128:2	UP-436B	ATSF-128:2	09/59	08/79	25425	5,12,19,55,63,93
1129:2	UP-420B	ATSF-129:2	07/59	10/79	25408	5,12,19,55,63,93

Slug — 1140 Class — 7 units

400,620 lbs

Road#	1st#	2nd#	3rd#	Built	Rebuilt	Build#	Notes
1140:2	IT-2304	N&W-2964	ATSF-140:3	05/69	02/86	34886	5,12,19,56,64,93
1141:2	1715	5015	141:3	03/66	06/87	32051	5,12,19,56,65,93
1142:3	5208	142:3		10/78	09/87	786153-9	6,17,19,54,66,86,93
1143:2	SP-8644	ATSF-143:3		05/69	12/87	37046	10,12,19,56,67,93
1144:2	SP-8626	ATSF-144:3		04/69	03/88	36925	10,12,19,56,67,93
1145:2	SP-5303	ATSF-145:3		08/68	03/86	34001	5,12,19,56,64,93
1146:2	SP-?	ATSF-146:3			03/86		5,12,19,56,68,93

GP7 — 1310 Class — 1,500 hp — 19 units

16-567BC engine — 41,300 lbs T.E. @ 11 mph — 249,000 lbs

Road#	1st#	2nd#	Built	Rebuilt	Build#	Notes
1310:2	2829:1	2246:2	12/52	06/73	17640	2,12,19,23,78,94,95
1311:2	2879:1	2247:2	11/53	04/73	18896	2,12,19,23,78,94,95
1312:2	2830:1		12/52	04/80	17641	2,12,19,23,78,94,95
1313:2	2702:1		01/52	06/80	15802	2,12,19,23,78,94,95
1314:2	2734:1		06/52	07/80	16378	2,12,19,23,78,94,95
1315:2	2826:1		12/52	09/80	17637	2,12,19,23,78,94,95
1316:2	2853:1		06/53	06/81	18558	2,12,19,23,78,94,95
1317:2	2822:1		12/52	06/81	17633	2,12,19,23,78,94,95
1318:2	2750:1		08/52	07/81	16977	2,12,19,23,78,94,95
1319:2	2872:1		11/53	09/81	18889	2,12,19,23,78,94,95
1320:2	2796		10/52	10/81	17451	2,12,19,23,78,94,95
1321:2	2846:1		12/52	11/81	17707	2,12,19,23,78,94
1322:2	2866:1		10/53	11/81	18883	2,12,19,23,78,94
1323:2	2752:1		08/52	11/81	16979	2,12,19,23,78,94
1324:2	2721:1		02/52	12/81	15821	2,12,19,23,78,94
1325:2	2749:1		08/52	12/81	16976	2,12,19,23,78,94
1327:2	2843:1		12/52	12/81	17704	2,12,19,23,78,94
1328:2	2651		10/50	12/81	12197	2,12,19,23,78,94
1329:2	2838:1		12/52	12/81	17699	2,12,19,23,78,94

1116, Topeka, Kansas, April 6, 1990. *Thomas Chenoweth*

1328, Chicago, Illinois, August 28, 1983. *George Horna*

1128, Topeka, Kansas, April 4, 1991. *Thomas Chenoweth*

1460, Cleburne, Texas, April, 1983. *Keith Wilhite*

1561, San Bernardino, California, November 2, 1985. *Gary Sugg*

2019, McCook, Illinois, August 6, 1987. *George Horna*

2084, Pueblo, Colorado, September 28, 1991. *Bruce Barrett*

112

Switcher	1460 Class		1,500 hp		1 unit
16-567BC engine		41,300 lbs T.E. @ 11 mph			262,500 lbs

Road#	1st#	2nd#	3rd#	Built	Rebuilt	Build#	Notes
1460	2220:1	2450	1160:2	06/43	12/70	67729	2,12,19,21,69

SD39	1556 Class		2,500 hp		20 units
12-645E3 engine		82,284 lbs T.E. @ 8.0 mph			389,000 lbs

Road#	1st#	Built	Rebuilt	Build#	Notes
1556	4004:1	05/69	11/85	35024	5,12,19,34,45,77,94,95
1557	4019:1	06/69	10/85	35039	5,12,19,34,45,77,94,95
1558	4010:1	05/69	11/85	35030	5,12,19,34,45,77,94,95
1559	4001:1	05/69	10/85	35021	5,12,19,34,45,77,94,95
1560	4006:1	05/69	11/85	35026	5,12,19,34,45,77,94,95
1561	4011:1	05/69	10/85	35031	5,12,19,34,45,77,94,95
1562	4002:1	05/69	12/85	35022	5,12,19,34,45,77,94,95
1563	4005:1	05/69	10/85	35025	5,12,19,34,45,77,94,95
1564	4018:1	06/69	12/85	35038	5,12,19,34,45,77,94,95
1565	4017:1	05/69	11/85	35037	5,12,19,34,45,77,94,95
1566	4000:1	05/69	12/85	35020	5,12,19,34,45,77,94,95
1567	4009:1	05/69	10/85	35029	5,12,19,34,45,77,94,95
1568	4016:1	05/69	01/86	35036	5,12,19,34,45,77,94,95
1569	4015:1	06/69	12/85	35035	5,12,19,34,45,77,94,95
1570	4014:1	06/69	01/86	35034	5,12,19,34,45,77,94,95
1571	4003:1	05/69	12/85	35023	5,12,19,34,45,77,94,95
1572	4008:1	05/69	01/86	35028	5,12,19,34,45,77,94,95
1573	4013:1	06/69	01/86	35033	5,12,19,34,45,77,94,95
1574	4012:1	05/69	01/86	35032	5,12,19,34,45,77,94,95
1575	4007:1	05/69	02/86	35027	5,12,19,34,45,77,94,95

GP7	2000 Class		1,500 hp		11 units
16-567BC engine		41,300 lbs T.E. @ 11 mph			249,000 lbs

Road#	1st#	Built	Rebuilt	Build#	Notes
2000	2671	01/51	09/73	13192	2,12,19,22,78
2009	2703:1	01/52	06/81	15803	2,12,19,23,78
2010	2764:1	09/52	06/81	16991	2,12,19,23,78
2011	2787	10/52	07/81	17014	2,12,19,23,78
2012	2777:1	09/52	07/81	17004	2,12,19,23,78
2014	2835:1	12/52	07/81	17646	2,12,19,23,78
2016	2870:1	11/53	08/81	18887	2,12,19,23,78
2017	2850:1	06/53	08/81	18555	2,12,19,23,78
2019	2673	02/51	08/81	12201	2,12,19,22,78
2020	2714:1	02/52	08/81	15814	2,12,19,23,78
2026	2769:1	09/52	10/81	16996	2,12,19,23,78

GP7	2050 Class		1,500 hp		81 units
16-567BC engine		41,300 lbs T.E. @ 11 mph			249,000 lbs

Road#	1st#	Built	Rebuilt	Build#	Notes
2052	2885:1	11/53	06/73	18902	2,12,19,23,78
2055	2801:2	10/52	08/73	17456	2,12,19,23,78
2079	2856:1	07/53	09/74	18561	2,12,19,23,78
2080	2833:1	12/52	09/74	17644	2,12,19,23,78
2083	2883:1	11/53	12/74	18900	2,12,19,23,78
2084	2772:1	09/52	12/74	16999	2,12,19,23,78
2087	2839:1	12/52	01/75	17700	2,12,19,23,78
2089	2704:1	01/52	03/76	15804	2,12,19,23,78
2091	2851:1	06/53	02/77	18556	2,12,19,23,78
2092	2824:1	12/52	03/77	17635	2,12,19,23,78
2095	2865:1	10/53	05/77	18882	2,12,19,23,78
2096	2675	02/51	05/77	13196	2,12,19,23,78
2098	2737:1	06/52	06/77	16381	2,12,19,23,78
2102:2	2812:2	10/52	08/77	17467	2,12,19,23,78
2103:2	2771:1	09/52	08/77	16998	2,12,19,23,78
2104:2	2873:1	11/53	09/77	18890	2,12,19,23,78
2107:2	2857:1	07/53	10/77	18562	2,12,19,23,78
2108:2	2886:1	11/53	10/77	18903	2,12,19,23,78
2109:2	2699	01/52	11/77	15799	2,12,19,22,78
2113:2	2724:1	05/52	12/77	16368	2,12,19,23,78
2115:2	2794	10/52	04/78	17449	2,12,19,23,78
2117:2	2747:1	08/52	04/78	16391	2,12,19,23,78
2119:2	2831:1	12/52	05/78	17642	2,12,19,23,78
2120:2	2815:2	11/52	05/78	17626	2,12,19,23,78
2122:2	2874:1	11/53	07/78	18891	2,12,19,23,78
2123:2	2892:1	12/53	07/78	18909	2,12,19,23,78
2124:2	2844:1	12/52	07/78	17705	2,12,19,23,78

Road#	1st#	Built	Rebuilt	Build#	Notes
2125:2	2820:1	12/52	08/78	17631	2,12,19,23,78
2131:2	2731:1	05/52	10/78	16375	2,12,19,23,78
2132:2	2864:1	10/53	10/78	18881	2,12,19,23,78
2135:2	2693	05/51	06/78	13204	2,12,19,22,78
2136:2	2689	05/51	07/78	13200	2,12,19,22,78
2137:2	2696	05/51	08/78	13207	2,12,19,22,78
2138:2	2697	05/51	10/78	13208	2,12,19,22,78
2140:2	2684	05/51	11/78	13195	2,12,19,22,78
2141:2	2713:1	02/52	11/78	15813	2,12,19,23,78
2142:2	2819:2	12/52	11/78	17630	2,12,19,23,78
2143:2	2858:1	07/53	12/78	18563	2,12,19,23,78
2145:2	2869:1	11/53	12/78	18886	2,12,19,23,78
2147:2	2705:1	01/52	01/79	15805	2,12,19,23,78
2148:2	2757:1	09/52	01/79	16984	2,12,19,23,78
2149:2	2816:2	11/52	01/79	17627	2,12,19,23,78
2159:2	2841:1	12/52	05/79	17702	2,12,19,23,78
2172	2711:1	02/52	10/79	15811	2,12,19,23,78
2181	2860:1	07/53	01/80	18565	2,12,19,23,78
2183	2878:1	10/53	02/80	18895	2,12,19,23,78
2192	2854:1	06/53	05/80	18559	2,12,19,23,78
2193	2670:1	01/51	05/80	13191	2,12,19,23,78
2194	2712:1	02/52	05/80	15812	2,12,19,23,78
2195	2770:1	09/52	05/80	16997	2,12,19,23,78
2199	2788	03/53	07/80	17015	2,12,19,23,78
2200:3	2654	12/50	07/80	12200	2,12,19,22,78
2201:2	2659	10/50	07/80	13163	2,12,19,22,78
2204:2	2672	01/51	08/80	13193	2,12,19,22,78
2208:2	2740:1	08/52	09/80	16384	2,12,19,23,78
2209:2	2694	05/51	10/80	13205	2,12,19,22,78
2212:2	2859:1	07/53	10/80	18564	2,12,19,23,78
2213:2	2798	10/52	11/80	17453	2,12,19,23,78
2215:2	2732:1	05/52	11/80	16376	2,12,19,23,78
2216:2	2746:1	08/52	12/80	16390	2,12,19,23,78
2217:2	2726:1	05/52	12/80	16370	2,12,19,23,78
2218:2	2717:1	02/52	12/80	15817	2,12,19,23,78
2220:2	2765:1	09/52	01/81	16992	2,12,19,23,78
2221:2	2795	10/52	01/81	17450	2,12,19,22,78
2222:2	2723:1	05/52	01/81	16367	2,12,19,23,78
2224:2	2716:1	02/52	02/81	15816	2,12,19,23,78
2228:2	2776:1	09/52	03/81	17001	2,12,19,23,78
2229:2	2709:1	01/52	03/81	15809	2,12,19,23,78
2230:2	2803:2	10/52	03/81	17458	2,12,19,23,78
2231:2	2837:1	12/52	03/81	17648	2,12,19,23,78
2232:2	2780:1	09/52	04/81	17007	2,12,19,23,78
2233:2	2718:1	02/52	04/81	15818	2,12,19,23,78
2235:2	2775:1	09/52	04/81	17002	2,12,19,23,78
2236:2	2681	02/51	04/81	12209	2,12,19,22,78
2237:2	2862:1	07/53	05/81	18567	2,12,19,23,78
2238:2	2676	02/51	05/81	12204	2,12,19,22,78
2239:2	2814:2	11/52	05/81	17625	2,12,19,23,78
2240:2	2679	02/51	05/81	12207	2,12,19,22,78
2241:2	2669	01/51	06/81	13190	2,12,19,22,78
2242:2	2715:1	02/52	06/81	15815	2,12,19,23,78
2243:2	2802:2	10/52	06/81	17457	2,12,19,23,78

GP9   2244 Class   1,750 hp   50 units

16-567C engine   45,200 lbs T.E. @ 11.8 mph   249,000 lbs

Road#	1st#	2nd#	Built	Rebuilt	Build#	Notes
2244:2	2789A		03/53	05/80	17021	2,12,19,23,70
2245:2	704	2904:1	05/56	03/80	21574	2,12,19,23,78
2246:2	734	2934:1	02/57	03/80	23469	2,12,19,23,78
2247:2	739	2939:1	04/57	03/80	23142	2,12,19,23,78
2250:2	702	2902:1	05/56	04/78	21572	2,12,19,23,78
2251:2	703	2903:1	05/56	05/78	21573	2,12,19,23,78
2252:2	726	2926:1	05/56	06/78	21564	2,12,19,23,78
2253:2	740	2940:1	04/57	06/78	23143	2,12,19,23,78
2254:2	706	2906:1	05/56	07/78	21576	2,12,19,23,78
2255:2	747	2947:1	04/57	07/78	23150	2,12,19,23,78
2256:2	710	2910:1	05/56	08/78	21580	2,12,19,23,78
2257:2	744	2944:1	04/57	08/78	23147	2,12,19,23,78
2258:2	2790A		03/53	08/78	17022	2,12,19,23,70
2259:2	717	2917:1	05/56	09/78	21587	2,12,19,23,78
2260:2	700	2900:1	05/56	10/78	21570	2,12,19,23,78
2261:2	724	2924:1	05/56	10/78	21594	2,12,19,23,78
2262:2	709	2909:1	05/56	11/78	21579	2,12,19,23,78

2212, Amarillo, Texas, March 28, 1992. *George Horna*

2281, Chicago, Illinois, June 9, 1991. *George Horna*

Road#	1st#	2nd#	Built	Rebuilt	Build#	Notes
2263:2	751	2951:1	04/57	11/78	23154	2,12,19,23,78
2265:2	725	2925:1	05/56	12/78	21595	2,12,19,23,78
2266:2	723	2923:1	05/56	01/79	21593	2,12,19,23,78
2267:2	711	2911:1	05/56	01/79	21581	2,12,19,23,78
2268:2	746	2946:1	04/57	02/79	23149	2,12,19,23,78
2269:2	745	2945:1	04/57	03/79	23148	2,12,19,23,78
2270:2	2791A		04/53	04/79	17023	2,12,19,23,70
2271:2	748	2948:1	04/57	05/79	23151	2,12,19,23,78
2272:2	714	2914:1	05/56	05/79	21584	2,12,19,23,78
2273:2	722	2922:1	05/56	05/79	21592	2,12,19,23,78
2274:2	716	2916:1	05/56	05/79	21586	2,12,19,23,78
2275:2	732	2932:1	02/57	06/79	23467	2,12,19,23,78
2276:2	701	2901:1	05/56	07/79	21571	2,12,19,23,78
2277:2	741	2941:1	04/57	07/79	23144	2,12,19,23,78
2279:2	738	2938:1	04/57	07/79	23141	2,12,19,23,78
2280:2	735	2935:1	02/57	07/79	23470	2,12,19,23,78
2281:2	736	2936:1	04/57	08/79	23139	2,12,19,23,78
2282:2	729	2929:1	05/56	08/79	21567	2,12,19,23,78
2283:2	750	2950:1	04/57	08/79	23153	2,12,19,23,78
2285:2	708	2908:1	05/56	09/79	21578	2,12,19,23,78
2286:2	727	2927:1	05/56	10/79	21565	2,12,19,23,78
2287:2	749	2949:1	04/57	10/79	23152	2,12,19,23,78
2288:2	2792A		04/53	10/79	17024	2,12,19,23,70
2289:2	720	2920:1	05/56	11/79	21590	2,12,19,23,70
2291:2	731	2931:1	05/56	11/79	21569	2,12,19,23,78
2292:2	712	2912:1	05/56	12/79	21582	2,12,19,23,78
2293:2	733	2933:1	02/57	12/79	23468	2,12,19,23,78
2294:2	719	2919:1	05/56	12/79	21589	2,12,19,23,78
2295:2	742	2942:1	04/57	01/80	23145	2,12,19,23,78
2296:2	721	2921:1	05/56	01/80	21591	2,12,19,23,78
2297:2	728	2928:1	05/56	01/80	21566	2,12,19,23,78
2298:2	713	2913:1	05/56	02/80	21583	2,12,19,23,78
2299:2	730	2930:1	05/56	02/80	21568	2,12,19,23,78

GP38	2300 Class	2,000 hp		58 units

16-645E engine   55,460 lbs T.E. @ 10.5 mph   262,500 lbs

Road#	1st#	Built	Rebuilt	Build#	Notes
2300:2	3500	06/70	09/84	36536	2,12,19,28,53,78
2301:3	3501	06/70	04/85	36537	2,12,19,28,53,78
2302:2	3502	06/70	05/85	36538	2,12,19,28,53,78
2303:2	3503	06/70	02/85	36539	2,12,19,28,53,78
2304:2	3504	06/70	02/85	36540	2,12,19,28,53,78
2305:2	3505	06/70	09/84	36541	2,12,19,28,53,78
2306:2	3506	06/70	01/85	36542	2,12,19,28,53,78
2307:2	3507	06/70	06/85	36543	2,12,19,28,53,78
2308:2	3508	06/70	01/85	36544	2,12,19,28,53,78
2309:2	3509	06/70	05/85	36545	2,12,19,28,53,78
2310:2	3510	06/70	10/84	36546	2,12,19,28,53,78
2311:2	3511	06/70	08/85	36547	2,12,19,28,53,78
2312:2	3512	06/70	10/82	36548	2,12,19,28,53,78
2313:2	3513	06/70	06/85	36549	2,12,19,28,53,78
2314:2	3514	06/70	01/85	36550	2,12,19,28,53,78
2315:2	3515	06/70	03/85	36551	2,12,19,28,53,78
2316:2	3516	06/70	12/84	36552	2,12,19,28,53,78
2317:2	3517	06/70	12/84	36553	2,12,19,28,53,78
2318:2	3518	06/70	03/85	36554	2,12,19,28,53,78
2319:2	3519	06/70	11/84	36555	2,12,19,28,53,78
2320:2	3520	06/70	10/84	36556	2,12,19,28,53,78
2321:2	3521	06/70	06/85	36557	2,12,19,28,53,78
2322:2	3522	06/70	07/85	36558	2,12,19,28,53,78
2324:2	3524	06/70	10/84	36560	2,12,19,28,53,78
2325:2	3525	06/70	10/84	36561	2,12,19,28,53,78
2326:2	3526	06/70	05/85	36562	2,12,19,28,53,78
2327:2	3527	06/70	04/85	36563	2,12,19,28,53,78
2328:2	3528	06/70	12/84	36564	2,12,19,28,53,78
2329:2	3529	08/70	05/85	36565	2,12,19,28,53,78
2330:2	3530	08/70	10/84	36566	2,12,19,28,53,78
2331:2	3531	08/70	11/84	36567	2,12,19,28,53,78
2332:2	3532	08/70	03/83	36568	2,12,19,28,53,78
2333:2	3533	08/70	03/85	36569	2,12,19,28,53,78
2334:2	3534	08/70	02/85	36570	2,12,19,28,53,78
2335:2	3535	08/70	04/85	36571	2,12,19,28,53,78

GP38	2300 Class		Continued	

Road#	1st#	Built	Rebuilt	Build#	Notes
2336:2	3536	08/70	04/85	36572	2,12,19,28,53,78
2337:2	3537	08/70	03/85	36573	2,12,19,28,53,78
2338:2	3538	08/70	03/85	36574	2,12,19,28,53,78
2339:2	3539	08/70	05/85	36575	2,12,19,28,53,78
2340:2	3540	08/70	07/85	36576	2,12,19,28,53,78
2341:2	3541	08/70	07/85	36577	2,12,19,28,53,78
2342:2	3542	08/70	12/84	36578	2,12,19,28,53,78
2343:2	3543	08/70	06/85	36579	2,12,19,28,53,78
2344:2	3544	08/70	10/84	36580	2,12,19,28,53,78
2345:2	3545	08/70	04/85	36581	2,12,19,28,53,78
2346:2	3546	08/70	01/85	36582	2,12,19,28,53,78
2347:2	3547	08/70	11/84	36583	2,12,19,28,53,78
2349:2	3549	08/70	07/85	36585	2,12,19,28,53,78
2350:3	3550	09/70	01/85	36586	2,12,19,28,53,78
2351:3	3551	09/70	11/84	36587	2,12,19,28,53,78
2353:3	3553	09/70	06/85	36589	2,12,19,28,53,78
2354:3	3554	09/70	09/84	36590	2,12,19,28,53,78
2355:3	3555	09/70	05/85	36591	2,12,19,28,53,78
2356:3	3556	09/70	02/85	36592	2,12,19,28,53,78
2357:3	3557	09/70	02/85	36593	2,12,19,28,53,78
2358:3	3558	09/70	07/85	36594	2,12,19,28,53,78
2359:3	3559	09/70	01/85	36595	2,12,19,28,53,78
2360:3	3560	09/70	11/84	36596	2,12,19,28,53,78

GP38-2	2370 Class		2,000 hp		11 units

16-645E engine   55,400 lbs T.E. @ 10.8 mph   260,800 lbs

Road#	1st#	2nd#	Built	Build#	Notes
2370:2	TPW-2001	ATSF-3561	05/77	766058-1	2,12,19,26
2371:2	TPW-2002	ATSF-3562	05/77	766058-2	2,12,19,26
2372:2	TPW-2003	ATSF-3563	05/77	766058-3	2,12,19,26
2373:2	TPW-2004	ATSF-3564	05/77	766058-4	2,12,19,26
2374:2	TPW-2005	ATSF-3565	10/78	776122-1	2,12,19,26
2375:2	TPW-2006	ATSF-3566	10/78	776122-2	2,12,19,26
2376:2	TPW-2007	ATSF-3567	10/78	776122-3	2,12,19,26
2377:2	TPW-2008	ATSF-3568	10/78	776122-4	2,12,19,26
2378:2	TPW-2009	ATSF-3569	10/78	776122-5	2,12,19,26
2379:3	TPW-2010	ATSF-3570	10/78	776122-6	2,12,19,26
2380:3	TPW-2011	ATSF-3571	10/78	776122-7	2,12,19,26

GP30	2700 Class		2,500 hp		78 units

16-645D3 engine   51,400 lbs T.E. @ 12 mph   262,900 lbs

Road#	1st#	2nd#	Built	Rebuilt	Build#	Notes
2700:2	1200	3200:1	04/62	02/81	27187	2,12,19,26,44,78
2701:2	1201	3201:1	04/62	03/84	27188	2,12,19,26,44,78
2702:2	1202	3202	04/62	08/83	27189	2,12,19,26,44,78
2703:2	1203	3203	04/62	01/84	27190	2,12,19,26,44,78
2704:2	1204	3204	04/62	10/82	27191	2,12,19,26,44,78
2705:2	1205	3205	04/62	08/82	27192	2,12,19,26,44,78
2707:2	1207	3207	05/62	01/83	27194	2,12,19,26,44,78
2708:2	1208	3208	05/62	01/84	27195	2,12,19,26,44,78
2709:2	1209	3209	05/62	01/83	27196	2,12,19,26,44,78
2710:2	1210	3210	05/62	07/80	27197	2,12,19,26,44,77
2711:2	1211	3211	05/62	01/83	27198	2,12,19,26,44,78
2712:2	1212	3212	05/62	02/84	27199	2,12,19,26,44,78
2713:2	1213	3213	05/62	10/80	27200	2,12,19,26,44,77
2714:2	1214	3214	05/62	11/83	27201	2,12,19,26,44,78
2715:2	1215	3215	05/62	08/83	27202	2,12,19,26,44,78
2716:2	1216	3216	05/62	11/82	27203	2,12,19,26,44,78
2717:2	1217	3217	05/62	06/81	27204	2,12,19,26,44,77
2718:2	1218	3218	05/62	07/81	27205	2,12,19,26,44,77
2719:2	1219	3219	05/62	07/83	27206	2,12,19,26,44,78
2720:2	1220	3220	05/62	11/83	27207	2,12,19,26,44,78
2721:2	1221	3221	05/62	11/82	27208	2,12,19,26,44,78
2722:2	1222	3222	06/62	08/83	27209	2,12,19,26,44,78
2723:2	1223	3223	06/62	07/80	27210	2,12,19,26,44,77
2724:2	1224	3224	06/62	08/81	27211	2,12,19,26,44,77
2725:2	1225	3225	06/62	04/84	27212	2,12,19,26,44,78
2726:2	1226	3226	06/62	07/83	27213	2,12,19,26,44,78
2727:2	1227	3227	06/62	11/82	27214	2,12,19,26,44,78
2728:2	1228	3228	06/62	03/84	27215	2,12,19,26,44,78
2729:2	1229	3229	06/62	12/83	27216	2,12,19,26,44,78
2731:2	1231	3231	06/62	11/82	27218	2,12,19,26,44,78
2732:2	1232	3232	06/62	07/82	27219	2,12,19,26,44,78

2357, Chicago, Illinois, August 4, 1991. *George Horna*

2371, Topeka, Kansas, May 3, 1991. *Tom Chenoweth*

Road#	1st#	2nd#	Built	Rebuilt	Build#	Notes
2734:2	1234	3234	06/62	10/82	27221	2,12,19,26,44,78
2735:2	1235	3235	01/63	07/83	28058	2,12,19,26,44,78
2736:2	1236	3236	01/63	06/82	28059	2,12,19,26,44,78
2737:2	1237	3237	01/63	06/83	28060	2,12,19,26,44,78
2738:2	1238	3238	01/63	11/83	28061	2,12,19,26,44,78
2739:2	1239	3239	01/63	02/83	28062	2,12,19,26,44,78
2740:2	1240	3240	01/63	02/83	28063	2,12,19,26,44,78
2741:2	1241	3241	01/63	02/84	28064	2,12,19,26,44,78
2742:2	1242	3242	01/63	04/84	28065	2,12,19,26,44,78
2743:2	1243	3243	02/63	07/82	28066	2,12,19,26,44,78
2744:2	1244	3244	02/63	01/84	28067	2,12,19,26,44,78
2745:2	1245	3245	02/63	07/82	28068	2,12,19,26,44,78
2746:2	1246	3246	02/63	02/84	28069	2,12,19,26,44,78
2747:2	1247	3247	02/63	10/82	28070	2,12,19,26,44,78
2748:2	1248	3248	02/63	06/82	28071	2,12,19,26,44,78
2750:2	1250	3250	02/63	04/84	28073	2,12,19,26,44,78
2751:2	1251	3251	03/63	02/83	28074	2,12,19,26,44,78
2753:2	1253	3253	03/63	08/82	28076	2,12,19,26,44,78
2754:2	1254	3254	03/63	10/82	28077	2,12,19,26,44,78
2755:2	1255	3255	03/63	01/83	28078	2,12,19,26,44,78
2756:2	1256	3256	03/63	07/83	28079	2,12,19,26,44,78
2757:2	1257	3257	03/63	03/84	28080	2,12,19,26,44,78
2759:2	1259	3259	03/63	08/81	28082	2,12,19,26,44,77
2760:2	1260	3260	03/63	03/84	28083	2,12,19,26,44,78
2762:2	1262	3262	03/63	03/84	28085	2,12,19,26,44,78
2763:2	1263	3263	04/63	03/84	28086	2,12,19,26,44,78
2764:2	1264	3264	04/63	10/82	28087	2,12,19,26,44,78
2765:2	1265	3265	04/63	12/83	28088	2,12,19,26,44,78
2767:2	1267	3267	04/63	02/84	28090	2,12,19,26,44,78
2768:2	1268	3268	04/63	12/80	28091	2,12,19,26,44,77
2769:2	1269	3269	05/63	08/83	28092	2,12,19,26,44,78
2770:2	1270	3270	05/63	06/82	28093	2,12,19,26,44,78
2771:2	1271	3271	05/63	02/83	28094	2,12,19,26,44,78
2772:2	1272	3272	05/63	01/83	28095	2,12,19,26,44,78

Road#	1st#	2nd#	Built	Rebuilt	Build#	Notes
2773:2	1273	3273	05/63	08/82	28096	2,12,19,26,44,78
2774:2	1274	3274	05/63	01/84	28097	2,12,19,26,44,78
2775:2	1275	3275	05/63	08/83	28098	2,12,19,26,44,78
2776:2	1276	3276	05/63	07/78	28099	2,12,19,26,44,78
2777:2	1277	3277	06/63	04/84	28100	2,12,19,26,44,78
2778:2	1278	3278	06/63	11/83	28101	2,12,19,26,44,78
2779:2	1279	3279	06/63	12/83	28102	2,12,19,26,44,78
2780:2	1280	3280	06/63	07/82	28103	2,12,19,26,44,78
2781:2	1281	3281	06/63	02/83	28104	2,12,19,26,44,78
2782:2	1282	3282	06/63	01/84	28105	2,12,19,26,44,78
2783:2	1283	3283	06/63	11/82	28106	2,12,19,26,44,78
2784:2	1284	3284	06/63	02/82	28107	2,12,19,26,44,78
2785:2	TPW-700	ATSF-3285	09/63	07/84	28354	2,12,19,26,44,78

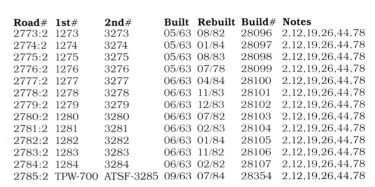

2716, San Bernardino, California, February 3, 1991. *George Horna*

GP35   2800 Class   2,500 hp   150 units

16-645D3 engine   51,400 lbs T.E. @ 12 mph   266,000 lbs

Road#	1st#	2nd#	3rd#	4th#	Built	Rebuilt	Build#	Notes
2801:4	1301:1	3301	2801:3	3561	03/64	07/84	28698	2,12,19,26,44,77
2802:4	1302:1	3302	2802:3	3562	03/64	08/84	28699	2,12,19,26,44,78
2804:4	1304	3304	2804:3	3563	03/64	11/84	28701	2,12,19,26,44,77
2805:4	1305	3305	2805:3	3564	03/64	08/82	28702	2,12,19,26,44,78
2806:4	1306	3306	2806:3	3565	03/64	02/82	28703	2,12,19,26,44,78
2807:4	1307	3307	2807:3	3566	03/64	03/83	28704	2,12,19,26,44,78
2808:4	1308	3308	2808:3	3567	03/64	08/84	28705	2,12,19,26,44,77
2809:4	1309	3309	2809:3	3568	03/64	02/84	28706	2,12,19,26,44,77
2810:4	1310:1	3310	2810:3	3569	03/64	07/84	28707	2,12,19,26,44,78
2811:4	1311:1	3311	2811:3	3570	03/64	08/82	28708	2,12,19,26,44,78
2812:4	1312:1	3312	2812:3	3571	03/64	06/84	28709	2,12,19,26,44,77
2813:4	1313:1	3313	2813:3	3572	03/64	01/85	28710	2,12,19,26,44,77
2814:4	1314:1	3314			03/64	09/84	28711	2,12,19,26,44,78
2815:4	1315:1	3315	2815:3	3574	03/64	04/84	28712	2,12,19,26,44,77
2816:4	1316:1	3316	2816:3	3575	03/64	02/82	28713	2,12,19,26,44,78
2818:4	1318:1	3318			03/64	11/84	28715	2,12,19,26,44,77
2819:4	1319:1	3319	2819:3	3577	03/64	05/83	28716	2,12,19,26,44,78
2821:3	1321:1	3321	2821:2	3578	03/64	07/82	28718	2,12,19,26,44,78
2822:3	1322:1	3322	2822:2	3579	03/64	05/84	28719	2,12,19,26,44,77
2823:3	1323:1	3323			03/64	09/82	28720	2,12,19,26,44,78
2824:3	1324:1	3324	2824:2	3581	04/64	09/84	28721	2,12,19,26,44,77
2825:3	1325:1	3325	2825:2	3582	04/64	11/82	28722	2,12,19,26,44,78
2826:3	1326:1	3326	2826:2	3583	04/64	11/84	28723	2,12,19,26,44,77
2827:3	1327:1	3327	2827:2	3584	04/64	02/84	28724	2,12,19,26,44,77
2828:3	1328:1	3328	2828:2	3585	04/64	07/84	28725	2,12,19,26,44,78
2829:3	1329:1	3329	2829:2	3586	04/64	12/84	28726	2,12,19,26,44,77
2830:3	1330	3330			04/64	06/83	28727	2,12,19,26,44,78
2831:3	1331	3331			04/64	03/83	28728	2,12,19,26,44,78
2832:3	1332	3332			04/64	02/84	28729	2,12,19,26,44,77
2833:3	1333	3333	2833:2	3590	04/64	03/79	28730	2,12,19,26,44,77
2834:3	1334	3334	2834:2	3591	04/64	06/83	28731	2,12,19,26,44,78
2835:3	1335	3335	2835:2	3592	04/64	12/78	28732	2,12,19,26,44,77
2836:3	1336	3336	2836:2	3593	04/64	04/83	28733	2,12,19,26,44,78
2837:3	1337	3337	2837:2	3594	05/64	08/82	28734	2,12,19,26,44,78
2838:3	1338	3338	2838:2	3595	05/64	09/83	28735	2,12,19,26,44,78
2839:3	1339	3339	2839:2	3596	05/64	09/82	28736	2,12,19,26,44,78

Road#	1st#	2nd#	Built	Rebuilt	Build#	Notes
2840:2	1340	3340	05/64	02/82	28737	2,12,19,26,44,78
2841:2	1341	3341	05/64	08/83	28738	2,12,19,26,44,78
2842:2	1342	3342	05/64	05/82	28739	2,12,19,26,44,78
2843:2	1343	3343	06/64	06/83	28740	2,12,19,26,44,78
2844:2	1344	3344	06/64	07/81	28741	2,12,19,26,44,77
2845:2	1345	3345	06/64	12/82	28742	2,12,19,26,44,78
2847:2	1347	3347	06/64	05/84	28744	2,12,19,26,44,78
2848:2	1348	3348	06/64	06/81	28745	2,12,19,26,44,77
2849:2	1349	3349	06/64	05/83	28746	2,12,19,26,44,78
2850:2	1350	3350	04/65	06/82	30064	2,12,19,26,44,78
2851:2	1351	3351	04/65	12/82	30065	2,12,19,26,44,78
2852:2	1352	3352	04/65	03/83	30066	2,12,19,26,44,78
2853:2	1353	3353	04/65	12/82	30067	2,12,19,26,44,78
2854:2	1354	3354	04/65	06/83	30068	2,12,19,26,44,78

2850, Barstow, California, June 7, 1984. *Gary Zuters*

2857, San Bernardino, California, November 2, 1985. *Gary Sugg*

2903, Temple, Texas, September 21, 1991. *Rick Bartoskewitz*

Road#	1st#	2nd#	Built	Rebuilt	Build#	Notes
2855:2	1355	3355	04/65	03/84	30069	2,12,19,26,44,77
2857:2	1357	3357	04/65	10/83	30071	2,12,19,26,44,78
2858:2	1358	3358	05/65	08/84	30072	2,12,19,26,44,77
2859:2	1359	3359	04/65	12/82	30073	2,12,19,26,44,78
2860:2	1360	3360	04/65	10/84	30074	2,12,19,26,44,77
2861:2	1361	3361	04/65	10/84	30075	2,12,19,26,44,77
2862:2	1362	3362	05/65	03/83	30076	2,12,19,26,44,78
2863:2	1363	3363	05/65	09/82	30077	2,12,19,26,44,78
2864:2	1364	3364	05/65	03/84	30078	2,12,19,26,44,77
2865:2	1365	3365	05/65	09/82	30079	2,12,19,26,44,78
2866:2	1366	3366	05/65	06/84	30080	2,12,19,26,44,78
2867:2	1367	3367	05/65	10/82	30081	2,12,19,26,44,78
2868:2	1368	3368	05/65	11/84	30082	2,12,19,26,44,77
2869:2	1369	3369	05/65	07/80	30083	2,12,19,26,44,77
2870:2	1370	3370	05/65	03/84	30084	2,12,19,26,44,78
2871:2	1371	3371	05/65	10/82	30085	2,12,19,26,44,78
2872:2	1372	3372	05/65	05/82	30086	2,12,19,26,44,78
2873:2	1373	3373	05/65	10/83	30087	2,12,19,26,44,78
2874:2	1374	3374	05/65	09/81	30088	2,12,19,26,44,77
2875:2	1375	3375	06/65	03/83	30089	2,12,19,26,44,78
2876:2	1376	3376	06/65	04/83	30090	2,12,19,26,44,78
2877:2	1377	3377	06/65	09/84	30091	2,12,19,26,44,78
2878:2	1378	3378	06/65	12/81	30092	2,12,19,26,44,78
2880:2	1380	3380	06/65	04/83	30094	2,12,19,26,44,78
2882:2	1382	3382	06/65	05/84	30096	2,12,19,26,44,78
2883:2	1383	3383	06/65	04/84	30097	2,12,19,26,44,77
2884:2	1384	3384	06/65	11/84	30098	2,12,19,26,44,77
2885:2	1385	3385	06/65	08/84	30099	2,12,19,26,44,77
2886:2	1386	3386	07/65	08/84	30100	2,12,19,26,44,78
2887:2	1387	3387	06/65	08/84	30101	2,12,19,26,44,78
2888:2	1388	3388	06/65	04/83	30102	2,12,19,26,44,78
2889:2	1389	3389	06/65	05/84	30103	2,12,19,26,44,78
2890:2	1390	3390	06/65	10/83	30104	2,12,19,26,44,78
2891:2	1391	3391	07/65	04/84	30105	2,12,19,26,44,78
2892:2	1392	3392	06/65	09/83	30106	2,12,19,26,44,78
2893:2	1393	3393	07/65	07/84	30107	2,12,19,26,44,77
2894	1394	3394	07/65	05/84	30108	2,12,19,26,44,78
2896	1396	3396	07/65	06/82	30110	2,12,19,26,44,78
2897	1397	3397	07/65	12/82	30111	2,12,19,26,44,78
2898	1398	3398	07/65	10/81	30112	2,12,19,26,44,77
2899:2	1399	3399	07/65	10/79	30113	2,12,19,26,44,77
2901:2	1401	3401:1	08/65	04/84	30546	2,12,19,26,44,77
2902:2	1402	3402:1	08/65	07/84	30547	2,12,19,26,44,77
2903:2	1403	3403:1	08/65	03/84	30548	2,12,19,26,44,77
2904:2	1404	3404:1	08/65	04/84	30549	2,12,19,26,44,77
2905:2	1405	3405:1	08/65	05/84	30550	2,12,19,26,44,77
2906:2	1406	3406:1	08/65	10/83	30551	2,12,19,26,44,78
2907:2	1407	3407:1	08/65	07/84	30552	2,12,19,26,44,77
2908:2	1408	3408:1	08/65	01/85	30553	2,12,19,26,44,77
2909:2	1409	3409:1	08/65	05/84	30554	2,12,19,26,44,77
2910:2	1110	3110:1	08/65	10/84	30555	2,12,19,26,44,77
2911:2	1411	3411:1	08/65	09/82	30556	2,12,19,26,44,78
2912:2	1412	3412:1	08/65	09/84	30557	2,12,19,26,44,77
2913:2	1413	3413:1	08/65	10/83	30558	2,12,19,26,44,78
2914:2	1414	3414:1	08/65	02/84	30559	2,12,19,26,44,77
2915:2	1415	3415:1	08/65	12/84	30560	2,12,19,26,44,77
2916:2	1416	3416:1	08/65	09/83	30561	2,12,19,26,44,78
2917:2	1417	3417:1	08/65	05/84	30562	2,12,19,26,44,78
2918:2	1418	3418:1	09/65	12/84	30563	2,12,19,26,44,77
2919:2	1419	3419:1	09/65	01/84	30564	2,12,19,26,44,77
2920:2	1420	3420:1	09/65	06/83	30565	2,12,19,26,44,78
2921:2	1421	3421:1	09/65	06/84	30566	2,12,19,26,44,78
2922:2	1422	3422:1	09/65	07/84	30567	2,12,19,26,44,78
2923:2	1423	3423:1	09/65	03/81	30568	2,12,19,26,44,77
2924:2	1424	3424:1	09/65	06/84	30569	2,12,19,26,44,77
2925:2	1425	3425:1	09/65	07/84	30570	2,12,19,26,44,78
2927:2	1427	3427:1	09/65	08/84	30572	2,12,19,26,44,78
2928:2	1428	3428:1	09/65	05/83	30573	2,12,19,26,44,78
2929:2	1429	3429:1	09/65	12/84	30574	2,12,19,26,44,77
2930:2	1430	3430:1	09/65	04/84	30575	2,12,19,26,44,77
2931:2	1431	3431:1	09/65	06/84	30576	2,12,19,26,44,78
2932:2	1432	3432:1	09/65	04/81	30577	2,12,19,26,44,77
2933:2	1433	3433:1	09/65	08/84	30578	2,12,19,26,44,78
2934:2	1434	3434:1	09/65	12/82	30579	2,12,19,26,44,78
2935:2	1435	3435:1	09/65	04/83	30580	2,12,19,26,44,78
2936:2	1436	3436:1	09/65	03/84	30581	2,12,19,26,44,77
2937:2	1437	3437:1	09/65	02/84	30582	2,12,19,26,44,77

GP35	2800 Class	Continued				

Road#	1st#	2nd#	Built	Rebuilt	Build#	Notes
2938:2	1438	3438:1	09/65	12/81	30583	2,12,19,26,44,78
2940:2	1440	3440:1	09/65	02/82	30585	2,12,19,26,44,78
2941:2	1441	3441:1	10/65	08/84	30586	2,12,19,26,44,77
2942:2	1442	3442:1	10/65	06/82	30587	2,12,19,26,44,78
2943:2	1443	3443:1	10/65	10/83	30588	2,12,19,26,44,78
2944:2	1444	3444:1	10/65	05/83	30589	2,12,19,26,44,78
2946:2	1446	3446:1	10/65	11/78	30591	2,12,19,26,44,77
2947:2	1447	3447:1	10/65	05/84	30592	2,12,19,26,44,77
2948:2	1448	3448:1	10/65	01/85	30593	2,12,19,26,44,77
2949:2	1449	3449:1	10/65	10/84	30594	2,12,19,26,44,77
2951:2	1451	3451:1	10/65	09/84	30927	2,12,19,26,44,77
2952	1452	3452	10/65	06/84	30928	2,12,19,26,44,77
2953	1453	3453	10/65	07/79	30929	2,12,19,26,44,77
2954	1454	3454	10/65	05/81	30930	2,12,19,26,44,77
2955	1455	3455	11/65	11/81	30931	2,12,19,26,44,77
2956	1456	3456	11/65	09/84	30932	2,12,19,26,44,77
2957	1457	3457	11/65	06/84	30933	2,12,19,26,44,77
2958	1458	3458	11/65	05/81	30934	2,12,19,26,44,77
2959	1459	3459	11/65	01/79	30935	2,12,19,26,44,77
2960	1460	3460	11/65	07/84	30936	2,12,19,26,44,77
2961	TPW-900	ATSF-3461	11/65	01/85	31061	2,12,19,26,44,77,101
2962	TPW-901	ATSF-3462	11/65	10/84	31062	2,12,19,26,44,77,101
2963	TPW-902	ATSF-3463	11/65	12/84	31063	2,12,19,26,44,77,101

GP20	3000 Class	2,000 hp	52 units
16-567D2 engine		44,800 lbs T.E. @ 13.7 mph	265,000 lbs

Road#	1st#	2nd#	Built	Rebuilt	Build#	Notes
3000:2	1100	3100:1	05/60	11/80	25573	2,12,19,24,52,77
3001:2	1101:1	3101:1	05/60	03/78	25574	2,12,19,24,52,77
3002:2	1102:1	3102:1	05/60	07/78	25575	2,12,19,24,52,77
3005:2	1105:1	3105:1	05/60	07/81	25578	2,12,19,24,52,77
3006:2	1106:1	3106:1	05/60	09/77	25579	2,12,19,24,52,77
3007:2	1107:1	3107:1	05/60	04/78	25580	2,12,19,24,52,77
3008:2	1108:1	3108:1	06/60	05/79	25581	2,12,19,24,52,77
3009:2	1109:1	3109:1	06/60	06/79	25582	2,12,19,24,52,77
3010:2	1110	3110:1	06/60	06/78	25583	2,12,19,24,52,77
3012:2	1112	3112:1	06/60	02/81	25585	2,12,19,24,52,77
3017:2	1117:1	3117:1	07/60	10/77	25590	2,12,19,24,52,77
3018:2	1118:1	3118:1	07/60	06/78	25591	2,12,19,24,52,77
3020	1120:1	3120:1	07/60	05/78	25593	2,12,19,24,52,77
3021	1121	3121:1	07/60	03/77	25594	2,12,19,24,52,77
3023	1123:1	3123:1	07/60	02/77	25596	2,12,19,24,52,77
3024	1124:1	3124:1	07/60	07/77	25597	2,12,19,24,52,77
3025	1125:1	3125	08/61	02/78	26831	2,12,19,24,52,77
3026	1126:1	3126:1	08/61	03/81	26832	2,12,19,24,52,77
3028	1128:1	3128:1	08/61	09/78	26834	2,12,19,24,52,77
3029	1129:1	3129:1	08/61	08/78	26835	2,12,19,24,52,77
3030	1130	3130:1	08/61	04/81	26836	2,12,19,24,52,77
3031	1131	3131:1	08/61	06/79	26837	2,12,19,24,52,77
3032	1132	3132	08/61	06/81	26838	2,12,19,24,52,77
3033	1133	3133:1	09/61	01/77	26839	2,12,19,24,52,77
3035	1135	3135:1	09/61	05/79	26841	2,12,19,24,52,77

3421, Topeka, Kansas, January 3, 1991. *Thomas Chenoweth*

3018, Chicago, Illinois, June 17, 1991. *George Horna*

GP20	3000 Class	Continued			

Road#	1st#	2nd#	Built	Rebuilt	Build#	Notes
3036	1136	3136:1	09/61	05/79	26842	2,12,19,24,52,77
3038	1138	3138:1	09/61	11/77	26844	2,12,19,24,52,77
3041	1141:1	3141:1	09/61	07/81	26847	2,12,19,24,52,77
3043	1143:1	3143:1	10/61	03/78	26849	2,12,19,24,52,77
3044	1144:1	3144:1	10/61	02/79	26850	2,12,19,24,52,77
3045	1145:1	3145:1	10/61	06/77	26851	2,12,19,24,52,77
3046	1146:1	3146:1	10/61	08/77	26852	2,12,19,24,52,77
3047	1147	3147:1	10/61	04/79	26853	2,12,19,24,52,77
3048	1148	3148:1	10/61	11/78	26854	2,12,19,24,52,77
3049	1149	3149:1	10/61	03/81	26855	2,12,19,24,52,77
3050	1150	3150:1	10/61	12/77	26856	2,12,19,24,52,77
3052	1152	3152	10/61	08/81	26858	2,12,19,24,52,77
3054	1154	3154:1	11/61	04/81	26860	2,12,19,24,52,77
3055	1155	3155:1	11/61	12/78	26861	2,12,19,24,52,77
3056	1156	3156:1	11/61	03/79	26862	2,12,19,24,52,77
3057	1157	3157:1	11/61	05/77	26863	2,12,19,24,52,77
3058	1158	3158	11/61	08/78	26864	2,12,19,24,52,77
3060	1160	3160	11/61	06/81	26866	2,12,19,24,52,77
3061	1161	3161:1	11/61	11/78	26867	2,12,19,24,52,77
3062	1162	3162:1	11/61	10/78	26868	2,12,19,24,52,77
3064	1164	3164:1	12/61	02/78	26870	2,12,19,24,52,77
3065	1165	3165	12/61	04/78	26871	2,12,19,24,52,77
3066	1166	3166:1	12/61	04/77	26872	2,12,19,24,52,77
3067	1167	3167:1	12/61	01/80	26873	2,12,19,24,52,77
3069	1169	3169	12/61	01/79	26875	2,12,19,24,52,77
3070	1170	3170:1	12/61	09/78	26876	2,12,19,24,52,77
3072	1172	3172:1	12/61	07/78	26878	2,12,19,24,52,77

GP39-2	3400 Class	2,300 hp	50 units
12 645E3B engine		55,400 lbs T.E. @ 11.3 mph	270,000 lbs

Road#	1st#	2nd#	3rd#	Built	Rebuilt	Build#	Notes
3400:2	3631			02/75	08/86	74664-15	3,12,19,25,45,78
3401:2	3645	3145:2	3645	03/75	11/86	74664-29	3,12,19,25,45,78
3402:2	3622			01/75	11/86	74664-6	3,12,19,25,45,78
3403:2	3625			01/75	12/86	74664-9	3,12,19,25,45,78
3404:2	3655	3154:2	3655	04/75	12/86	74664-39	3,12,19,25,45,78
3405:2	3653			04/75	12/86	74664-37	3,12,19,25,45,78
3406:2	3637	3137:2		02/75	12/86	74664-21	3,12,19,25,45,78
3407:2	3644	3144:2		03/75	12/86	74664-28	3,12,19,25,45,78
3408:2	3634	3134:2		02/75	01/87	74664-18	3,12,19,25,45,78
3409:2	3619	3119:2		01/75	01/87	74664-3	3,12,19,25,45,78
3410:2	3627	3127:2		02/75	01/87	74664-11	3,12,19,25,45,78
3411:2	3628	3128:2		02/75	02/87	74664-12	3,12,19,25,45,78
3412:2	3639	3139:2		02/75	02/87	74664-23	3,12,19,25,45,78
3413:2	3664	3163:2		04/75	03/87	74664-48	3,12,19,25,45,78
3414:2	3618	3118:2	3618	01/75	03/87	74664-2	3,12,19,25,45,78
3415:2	3623	3123:2	3623	01/75	03/87	74664-7	3,12,19,25,45,78
3416:2	3668	3167:2	3668	04/75	04/87	74664-52	3,12,19,25,45,78
3417:2	3662	3161:2	3662	04/75	04/87	74664-46	3,12,19,25,45,78
3418:2	3663	3162:2	3663	04/75	04/87	74664-47	3,12,19,25,45,78
3419:2	3651	3150:2	3651	04/75	04/87	74664-35	3,12,19,25,45,78
3420:2	3617	3117:2	3617	01/75	05/87	74664-1	3,12,19,25,45,78
3421:2	3650	3149:2	3650	03/75	05/87	74664-34	3,12,19,25,45,78

Road#	1st#	2nd#	3rd#	Built	Rebuilt	Build#	Notes
3422:2	3626	3126:2	3626	01/75	06/87	74664-10	3,12,19,25,45,78
3423:2	3665	3164:2	3665	04/75	06/87	74664-49	3,12,19,25,45,78
3424:2	3642	3142:2	3642	03/75	06/87	74664-26	3,12,19,25,45,78
3425:2	3620	3120:2	3620	01/75	07/87	74664-4	3,12,19,25,45,78
3426:2	3666			04/75	07/87	74664-50	3,12,19,25,45,78
3427:2	3660	3159:2	3660	04/75	08/87	74664-44	3,12,19,25,45,78
3428:2	3643	3143:2	3643	03/75	08/87	74664-27	3,12,19,25,45,78
3429:2	3658	3157:2	3658	04/75	08/87	74664-42	3,12,19,25,45,78
3430:2	3630	3130:2	3630	02/75	09/87	74664-14	3,12,19,25,45,78
3431:2	3646	3146:2	3646	03/75	09/87	74664-30	3,12,19,25,45,78
3432:2	3647	3147:2	3647	03/75	09/87	74664-31	3,12,19,25,45,78
3433:2	3624	3124:2	3624	01/75	10/87	74664-8	3,12,19,25,45,78
3434:2	3633	3133:2	3633	02/75	10/87	74664-17	3,12,19,25,45,78
3435:2	3641	3141:2	3641	03/75	10/87	74664-25	3,12,19,25,45,78
3436:2	3621	3121:2	3621	01/75	11/87	74664-5	3,12,19,25,45,78
3437:2	3636	3136:2	3636	02/75	11/87	74664-20	3,12,19,25,45,78
3438:2	3638	3138:2	3638	02/75	11/87	74664-22	3,12,19,25,45,78
3439:2	3657	3156:2	3657	04/75	12/87	74664-41	3,12,19,25,45,78
3440:2	3654			04/75	12/87	74664-38	3,12,19,25,45,78
3441:2	3659			04/75	12/87	74664-43	3,12,19,25,45,78
3442:2	3632	3131:2	3652	02/75	12/87	74664-32	3,12,19,25,45,78
3443:2	3629	3129:2	3629	02/75	12/87	74664-13	3,12,19,25,45,78
3444:2	3656	3155:2	3656	04/75	12/87	74664-40	3,12,19,25,45,78
3445:2	3649	3148:2	3649	03/75	12/87	74664-33	3,12,19,25,45,78
3446:2	3661			04/75	01/88	74664-45	3,12,19,25,45,78
3447:2	3635	3135:2	3635	02/75	01/88	74664-19	3,12,19,25,45,78
3448:2	3667	3166:2	3667	04/75	01/88	74664-51	3,12,19,25,45,78
3449:2	3652	3151:2	3652	04/75	01/88	74664-36	3,12,19,25,45,78

GP39-2   3600 Class   2,300 hp   17 units

12-645E3 engine   55,400 lbs T.E. @ 11.3 mph   264,400 lbs

Road#	1st#	2nd#	Built	Build#	Notes
3600:2	3600:1	3100:2	08/74	74602-1	3,12,19,27,45
3601:2	3601:1	3101:2	08/74	74602-2	3,12,19,27,45
3602:2	3602:1	3102:2	08/74	74602-3	3,12,19,27,45
3603:2	3603:1	3103:2	08/74	74602-4	3,12,19,27,45
3604:2	3604:1	3104:2	08/74	74602-5	3,12,19,27,45
3605:2	3605:1	3105:2	08/74	74602-6	3,12,19,27,45
3606:2	3606:1	3106:2	08/74	74602-7	3,12,19,27,45
3607:2	3607:1	3107:2	08/74	74602-8	3,12,19,27,45
3608:2	3608:1	3108:2	08/74	74602-9	3,12,19,27,45
3609:2	3609:1	3109:2	08/74	74602-10	3,12,19,27,45
3610.2	3610:1	3110:2	08/74	74602-11	3,12,19,27,45
3611:2	3611:1	3111:2	08/74	74602-12	3,12,19,27,45
3612:2	3612:1	3112:2	08/74	74602-13	3,12,19,27,45
3613:2	3613:1	3113:2	08/74	74602-14	3,12,19,27,45
3614:2	3614:1	3114:2	08/74	74602-15	3,12,19,27,45
3615:2	3615:1	3115:2	08/74	74602-16	3,12,19,27,45
3616:2	3616:1	3116:2	08/74	74602-17	3,12,19,27,45

GP39-2   3640 Class   2,300 hp   1 unit

12-645E3B engine   55,400 lbs T.E. @ 11.3 mph   264,400 lbs

Road#	1st#	2nd#	Built	Build#	Notes
3640:2	3640:1	3140:2	02/75	74664-24	3,12,19,25,44

GP39-2   3669 Class   2,300 hp   13 units

12-645E3 engine   55,400 lbs T.E. @ 11.3 mph   264,000 lbs

Road#	1st#	2nd#	Built	Build#	Notes
3669			11/77	776028-1	3,12,19,25,44
3670			11/77	776028-2	3,12,19,25,44
3671:2	3671:1	3170:2	11/77	776028-3	3,12,19,25,44
3673:2	3673:1	3171:2	11/77	776028-5	3,12,19,25,44
3674:2	3674:1	3172:2	11/77	776028-6	3,12,19,25,44
3675:2	3675:1	3173:2	11/77	776028-7	3,12,19,25,44
3676			11/77	776028-8	3,12,19,25,44
3677:2	3677:1	3175	11/77	776028-9	3,12,19,25,44
3678			11/77	776028-10	3,12,19,25,44
3679:2	3679:1	3177	11/77	776028-11	3,12,19,25,44
3680:2	3680:1	3178	11/77	776028-12	3,12,19,25,44
3681:2	3681:1	3179	11/77	776028-13	3,12,19,25,44
3682:2	3682:1	3180	11/77	776028-14	3,12,19,25,44

3442, Chicago, Illinois, March 24, 1991. *George Horna*

3609, Lubbock, Texas, December 24, 1989. *Marshall Higgins*

3640, Topeka, Kansas, July 20, 1990. *Thomas Chenoweth*

3676, Chicago, Illinois, June 8, 1978. *George Horna*

GP39-2	3683 Class		2,300 hp		11 units
12-645E3 engine		55,400 lbs T.E. @ 11.3 mph			264,000 lbs

Road#	1st#	2nd#	Built	Build#	Notes
3683:2	3683:1	3181	05/79	786224-1	3,12,19,27,45
3684			05/79	786224-2	3,12,19,27,45
3685:2	3685:1	3183	05/79	786224-3	3,12,19,27,45
3686:2	3686:1	3184	05/79	786224-4	3,12,19,27,45
3687:2	3687:1	3185	05/79	786224-5	3,12,19,27,45
3688			05/79	786224-6	3,12,19,27,45
3689			05/79	786224-7	3,12,19,27,45
3690			05/79	786224-8	3,12,19,27,45
3693:2	3693:1	3190	05/79	786224-11	3,12,19,27,45
3694			05/79	786224-12	3,12,19,27,45
3695			05/79	786224-13	3,12,19,27,45

3689, Pueblo, Colorado, August, 1987. *Bruce Barrett*

GP39-2	3696 Class		2,300 hp		10 units
12-645E3B engine		55,400 lbs T.E. @ 11.3 mph			264,000 lbs

Road#	1st#	2nd#	Built	Build#	Notes
3696			04/80	796314-1	3,12,19,27,46
3697:2	3697:1	3194	04/80	796314-2	3,12,19,27,46
3698:2	3698:1	3195	04/80	796314-3	3,12,19,27,46
3699:2	3699:1	3196	04/80	796314-4	3,12,19,27,46
3700:2	3690:1	3197	04/80	796314-5	3,12,19,27,46
3701:2	3701:1	3198	04/80	796314-6	3,12,19,27,46
3702:2	3702:1	3199	04/80	796314-7	3,12,19,27,46
3703:2	3703:1	3200:2	04/80	796314-8	3,12,19,27,46
3704:2	3704:1	3201:2	04/80	796314-9	3,12,19,27,46
3705			04/80	796314-10	3,12,19,27,46

3704, San Bernardino, California, February 4, 1987. *George Horna*

GP4OX	3800 Class	3,500 hp		10 units
16-645F3 engine		62,685 lbs T.E. @ 9.9 mph		264,400 lbs

Road#	Built	Build#	Notes
3800	08/78	776008-1	3,13,19,27,41,96
3801	06/78	776009-1	3,13,19,27,41,97
3802	04/78	776054-1	3,13,19,27,41
3803	04/78	776054-2	3,13,19,27,41
3804	04/78	776054-3	3,13,19,27,41
3805	04/78	776054-4	3,13,19,27,41
3806	04/78	776054-5	3,13,19,27,41
3807	05/78	776054-6	3,13,19,27,41
3808	05/78	776054-7	3,13,19,27,41
3809	05/78	776054-8	3,13,19,27,41

3803, Chicago, Illinois, June 9, 1991. *George Horna*

GP50	3810 Class	3,500 hp		30 units
16-645F3 engine		64,200 lbs T.E. @ 9.7 mph		271,663 lbs

Road#	Built	Build#	Notes
3810	02/81	806005-1	3,13,19,32,41,96,103
3811	02/81	806006-1	3,13,19,32,41,97
3812	02/81	806005-2	3,13,19,32,41,96
3813	02/81	806006-2	3,13,19,32,41,97
3814	02/81	806005-3	3,13,19,32,41,96
3815	02/81	806006-3	3,13,19,32,41,97
3816	02/81	806005-4	3,13,19,32,41,96
3817	02/81	806006-4	3,13,19,32,41,97
3818	02/81	806005-5	13,19,32,41,96
3819	02/81	806006-5	3,13,19,32,41,97
3820	02/81	806005-6	3,13,19,32,41,96
3821	02/81	806006-6	3,13,19,32,41,97
3822	02/81	806005-7	3,13,19,32,41,96
3823	02/81	806006-7	3,13,19,32,41
3824	03/81	796317-1	3,13,19,32,41
3825	03/81	796317-2	3,13,19,32,41
3826	03/81	796317-3	3,13,19,32,41
3827	03/81	796317-4	3,13,19,32,41
3828	03/81	796317-5	3,13,19,32,41

3817, Chicago, Illinois, October 7, 1986. *George Horna*

3830, Chicago, Illinois, September 15, 1985. *George Horna*

3854, Chicago, Illinois, June 26, 1988. *George Horna*

4019, Chicago, Illinois, June 17, 1991. *George Horna*

4034, Chicago, Illinois, July 27, 1991. *George Horna*

GP50	3810 Class	Continued	

Road#	Built	Build#	Notes
3829	03/81	796317-6	3,13,19,32,41
3830	03/81	796317-7	3,13,19,32,41
3831	04/81	796317-8	3,13,19,32,41
3832	04/81	796317-9	3,13,19,32,41
3833	04/81	796317-10	3,13,19,32,41
3834	04/81	796317-11	3,13,19,32,41
3835	04/81	796317-12	3,13,19,32,41
3836	04/81	796317-13	3,13,19,32,41
3837	04/81	796317-14	3,13,19,32,41
3838	04/81	796317-15	3,13,19,32,41
3839	04/81	796317-16	3,13,19,32,41

GP50	3840 Class	3,600 hp	15 units
16-645F3B engine	64,200 lbs T.E. @ 9.8 mph		273,120 lbs

Road#	Built	Build#	Notes
3840	04/85	847057-1	3,13,19,32,41
3841	04/85	847057-2	3,13,19,32,41
3842	04/85	847057-3	3,13,19,32,41
3843	04/85	847057-4	3,13,19,32,41
3844	04/85	847057-5	3,13,19,32,41
3845	04/85	847057-6	3,13,19,32,41
3846	04/85	847057-7	3,13,19,32,41
3847	04/85	847057-8	3,13,19,32,41
3848	04/85	847057-9	3,13,19,32,41
3849	04/85	847057-10	3,13,19,32,41
3850	04/85	847057-11	3,13,19,32,41
3851	04/85	847057-12	3,13,19,32,41
3852	04/85	847057-13	3,13,19,32,41
3853	04/85	847057-14	3,13,19,32,41
3854	04/85	847057-15	3,13,19,32,41

GP60	4000 Class	3,800 hp	40 units
16-710G3 engine	62,070 lbs T.E. @ 10.5 mph		276,000 lbs

Road#	Built	Build#	Notes
4000:2	05/88	876031-2	4,15,20,30,41
4001:2	05/88	876031-1	4,15,20,30,41
4002:2	05/88	876031-4	4,15,20,30,41
4003:2	06/88	876031-3	4,15,20,30,41
4004:2	06/88	876031-5	4,15,20,30,41
4005:2	06/88	876031-6	4,15,20,30,41
4006:2	06/88	876031-8	4,15,20,30,41
4007:2	06/88	876031-7	4,15,20,30,41
4008:2	06/88	876031-10	4,15,20,30,41
4009:2	06/88	876031-9	4,15,20,30,41
4010:2	06/88	876031-11	4,15,20,30,41
4011.2	06/88	876031-12	4,15,20,30,41
4012:2	06/88	876031-13	4,15,20,30,41
4013:2	06/88	876031-14	4,15,20,30,41
4014:2	06/88	876031-15	4,15,20,30,41
4015:2	06/88	876031-16	4,15,20,30,41
4016:2	07/88	876031-17	4,15,20,30,41
4017:2	07/88	876031-18	4,15,20,30,41
4018:2	07/88	876031-19	4,15,20,30,41
4019:2	07/88	876031-20	4,15,20,30,41
4020	07/89	886012-1	4,15,20,30,41
4021	07/89	886012-2	4,15,20,30,41
4022	07/89	886012-3	4,15,20,30,41
4023	07/89	886012-4	4,15,20,30,41
4024	07/89	886012-5	4,15,20,30,41
4025	07/89	886012-6	4,15,20,30,41
4026	07/89	886012-7	4,15,20,30,41
4027	07/89	886012-8	4,15,20,30,41
4028	07/89	886012-9	4,15,20,30,41
4029	07/89	886012-10	4,15,20,30,41
4030	07/89	886012-11	4,15,20,30,41
4031	07/89	886012-12	4,15,20,30,41
4032	08/89	886012-13	4,15,20,30,41
4033	08/89	886012-14	4,15,20,30,41
4034	08/89	886012-15	4,15,20,30,41
4035	08/89	886012-16	4,15,20,30,41
4036	08/89	886012-17	4,15,20,30,41
4037	08/89	886012-18	4,15,20,30,41
4038	08/89	886012-19	4,15,20,30,41
4039	08/89	886012-20	4,15,20,30,41

5008, Barstow, California, September 25, 1981. *Gary Zuters*

SD40		5000 Class		3,000 hp	18 units
16-645E3 engine		82,107 lbs T.E. @ 11.1 mph			391,500 lbs

Road#	1st#	Built	Rebuilt	Build#	Notes
5000	1700	03/66	06/81	32036	5,12,19,34,44,77
5001	1701	04/66	09/81	32037	5,12,19,34,44,77
5002	1702	04/66	10/81	32038	5,12,19,34,44,77
5003	1703	04/66	01/81	32039	5,12,19,34,44,77
5004	1704	04/66	12/81	32040	5,12,19,34,44,77
5005	1705	04/66	08/81	32041	5,12,19,34,44,77
5006	1706	04/66	11/81	32042	5,12,19,34,44,77
5007	1707	04/66	12/81	32043	5,12,19,34,44,77
5008	1708	05/66	09/81	32044	5,12,19,34,44,77
5009	1709	04/66	11/81	32045	5,12,19,34,44,77
5010	1710	04/66	12/81	32046	5,12,19,34,44,77
5012	1712	03/66	02/81	32048	5,12,19,34,44,77
5013	1713	03/66	04/81	32049	5,12,19,34,44,77
5014	1714	03/66	10/81	32050	5,12,19,34,44,77
5016	1716	04/66	05/81	32052	5,12,19,34,44,77
5017	1717	04/66	12/80	32053	5,12,19,34,44,77
5018	1718	04/66	11/80	32054	5,12,19,34,44,77
5019	1719	04/66	07/81	32055	5,12,19,34,44,77

5066, Chicago, Illinois, June 21, 1979. *George Horna*

5051, Castle Rock, Colorado, April 18, 1985. *Bruce Barrett*

SD40-2	5020 Class	3,000 hp	37 units
16-645E3B engine	83,160 lbs T.E. @ 11.1 mph		391,500 lbs

Road#	Built	Rebuilt	Build#	Notes
5020	11/77	10/88	776029-1	6,12,19,33,45,77,96,100
5021	11/77	11/88	776030-1	6,12,19,33,45,77,97,100
5022	11/77	12/88	776029-2	6,12,19,33,45,77,96,100
5023	11/77	12/88	776030-2	6,12,19,33,45,77,97,100
5024	11/77	04/88	776029-3	6,12,19,33,45,77,96,100
5025	11/77	09/88	776030-3	6,12,19,33,45,77,97,100
5026	11/77	11/88	776029-4	6,12,19,33,45,77,96,100
5027	11/77	09/88	776030-4	6,12,19,33,45,77,97,100
5028	10/77	04/88	776031-1	6,12,19,33,45,77
5029	10/77	05/88	776031-2	6,12,19,33,45,77
5030	10/77	07/88	776031-3	6,12,19,33,45,77
5031	10/77	11/88	776031-4	6,12,19,33,45,77
5032	10/77	10/88	776031-5	6,12,19,33,45,77
5033	10/77	12/88	776031-6	6,12,19,33,45,77
5034	10/77	04/88	776031-7	6,12,19,33,45,77
5035	10/77	07/88	776031-8	6,12,19,33,45,77
5036	10/77	04/88	776031-9	6,12,19,33,45,77
5038	10/77	05/88	776031-11	6,12,19,33,45,77
5039	10/77	09/88	776031-12	6,12,19,33,45,77
5040	10/77	11/88	776031-13	6,12,19,33,45,77
5041	10/77	08/88	776031-14	6,12,19,33,45,77
5042	10/77	08/88	776031-15	6,12,19,33,45,77
5043	11/77	11/88	776031-16	6,12,19,33,45,77
5044	11/77	05/88	776031-17	6,12,19,33,45,77
5045	11/77	08/88	776031-18	6,12,19,33,45,77
5046	11/77	06/88	776031-19	6,12,19,33,45,77
5047	11/77	08/88	776031-20	6,12,19,33,45,77
5048	11/77	09/88	776031-21	6,12,19,33,45,77
5049	11/77	10/88	776031-22	6,12,19,33,45,77
5050	11/77	07/88	776031-23	6,12,19,33,45,77
5151	11/77	12/88	776031-24	6,12,19,33,45,77
5052	11/77	05/88	776031-25	6,12,19,33,45,77
5053	11/77	06/88	776031-26	6,12,19,33,45,77
5054	11/77	06/88	776031-27	6,12,19,33,45,77
5055	11/77	10/88	776031-28	6,12,19,33,45,77
5056	11/77	06/88	776031-29	6,12,19,33,45,77
5057	11/77	07/88	776031-30	6,12,19,33,45,77

SD40-2	5058 Class	3,000 hp	13 units
16-645E3 engine	83,160 lbs T.E. @ 11.1 mph		391,500 lbs

Road#	Built	Build#	Notes
5058	04/79	786225-1	6,12,19,33,45
5059	04/79	786225-2	6,12,19,33,45
5060	04/79	786225-3	6,12,19,33,45
5061	04/79	786225-4	6,12,19,33,45
5062	04/79	786225-5	6,12,19,33,45
5063	04/79	786225-6	6,12,19,33,45
5064	04/79	786225-7	6,12,19,33,45
5065	04/79	786225-8	6,12,19,33,45
5066	04/79	786225-9	6,12,19,33,45
5067	04/79	786225-10	6,12,19,33,45
5068	04/79	786225-11	6,12,19,33,45
5069	05/79	786225-12	6,12,19,33,45
5070	05/79	786225-13	6,12,19,33,45

SD40-2	5071 Class	3,000 hp	54 units
16-645E3B engine	83,160 lbs T.E. @ 11.1 mph		391,500 lbs

Road#	Built	Build#	Notes
5071	09/79	786219-1	6,12,19,33,45
5072	09/79	786219-2	6,12,19,33,45
5073	09/79	786219-3	6,12,19,33,45
5074	09/79	786219-4	6,12,19,33,45
5075	09/79	786219-5	6,12,19,33,45
5076	09/79	786219-6	6,12,19,33,45
5077	09/79	786219-7	6,12,19,33,45
5078	09/79	786219-8	6,12,19,33,45
5079	09/79	786219-9	6,12,19,33,45
5080	10/79	786219-10	6,12,19,33,45
5081	10/79	786219-11	6,12,19,33,45
5082	09/79	786219-12	6,12,19,33,45
5083	10/79	786219-13	6,12,19,33,45
5084	10/79	786219-14	6,12,19,33,45
5085	10/79	786219-15	6,12,19,33,45
5086	10/79	786219-16	6,12,19,33,45
5087	10/79	786219-17	6,12,19,33,45
5088	10/79	786219-18	6,12,19,33,45
5089	10/79	786219-19	6,12,19,33,45
5090	10/79	786219-20	6,12,19,33,45
5091	10/79	786219-21	6,12,19,33,45
5092	10/79	786219-22	6,12,19,33,45
5093	10/79	786219-23	6,12,19,33,45
5094	10/79	786219-24	6,12,19,33,45
5095	10/79	786219-25	6,12,19,33,45
5096	10/79	786219-26	6,12,19,33,45
5097	10/79	786219-27	6,12,19,33,45
5098	10/79	786219-28	6,12,19,33,45

SD40-2	5071 Class	Continued

Road#	Built	Build#	Notes
5099	10/79	786219-29	6,12,19,33,45
5100	10/79	786219-30	6,12,19,33,45
5101	10/79	786219-31	6,12,19,33,45
5102	10/79	786219-32	6,12,19,33,45
5103	10/79	786219-33	6,12,19,33,45
5104	10/79	786219-34	6,12,19,33,45
5105	10/79	786219-35	6,12,19,33,45
5106	10/79	786219-36	6,12,19,33,45
5107	10/79	786219-37	6,12,19,33,45
5108	10/79	786219-38	6,12,19,33,45
5109	10/79	786223-1	6,12,19,33,45,97,100
5110	10/79	786222-1	6,12,19,33,45,96,100
5111	10/79	786223-2	6,12,19,33,45,97,100
5112	10/79	786222-2	6,12,19,33,45,96,100
5113	10/79	786223-3	6,12,19,33,45,97,100
5114	10/79	786222-3	6,12,19,33,45,96,100
5115	10/79	786223-4	6,12,19,33,45,97,100
5116	10/79	786222-4	6,12,19,33,45,96,100
5117	10/79	786223-5	6,12,19,33,45,97,100
5118	10/79	786222-5	6,12,19,33,45,96,100
5119	10/79	786223-6	6,12,19,33,45,97,100
5120	10/79	786222-6	6,12,19,33,45,96,100
5121	10/79	786223-7	6,12,19,33,45,97,100
5122	10/79	786222-7	6,12,19,33,45,96,100
5123	10/79	786223-8	6,12,19,33,45,97,100
5124	10/79	786222-8	6,12,19,33,45,96,100

SD40-2	5125 Class	3,000 hp	45 units
16-645E3B engine	83,160 lbs T.E. @ 11.1 mph		391,500 lbs

Road#	Built	Build#	Notes
5125	11/80	796396-1	6,12,19,33,45,97,100
5126	11/80	796395-1	6,12,19,33,45,96,100
5127	12/80	796396-2	6,12,19,33,45,97,100
5128	11/80	796395-2	6,12,19,33,45,96,100
5129	12/80	796396-3	6,12,19,33,45,97,100
5130	11/80	796395-3	6,12,19,33,45,96,100
5131	12/80	796396-4	6,12,19,33,45,97,100
5132	11/80	796395-4	6,12,19,33,45,96,100
5133	12/80	796396-5	6,12,19,33,45,97,100
5134	11/80	796395-5	6,12,19,33,45,96,100
5135	12/80	796396-6	6,12,19,33,45,97,100
5136	11/80	796395-6	6,12,19,33,45,96,100
5137	12/80	796396-7	6,12,19,33,45,97,100
5138	11/80	796395-7	6,12,19,33,45,96,100
5139	12/80	796396-8	6,12,19,33,45,97,100
5140	11/80	796395-8	6,12,19,33,45,96,100
5141	09/80	796386-1	6,12,19,33,45
5142	09/80	796386-2	6,12,19,33,45
5143	09/80	796386-3	6,12,19,33,45
5144	09/80	796386-4	6,12,19,33,45
5145	09/80	796386-5	6,12,19,33,45
5146	09/80	796386-6	6,12,19,33,45
5147	09/80	796386-7	6,12,19,33,45
5148	09/80	796386-8	6,12,19,33,45
5149	09/80	796386-9	6,12,19,33,45
5150	09/80	796386-10	6,12,19,33,45
5151	10/80	796386-11	6,12,19,33,45
5152	09/80	796386-12	6,12,19,33,45
5153	10/80	796386-13	6,12,19,33,45
5154	10/80	796386-14	6,12,19,33,45
5155	10/80	796386-15	6,12,19,33,45
5156	10/80	796386-16	6,12,19,33,45
5157	10/80	796386-17	6,12,19,33,45
5158	10/80	796386-18	6,12,19,33,45
5159	10/80	796386-19	6,12,19,33,45
5160	10/80	796386-20	6,12,19,33,45
5161	10/80	796386-21	6,12,19,33,45
5162	10/80	796386-22	6,12,19,33,45
5163	10/80	796386-23	6,12,19,33,45
5164	10/80	796386-24	6,12,19,33,45
5165	10/80	796386-25	6,12,19,33,45
5166	10/80	796386-26	6,12,19,33,45
5167	10/80	796386-27	6,12,19,33,45
5168	10/80	796386-28	6,12,19,33,45
5169	10/80	796386-29	6,12,19,33,45

5113, Castle Rock, Colorado, April 20, 1985. *Bruce Barrett*

5168, Chicago, Illinois, December 9, 1990. *George Horna*

SD40-2	5170 Class		3,000 hp	23 units
16-645E3B engine		83,100 lbs T.E. @ 11.1 mph		391,500 lbs

Road#	Built	Build#	Notes
5170	11/81	816016-1	6,12,19,33,46
5171	11/81	816016-2	6,12,19,33,46
5172	11/81	816016-3	6,12,19,33,46
5173	11/81	816016-4	6,12,19,33,46
5174	11/81	816016-5	6,12,19,33,46
5175	11/81	816016-6	6,12,19,33,46
5176	11/81	816016-7	6,12,19,33,46
5177	11/81	816016-8	6,12,19,33,46
5178	11/81	816016-9	6,12,19,33,46
5179	11/81	816016-10	6,12,19,33,46
5180	11/81	816016-11	6,12,19,33,46
5181	11/81	816016-12	6,12,19,33,46
5182	11/81	816016-13	6,12,19,33,46
5183	11/81	816016-14	6,12,19,33,46
5184	12/81	816016-15	6,12,19,33,46
5185	12/81	816016-16	6,12,19,33,46
5186	12/81	816016-17	6,12,19,33,46
5187	12/81	816016-18	6,12,19,33,46
5188	12/81	816016-19	6,12,19,33,46
5189	12/81	816016-20	6,12,19,33,46
5190	12/81	816016-21	6,12,19,33,46
5191	12/81	816016-22	6,12,19,33,46
5192	12/81	816016-23	6,12,19,33,46

5173, Pueblo, Colorado, March 13, 1985. *Bruce Barrett*

SD40-2	5200 Class		3,000 hp	13 units
16-645E3 engine		90,475 lbs T.E. @ 8.5 mph		391,500 lbs

Road#	Built	Build#	Notes
5200	10/78	786153-1	6,12,19,33,45
5201	10/78	786153-2	6,12,19,33,45
5202	10/78	786153-3	6,12,19,33,45
5203	10/78	786153-4	6,12,19,33,45
5204	10/78	786153-5	6,12,19,33,45
5205	10/78	786153-6	6,12,19,33,45
5206	10/78	786153-7	6,12,19,33,45
5207	10/78	786153-8	6,12,19,33,45
5209	10/78	786153-10	6,12,19,33,45
5210	10/78	786153-11	6,12,19,33,45
5211	10/78	786153-12	6,12,19,33,45
5212	10/78	786153-13	6,12,19,33,45
5213	10/78	786153-14	6,12,19,33,45

5209, Saginaw, Texas, August 19, 1980. *Paul DeLuca*

SDF40-2	5250 Class		3,000 hp	18 units
16-645E3 engine		83,100 lbs T.E. @ 11.1 mph		388,000 lbs

Road#	1st#	2nd#	Built	Rebuilt	Build#	Notes
5250	AMTK-643	ATSF-643	11/74	01/85	74611-64	6,12,19,34,45,71
5251	AMTK-511	ATSF 511	03/73	04/85	72694-12	6,12,19,34,45,71
5252	AMTK-615	ATSF-615	01/74	02/85	74611-36	6,12,19,34,45,71
5253	AMTK-630	ATSF-630	06/74	02/85	74611-51	6,12,19,34,45,71
5254	AMTK-635	ATSF-635	07/74	03/85	74611-56	6,12,19,34,45,71
5255	AMTK-526	ATSF-526	06/73	02/85	72694-27	6,12,19,34,45,71
5256	AMTK-640	ATSF-640	06/74	03/85	74611-61	6,12,19,34,45,71
5257	AMTK-622	ATSF-622	01/74	03/85	74611-43	6,12,19,34,45,71
5258	AMTK-628	ATSF-628	03/74	03/85	74611-49	6,12,19,34,45,71
5259	AMTK-633	ATSF-633	07/74	03/85	74611-54	6,12,19,34,45,71
5260	AMTK-638	ATSF-638	06/74	03/85	74611-59	6,12,19,34,45,71
5261	AMTK-634	ATSF-634	04/74	04/85	74611-55	6,12,19,34,45,71
5262	AMTK-629	ATSF-629	03/74	04/85	74611-50	6,12,19,34,45,71
5263	AMTK-639	ATSF-639	05/74	04/85	74611-60	6,12,19,34,45,71
5264	AMTK-632	ATSF-632	04/74	04/85	74611-53	6,12,19,34,45,71
5265	AMTK-649	ATSF-649	09/74	04/85	74611-70	6,12,19,34,45,71
5266	AMTK-644	ATSF-644	08/74	05/85	74611-65	6,12,19,34,45,71
5267	AMTK-645	ATSF-645	10/74	05/85	74611-66	6,12,19,34,45,71

5258, Pueblo, Colorado, February 3, 1991. *Bruce Barrett*

SD45	5300 Class		3,600 hp	3 units
20-645E3 engine		82,100 lbs T.E. @ 11.3 mph		391,500 lbs

Road#	1st#	2nd#	Built	Rebuilt	Build#	Notes
5300	1883	5583	12/66	03/80	32599	5,12,19,34,38,77
5301	1869	5569	12/66	03/80	32545	5,12,19,34,38,77
5303	1821	5521	08/66	04/80	32077	5,12,19,34,38,77

5301, Topeka, Kansas, February 27, 1989. *Thomas Chenoweth*

20-645E3 engine   82,100 lbs T.E. @ 11.3 mph   391,500 lbs

Road#	1st#	2nd#	3rd#	Built	Rebuilt	Build#	Notes
5304	1865	5565		12/66	07/81	32541	5,12,19,34,38,77
5305	1870	5570		12/66	07/81	32546	5,12,19,34,38,77
5306	1873	5573		12/66	08/81	32549	5,12,19,34,38,77
5307	1808	5508		06/66	08/81	32064	5,12,19,34,38,77
5308	1842	5542		11/66	09/81	32518	5,12,19,34,38,77
5310	1820	5520		08/66	10/81	32076	5,12,19,34,38,77
5311	1825	5525		08/66	10/81	32081	5,12,19,34,38,77
5312	1866	5566		12/66	11/81	32542	5,12,19,34,38,77
5315	1871	5571		12/66	12/81	32547	5,12,19,34,38,77
5317	1817	5517		06/66	01/82	32071	5,12,19,34,38,77
5318	1852	5552		11/66	04/79	32528	5,12,19,34,38,77
5319	1807	5507		06/66	01/82	32063	5,12,19,34,38,77
5320	1834	5534		10/66	01/82	32510	5,12,19,34,38,77
5321	1844	5544		11/66	01/82	32520	5,12,19,34,38,77
5323	1853	5553		11/66	02/82	32529	5,12,19,34,38,77
5325	1828	5528		08/66	05/82	32084	5,12,19,34,38,77
5326	1857	5557		11/66	05/82	32533	5,12,19,34,38,77
5327	1816	5516		06/66	05/82	32072	5,12,19,34,38,77
5328	1887	5587		12/66	06/82	32563	5,12,19,34,38,77
5329	1837	5537		10/66	06/82	32513	5,12,19,34,38,77
5330	1854	5554		11/66	06/82	32530	5,12,19,34,38,77
5331	1861	5561		12/66	07/82	32537	5,12,19,34,38,77
5332	1880	5580		12/66	07/82	32556	5,12,19,34,38,77
5333	1810	5510		06/66	08/82	32066	5,12,19,34,38,77
5334	1822	5522		08/66	08/82	32078	5,12,19,34,38,77
5335	1800	5500		06/66	09/82	32056	5,12,19,34,38,77
5336	1874	5574		12/66	08/82	32550	5,12,19,34,38,77
5337	1875	5575		12/66	09/82	32551	5,12,19,34,38,77
5338	1863	5563		12/66	09/82	32539	5,12,19,34,38,77
5339	1819	5519		12/66	10/82	32075	5,12,19,34,38,77
5341	1849	5549		11/66	11/82	32525	5,12,19,34,38,77
5342	1802	5502		06/66	11/82	32058	5,12,19,34,38,77

5304, Chicago, Illinois, June 8, 1991. *George Horna*

5434, Topeka, Kansas, April 30, 1992. *Tom Chenoweth*

Road#	1st#	2nd#	3rd#	Built	Rebuilt	Build#	Notes
5343	1803	5503		06/66	11/82	32059	5,12,19,34,38,77
5344	1885	5585		12/66	12/82	32561	5,12,19,34,38,77
5345	1840	5540		10/66	12/82	32516	5,12,19,34,38,77
5346	1876	5576		12/66	12/82	32552	5,12,19,34,38,77
5347	1839	5539		10/66	12/82	32515	5,12,19,34,38,77
5348	1867	5567		12/66	01/83	32543	5,12,19,34,38,77
5349	1886	5586		12/66	01/83	32562	5,12,19,34,38,77
5350	1877	5577		12/66	03/83	32553	5,12,19,34,38,77
5351	1835	5535		10/66	03/83	31511	5,12,19,34,38,77
5352	1829	5529		08/66	03/83	32085	5,12,19,34,38,77
5353	1864	5564		12/66	04/83	32540	5,12,19,34,38,77
5354	1814	5514		06/66	04/83	32069	5,12,19,34,38,77
5355	1848	5548		11/66	04/83	32524	5,12,19,34,38,77
5356	1806	5506		06/66	05/83	32062	5,12,19,34,38,77
5357	1860	5560		12/66	05/83	32536	5,12,19,34,38,77
5358	1833	5533		10/66	05/83	32509	5,12,19,34,38,77
5359	1843	5543		11/66	06/83	32519	5,12,19,34,38,77
5360	1818	5518		07/66	06/83	32074	5,12,19,34,38,77
5361	1811	5511		06/66	07/83	32067	5,12,19,34,38,77
5362	1856	5556		11/66	07/83	32532	5,12,19,34,38,77
5364	1859	5559		12/66	08/83	32535	5,12,19,34,38,77
5365	1836	5536		10/66	08/83	32512	5,12,19,34,38,77
5366	1832	5532		10/66	09/83	32508	5,12,19,34,38,77
5367	1858	5558		11/66	09/83	32534	5,12,19,34,38,77
5368	1855	5555		11/66	09/83	32531	5,12,19,34,38,77
5369	1827	5527		08/66	10/83	32083	5,12,19,34,38,77
5370	1826	5526		08/66	10/83	32082	5,12,19,34,38,77
5371	5618			06/70	11/83	36497	5,12,19,34,38,77
5372	5616			06/70	11/83	36495	5,12,19,34,38,77
5373	5621			06/70	11/83	36500	5,12,19,34,38,77
5374	5620			06/70	12/83	36499	5,12,19,34,38,77
5375	5622			06/70	12/83	36491	5,12,19,34,38,77
5376	5624			06/70	12/83	36493	5,12,19,34,38,77
5377	5619			06/70	01/84	36498	5,12,19,34,38,77
5378	5623			06/70	01/84	36492	5,12,19,34,38,77
5379	5615			06/70	01/84	36494	5,12,19,34,38,77
5380	5617			06/70	01/84	36496	5,12,19,34,38,77
5381	5609			05/69	05/85	35014	5,12,19,34,39,77
5382	5600			05/69	05/85	35005	5,12,19,34,39,77
5383	5593			04/69	05/85	34998	5,12,19,34,39,77
5384	5598			05/69	06/85	35003	5,12,19,34,39,77
5385	5601			05/69	06/85	35006	5,12,19,34,39,77
5386	5590			04/69	06/85	34995	5,12,19,34,39,77
5387	5612			05/69	06/85	36481	5,12,19,34,39,77
5388	5591			04/69	06/85	34996	5,12,19,34,39,77
5389	5602			05/69	07/85	35007	5,12,19,34,39,77
5390	5611			05/69	07/85	36480	5,12,19,34,39,77
5391	5608			05/69	07/85	35013	5,12,19,34,39,77
5392	5607			05/69	07/85	35012	5,12,19,34,39,77
5393	5606			05/69	07/85	35011	5,12,19,34,39,77
5394	5597			04/69	08/85	35002	5,12,19,34,39,77
5395	5603			05/69	08/85	35008	5,12,19,34,39,77
5396	5604			05/69	08/85	35009	5,12,19,34,39,77
5397	5595			04/69	08/85	35000	5,12,19,34,39,77
5398	5614			05/69	08/85	36483	5,12,19,34,39,77
5399	5599			05/69	09/85	35004	5,12,19,34,39,77
5400	5594			04/69	09/85	34999	5,12,19,34,39,77
5401	5605			05/69	09/85	35010	5,12,19,34,39,77
5402	5596			04/69	09/85	35001	5,12,19,34,39,77
5403	5592			04/69	09/85	34997	5,12,19,34,39,77
5404	5613			05/69	10/85	36482	5,12,19,34,39,77
5405	1841	5541	5496	11/66	07/85	32517	5,12,19,34,38,77,81
5406	1815	5515	5497	06/66	06/85	32070	5,12,19,34,38,77,81
5407	1830	5530	5498	10/66	04/85	32506	5,12,19,34,38,77,81
5408	1851	5531	5499	11/66	02/85	32527	5,12,19,34,38,77,81

16-645F3 engine   82,100 lbs T.E. @ 11.3 mph   389,500 lbs

Road#	1st#	2nd#	Built	Rebuilt	Build#	Notes
5434	1888	5588	12/66	02/82	32564	5,12,19,34,38,77
5435	1804	5504	06/66	05/82	32060	5,12,19,34,38,77
5436	1884	5584	12/66	06/82	32560	5,12,19,34,38,77
5437	1809	5509	06/66	07/82	32065	5,12,19,34,38,77

SD45B	5500 Class	3,600 hp	2 units
20-645E3 engine	72,287 lbs T.E. @ 11.2 mph		392,860 lbs

Road#	1st#	2nd#	3rd#	Built	Rebuilt	Build#	Notes
5501	1881	5581		12/66	12/83	32557	5,18,19,34,38,72
5502:2	1847	5547	5340	11/66	10/82	32523	5,12,19,34,38,72,89

SD45-2B	5510 Class	3,600 hp	8 units
20-645E3 engine	83,100 lbs T.E. @ 11.3 mph		391,500 lbs

Road#	1st#	Built	Rebuilt	Build#	Notes
5510	5651	05/72	09/87	7391-27	6,12,19,34,40,73
5511	5676	06/73	10/87	72642-33	6,12,19,34,40,73
5512	5703	05/73	10/87	72642-17	6,12,19,34,40,73
5513	5626	05/72	11/87	7391-2	6,12,19,34,40,73
5514	5701	05/73	11/87	72642-15	6,12,19,34,40,73
5515	5633	05/72	12/87	7391-1	6,12,19,34,40,73
5516	5684	06/73	01/88	72642-41	6,12,19,34,40,73
5517	5700	04/73	01/88	72642-14	6,12,19,34,40,73

SD45-2	5705 Class	3,600 hp	9 units
20-645E3 engine	83,100 lbs T.E. @ 11.3 mph		391,500 lbs

Road#	Built	Build#	Notes
5705	05/74	74603-1	6,12,19,34,40
5707	05/74	74603-3	6,12,19,34,40
5708	05/74	74603-4	6,12,19,34,40
5709	05/74	74603-5	6,12,19,34,40
5710	05/74	74603-6	6,12,19,34,40
5711	05/74	74603-7	6,12,19,34,40
5712	05/74	74603-8	6,12,19,34,40
5713	05/74	74603-9	6,12,19,34,40
5714	05/74	74603-10	6,12,19,34,40

SD45-2	5800 Class	3,600 hp	68 units
20-645E3 engine	83,100 lbs T.E. @ 11.3 mph		395,500 lbs

Road#	1st#	2nd#	Built	Rebuilt	Build#	Notes
5800	5669	7200:1	06/73	02/86	72642-26	6,12,19,34,40,77,82
5801	5681	7201:1	06/73	02/86	72642-38	6,12,19,34,40,77,82
5802	5630	7202:1	05/72	02/86	7391-6	6,12,19,34,40,77
5803	5663	7203:1	06/73	02/86	72642-20	6,12,19,34,40,77,82
5804	5660	7204:1	05/72	03/86	7391-36	6,12,19,34,40,77
5805	5666	7205:1	05/72	03/86	72642-23	6,12,19,34,40,77,82
5806	5672	7206:1	06/73	03/86	72642-29	6,12,19,34,40,77,82
5807	5647	7207:1	05/72	03/86	7391-23	6,12,19,34,40,77
5808	5677	7208:1	06/73	03/86	72642-34	6,12,19,34,40,77,82
5809	5641	7209:1	05/72	04/86	7391-17	6,12,19,34,40,77
5810	5640	7210:1	05/72	04/86	7391-16	6,12,19,34,40,77
5811	5685	7211:1	06/73	04/86	72642-42	6,12,19,34,40,77,82
5812	5686	7212:1	06/73	04/86	72642-43	6,12,19,34,40,77,82
5813	5671	7213:1	06/73	04/86	72642-28	6,12,19,34,40,77,82
5814	5650	7214:1	05/72	05/86	7391-26	6,12,19,34,40,77
5815	5643	7215:1	05/72	05/86	7391-19	6,12,19,34,40,77
5816	5688	7216:1	05/73	05/86	72642-2	6,12,19,34,40,77,82
5817	5691	7217	05/73	05/86	72642-5	6,12,19,34,40,77,82
5818	5682	7218	06/73	05/86	72642-39	6,12,19,34,40,77,82
5819	5655	7219	05/72	06/86	7391-31	6,12,19,34,40,77
5820	5690	7220	05/73	06/86	72642-4	6,12,19,34,40,77,82
5821	5629	7221	05/72	06/86	7391-5	6,12,19,34,40,77
5822	5678	7222	06/73	06/86	72642-35	6,12,19,34,40,77,82
5823	5695	7223	05/73	06/86	72642-9	6,12,19,34,40,77,82
5824	5632	7224	05/72	07/86	7391-8	6,12,19,34,40,77
5825	5665	7225	05/72	07/86	72642-22	6,12,19,34,40,77
5826	5654	7226	05/72	07/86	7391-30	6,12,19,34,40,77
5827	5697	7227	05/73	07/86	72642-11	6,12,19,34,40,77,82
5828	5680	7228	06/73	07/86	72642-37	6,12,19,34,40,77,82
5829	5675	7229	06/73	08/86	72642-32	6,12,19,34,40,77,82
5830	5646		05/72	08/86	7391-22	6,12,19,34,40,77
5831	5667		05/72	08/86	72642-24	6,12,19,34,40,77
5832	5696		05/73	08/86	72642-10	6,12,19,34,40,77,82
5833	5634		05/72	08/86	7391-10	6,12,19,34,40,77
5834	5704		05/73	09/86	72642-18	6,12,19,34,40,77,82
5835	5631		05/72	09/86	7391-7	6,12,19,34,40,77
5836	5692		05/73	09/86	72642-6	6,12,19,34,40,77,82

5501, Chicago, Illinois, March 23, 1986. *David Fasules*

5515, Chicago, Illinois, June 26, 1988. *George Horna*

5711, Chicago, Illinois, October 2, 1990. *George Horna*

5803, Chicago, Illinois, June 17, 1991. *George Horna*

Road#	1st#	2nd#	Built	Rebuilt	Build#	Notes
5837	5699		05/73	09/86	72642-13	6,12,19,34,40,77,82
5838	5628		05/72	09/86	7391-4	6,12,19,34,40,77
5839	5657		05/72	10/86	7391-33	6,12,19,34,40,77
5840	5652		05/72	10/86	7391-28	6,12,19,34,40,77
5841	5659		05/72	10/86	7391-35	6,12,19,34,40,77
5842	5702		05/73	10/86	72642-16	6,12,19,34,40,77,82
5843	5653		05/72	10/86	7391-29	6,12,19,34,40,77
5844	5648		05/72	11/86	7391-24	6,12,19,34,40,77
5845	5635		05/72	11/86	7391-11	6,12,19,34,40,77
5846	5661		05/72	11/86	7391-37	6,12,19,34,40,77
5847	5649		05/72	12/86	7391-25	6,12,19,34,40,77
5848	5642		05/72	12/86	7391-18	6,12,19,34,40,77
5849	5698		05/73	01/87	72642-12	6,12,19,34,40,77,82
5850	5645		05/72	01/87	7391-21	6,12,19,34,40,77
5851	5639		05/72	02/87	7391-15	6,12,19,34,40,77
5852	5670		06/73	02/87	72642-27	6,12,19,34,40,77,82
5853	5694		05/73	03/87	72642-8	6,12,19,34,40,77,82
5854	5683		06/73	03/87	72642-40	6,12,19,34,40,77,82
5856	5637		05/72	04/87	7391-13	6,12,19,34,40,77
5857	5627		05/72	04/87	7391-3	6,12,19,34,40,77
5858	5689		05/73	05/87	72642-3	6,12,19,34,40,77,82
5859	5664		05/72	05/87	72642-21	6,12,19,34,40,77
5860	5667		06/73	06/87	72642-24	6,12,19,34,40,77,82
5861	5679		06/73	06/87	72642-36	6,12,19,34,40,77,82
5862	5668		06/73	07/87	72642-25	6,12,19,34,40,77,82
5863	5674		06/73	07/87	72642-31	6,12,19,34,40,77,82
5864	5673		06/73	08/87	72642-30	6,12,19,34,40,77,82
5865	5636		05/72	08/87	7391-12	6,12,19,34,40,77
5866	5656		05/72	02/88	7391-32	6,12,19,34,40,77
5867	5638		05/72	02/88	7391-14	6,12,19,34,40,77
5868	5693		05/73	03/88	72642-7	6,12,19,34,40,77,82

SD45-2	5855 Class	4,250 hp	1 unit

Caterpillar 3612 engine 96,950 lbs T.E. @ 11.3 mph 395,500 lbs

Road#	1st#	Built	Rebuilt	Build#	Notes
5855	5625	05/72	07/87	7391-1	6,12,19,34,40,77,83

5855, Topeka, Kansas, August 1, 1991. *Thomas Chenoweth*

SDF45	5950 Class	3,600 hp	40 units

20-645E3 engine 82,100 lbs T.E. @ 11.3 mph 395,000 lbs

Road#	1st#	2nd#	Built	Rebuilt	Build#	Notes
5950	1900	5900	06/68	02/83	34036	6,12,19,34,49,74
5951	1901	5901	06/68	08/83	34037	6,12,19,34,49,74
5952	1902	5902	06/68	09/83	34038	6,12,19,34,49,74
5953	1903	5903	06/68	08/82	34039	6,12,19,34,49,74
5954	1904	5904	06/68	04/83	34040	6,12,19,34,49,74
5955	1905	5905	06/68	09/82	34041	6,12,19,34,49,74
5956	1906	5906	06/68	05/82	34042	6,12,19,34,49,74
5957	1907	5907	06/68	06/83	34043	6,12,19,34,49,74
5958	1908	5908	06/68	06/83	34044	6,12,19,34,49,74
5959	1909	5909	06/68	11/82	34045	6,12,19,34,49,74
5960	1910	5910	06/68	02/83	34046	6,12,19,34,49,74
5961	1911	5911	06/68	03/83	34047	6,12,19,34,49,74
5962	1912	5912	06/68	03/83	34048	6,12,19,34,49,74
5963	1913	5913	06/68	02/82	34049	6,12,19,34,49,74
5061	1914	5014	06/68	02/83	34050	6,12,19,34,49,74
5965	1915	5915	06/68	09/82	34051	6,12,19,34,49,74
5966	1916	5916	06/68	01/83	34052	6,12,19,34,49,74
5967	1917	5917	06/68	11/83	34053	6,12,19,34,49,74
5968	1918	5918	06/68	10/83	34054	6,12,19,34,49,74
5969	1919	5919	06/68	06/83	34055	6,12,19,34,49,74
5970	1920	5920	06/68	07/82	34056	6,12,19,34,49,74
5971	1921	5921	06/68	11/83	34057	6,12,19,34,49,74
5972	1922	5922	06/68	01/82	34058	6,12,19,34,49,74
5973	1923	5923	06/68	02/83	34059	6,12,19,34,49,74
5974	1924	5924	06/68	10/83	34060	6,12,19,34,49,74
5975	1925	5925	07/68	07/82	34061	6,12,19,34,49,74
5976	1926	5926	07/68	12/82	34062	6,12,19,34,49,74
5977	1927	5927	07/68	01/83	34063	6,12,19,34,49,74
5978	1928	5928	07/68	05/83	34064	6,12,19,34,49,74
5979	1929	5929	07/68	09/83	34065	6,12,19,34,49,74
5980	1930	5930	07/68	08/83	34066	6,12,19,34,49,74
5981	1931	5931	07/68	08/82	34067	6,12,19,34,49,74
5982	1932	5932	07/68	04/83	34068	6,12,19,34,49,74
5983	1933	5933	07/68	08/83	34069	6,12,19,34,49,74
5984	1934	5934	07/68	07/83	34070	6,12,19,34,49,74
5985	1935	5935	07/68	07/83	34071	6,12,19,34,49,74
5986	1936	5936	07/68	01/83	34072	6,12,19,34,49,74
5987	1937	5937	07/68	10/83	34073	6,12,19,34,49,74
5988	1938	5938	07/68	05/83	34074	6,12,19,34,49,74
5989	1939	5939	08/68	12/82	34075	6,12,19,34,49,74

5860, Chicago, Illinois, August 23, 1987. *George Horna*

5985, Pueblo, Colorado, March 8, 1992. *Bruce Barrett*

6356, East Peoria, Illinois, March 3, 1987. *George Horna*

6372, Chriesman, Texas, October 14, 1989. *Rick Bartoskewitz*

6398, Phoenix, Arizona, March 24, 1992. *George Horna*

B23-7	6350 Class	2,250 hp	14 units
7FDL-12F9 engine	60,400 lbs T.E. @ 10.8 mph		268,000 lbs

Road#	Built	Build#	Notes
6350	03/78	41673	9,14,20,27,48,90
6351	04/78	41674	9,14,20,27,48,90
6352	04/78	41675	9,14,20,27,48,90
6353	04/78	41676	9,14,20,27,48,90
6354	04/78	41677	9,14,20,27,48,90
6355	04/78	41678	9,14,20,27,48,90
6356	04/78	41679	9,14,20,27,48,90
6357	04/78	41680	9,14,20,27,48,90
6358	04/78	41681	9,14,20,27,48,90
6359	04/78	41682	9,14,20,27,48,90
6360	04/78	41683	9,14,20,27,48,90
6361	04/78	41684	9,14,20,27,48,90
6362	04/78	41685	9,14,20,27,48,90
6363	04/78	41686	9,14,20,27,48,90

B23-7		6364 Class		2,250 hp		26 units
7FDL-12F16 engine		60,400 lbs T.E. @ 10.8 mph				265,000 lbs

Road#	1st#	2nd#	Built	Build#	Notes
6364			04/79	42410	9,14,20,27,48,90
6365			04/79	42411	9,14,20,27,48,90
6366	6366	7201:2	04/79	42412	9,14,20,27,48,80,90
6367	6367	7202:2	04/79	42413	9,14,20,27,48,90
6368	6368	7203:2	04/79	42414	9,14,20,27,48,90
6369	6369	7204:2	04/79	42415	9,14,20,27,48,80,90
6370	6370	7205:2	04/79	42416	9,14,20,27,48,80,90
6371			04/79	42417	9,14,20,27,48,90
6372	6372	7206:2	04/79	42418	9,14,20,27,48,80,90
6373	6373	7207:2	04/79	42419	9,14,20,27,48,80,90
6374	6374	7208:2	06/79	42420	9,14,20,27,48,88,90
6375	6375	7209:2	06/79	42421	9,14,20,27,48,88,90
6376	6376	7210:2	06/79	42422	9,14,20,27,48,80,88,90
6377	6377	7211:2	06/79	42423	9,14,20,27,48,88,90
6378	6378	7212:2	06/79	42424	9,14,20,27,48,88,90
6379	6379	7213:2	06/79	42425	9,14,20,27,48,80,88,90
6380			06/79	42426	9,14,20,27,48,88,90
6381			06/79	42427	9,14,20,27,48,88,90
6382			06/79	42428	9,14,20,27,48,88,90
6383			06/79	42429	9,14,20,27,48,88,90
6384			06/79	42430	9,14,20,27,48,88,90
6385			06/79	42431	9,14,20,27,48,88,90
6386			06/79	42432	9,14,20,27,48,88,90
6387			06/79	42433	9,14,20,27,48,88,90
6388			06/79	42434	9,14,20,27,48,88,90
6389	6389	7214:2	06/79	42435	9,14,20,27,48,80,88,90

B23-7			6390 Class		2,250 hp		29 units
7FDL-12F21 engine			61,000 lbs T.E. @ 10.7 mph				264,000 lbs

Road#	1st#	2nd#	Built	Build#	Notes
6390			04/80	42929	9,11,20,27,48
6391			04/80	42930	9,11,20,27,48
6392			04/80	42931	9,11,20,27,48
6393	6393	7215:2	04/80	42932	9,11,20,27,48,80
6394			04/80	42933	9,11,20,27,48
6395	6395	7216:2	04/80	42934	9,11,20,27,48,80
6396			04/80	42935	9,11,20,27,48
6397			04/80	42936	9,11,20,27,48
6398			04/80	42937	9,11,20,27,48
6399			04/80	42938	9,11,20,27,48
6400			04/80	42939	9,11,20,27,48
6401			04/80	42940	9,11,20,27,48
6402			04/80	42941	9,11,20,27,48
6403			04/80	42942	9,11,20,27,48
6404			04/80	42943	9,11,20,27,48
6405			12/84	44081	8,11,20,27,48,85
6406			12/84	44082	8,11,20,27,48,85
6407			12/84	44083	8,11,20,27,48,85
6408			12/84	44084	8,11,20,27,48,85
6409			12/84	44085	8,11,20,27,48,85
6410			12/84	44086	8,11,20,27,48,85
6411			12/84	44087	8,11,20,27,48,85
6412			12/84	44088	8,11,20,27,48,85
6413			12/84	44089	8,11,20,27,48,85
6414			12/84	44090	8,11,20,27,48,85
6415			12/84	44091	8,11,20,27,48,85
6416			12/84	44092	8,11,20,27,48,85
6417			12/84	44093	8,11,20,27,48,85
6418			12/84	44094	8,11,20,27,48,85

6419, Topeka, Kansas, October 25, 1990. *Tom Chenoweth*

7401, Argentine, Kansas, April 24, 1986. *Tom Chenoweth*

7415, Chicago, Illinois, August 10, 1991. *George Horna*

7487, Chicago, Illinois, January 7, 1987. *George Horna*

SF30B	6419 Class	2,300 hp	1 unit
7FDL-12F30UX engine	61,000 lbs T.E. @ 10.7 mph		277,000 lbs

Road#	1st#	2nd#	Built	Rebuilt	Build#	Notes
6419	6332	7200:2	12/70	07/87	37523	9,11,20,34,48,75

B39-8	7400 Class	3,900 hp	3 units
7FDL-16J2 engine	68,100 lbs T.E. @ 18.3 mph		285,940 lbs

Road#	Built	Build#	Notes
7400	01/84	43148	9,11,20,29,41,96
7401	12/84	44493	9,11,20,29,41
7402	09/84	44494	9,11,20,29,41

DASH 8-40B	7410 Class	4,000 hp	40 units
7FDL-16 engine	69,200 lbs T.E. @ 18.6 mph		282,500 lbs

Road#	Built	Build#	Notes
7410	06/88	45656	9,11,20,31,42
7411	06/88	45657	9,11,20,31,42
7412	06/88	45658	9,11,20,31,42
7413	06/88	45659	9,11,20,31,42
7414	06/88	45660	9,11,20,31,42
7415	06/88	45661	9,11,20,31,42
7416	06/88	45662	9,11,20,31,42
7417	06/88	45663	9,11,20,31,42
7418	06/88	45664	9,11,20,31,42
7419	06/88	45665	9,11,20,31,42
7420	06/88	45666	9,11,20,31,42
7421	06/88	45667	9,11,20,31,42
7422	06/88	45668	9,11,20,31,42
7423	06/88	45669	9,11,20,31,42
7424	06/88	45670	9,11,20,31,42
7425	06/88	45671	9,11,20,31,42
7426	06/88	45672	9,11,20,31,42
7427	06/88	45673	9,11,20,31,42
7428	06/88	45674	9,11,20,31,42
7429	06/88	45675	9,11,20,31,42
7430	04/89	45931	9,11,20,31,42
7431	04/89	45932	9,11,20,31,42
7432	04/89	45933	9,11,20,31,42
7433	01/89	45934	9,11,20,31,42
7434	04/89	45935	9,11,20,31,42
7435	04/89	45936	9,11,20,31,42
7436	04/89	45937	9,11,20,31,42
7437	04/89	45938	9,11,20,31,42
7438	04/89	45939	9,11,20,31,42
7439	04/89	45940	9,11,20,31,42
7440	04/89	45941	9,11,20,31,42
7441	04/89	45942	9,11,20,31,42
7442	04/89	45943	9,11,20,31,42
7443	04/89	45944	9,11,20,31,42
7444	04/89	45945	9,11,20,31,42
7445	04/89	45946	9,11,20,31,42
7446	04/89	45947	9,11,20,31,42
7447	04/89	45948	9,11,20,31,42
7448	04/89	45949	9,11,20,31,42
7449	04/89	45950	9,11,20,31,42

B36-7	7484 Class	3,600 hp	16 units
7FDL-16H9 engine	64,600 lbs T.E. @ 9.8 mph		274,500 lbs

Road#	Built	Build#	Notes
7484	12/80	43130	9,11,20,27,37,104
7485	11/80	43131	9,11,20,27,37,104
7486	12/80	43132	9,11,20,27,37,104
7487	12/80	43133	9,11,20,27,37,104
7488	10/80	43134	9,11,20,29,37,104
7489	10/80	43135	9,11,20,29,37,104
7490	10/80	43136	9,11,20,29,37,104
7491	10/80	43137	9,11,20,29,37,104
7492	10/80	43138	9,11,20,29,37,104
7493	10/80	43139	9,11,20,29,37,104
7494	11/80	43140	9,11,20,29,37,104
7495	11/80	43141	9,11,20,29,37,104
7496	11/80	43142	9,11,20,29,37,104
7497	11/80	43143	9,11,20,29,37,104
7498	11/80	43144	9,11,20,29,37,104
7499	11/80	43145	9,11,20,29,37,104

8024, San Bernardino, January 25, 1986. *Thomas Chenoweth*

8062, Topeka, Kansas, August 25, 1988. *Thomas Chenoweth*

8083, Chicago, Illinois, May, 1990. *George Horna*

C30-7	8010 Class	3,000 hp	46 units
7FDL-16G17 engine	90,600 lbs T.E. @ 9.6 mph		398,800 lbs

Road#	Built	Build#	Notes
8010	12/77	41663	10,14,19,34,48,91,104
8011	12/77	41664	10,14,19,34,48,91,104
8012	12/77	41665	10,14,19,34,48,91,104
8013	12/77	41666	10,14,19,34,48,91,104
8014	12/77	41667	10,14,19,34,48,91,104
8015	12/77	41668	10,14,19,34,48,91,104
8016	12/77	41669	10,14,19,34,48,91,104
8017	12/77	41670	10,14,19,34,48,91,104
8018	12/77	41671	10,14,19,34,48,91,104
8019	12/77	41672	10,14,19,34,48,91,104
8020	02/78	41687	10,14,19,34,48,87,91,104
8021	03/78	41688	10,14,19,34,48,87,91,104
8022	03/78	41689	10,14,19,34,48,87,91,104
8023	03/78	41690	10,14,19,34,48,87,91,104
8024	03/78	41691	10,14,19,34,48,87,91,104
8025	03/78	41692	10,14,19,34,48,87,91,104
8026	03/78	41693	10,14,19,34,48,87,91,104
8027	03/78	41694	10,14,19,34,48,87,91,104
8028	03/78	41695	10,14,19,34,48,87,91,104
8029	03/78	41696	10,14,19,34,48,87,91,104
8030	03/78	41697	10,14,19,34,48,87,91,104
8031	03/78	41698	10,14,19,34,48,87,91,104
8032	03/78	41699	10,14,19,34,48,87,91,104
8033	06/78	41700	10,14,19,34,48,87,91,104
8034	06/78	41701	10,14,19,34,48,87,91,104
8035	06/78	41702	10,14,19,34,48,87,91,104
8036	06/78	41703	10,14,19,34,48,87,91,104
8037	06/78	41704	10,14,19,34,48,87,91,104
8038	06/78	41705	10,14,19,34,48,87,91,104
8039	06/78	41706	10,14,19,34,48,87,91,104
8040	06/78	41707	10,14,19,34,48,87,91,104
8041	06/78	41708	10,14,19,34,48,87,91,104
8042	06/78	41709	10,14,19,34,48,87,91,104
8043	06/78	41710	10,14,19,34,48,87,91,104
8045	06/78	41712	10,14,19,34,48,87,91,104
8046	06/78	41713	10,14,19,34,48,87,91,104
8047	06/78	41714	10,14,19,34,48,87,91,104
8048	06/78	41715	10,14,19,34,48,87,91,104
8049	06/78	41716	10,14,19,34,48,87,91,104
8051	06/78	41718	10,14,19,34,48,87,91,104
8052	06/78	41719	10,14,19,34,48,87,91,104
8053	06/78	41720	10,14,19,34,48,87,91,104
8054	06/78	41721	10,14,19,34,48,87,91,104
8055	06/78	41722	10,14,19,34,48,87,91,104
8056	06/78	41723	10,14,19,34,48,87,91,104
8057	07/78	41724	10,14,19,34,48,87,91,104

C30-7	8058 Class	3,000 hp	6 units
7FDL-16G20 engine	90,600 lbs T.E. @ 8.4 mph		392,500 lbs

Road#	Built	Build#	Notes
8058	10/78	42080	10,14,20,34,48,91,104
8059	10/78	42081	10,14,20,34,48,91,104
8060	10/78	42082	10,14,20,34,48,91,104
8061	10/78	42083	10,14,20,34,48,91,104
8062	10/78	42084	10,14,20,34,48,91,104
8063	10/78	42085	10,14,20,34,48,91,104

C30-7	8064 Class	3,000 hp	34 units
7FDL-16G28 engine	90,600 lbs T.E. @ 8.4 mph		392,500 lbs

Road#	Built	Build#	Notes
8064	04/79	42375	10,14,20,33,48,91,104
8065	04/79	42376	10,14,20,33,48,91,104
8066	04/79	42377	10,14,20,33,48,91,104
8068	05/79	42379	10,14,20,33,48,91,104
8069	05/79	42380	10,14,20,33,48,91,104
8070	05/79	42381	10,14,20,33,48,91,104
8071	05/79	42382	10,14,20,33,48,91,104
8072	05/79	42383	10,14,20,33,48,91,104
8073	05/79	42384	10,14,20,33,48,91,104
8074	05/79	42385	10,14,20,33,48,91,104
8075	05/79	42386	10,14,20,33,48,91,104
8076	05/79	42387	10,14,20,33,48,91,104
8077	05/79	42388	10,14,20,33,48,91,104
8078	05/79	42389	10,14,20,33,48,91,104
8079	05/79	42390	10,14,20,33,48,91,104
8080	05/79	42391	10,14,20,33,48,91,104
8081	05/79	42392	10,14,20,33,48,91,104
8082	05/79	42393	10,14,20,33,48,91,104
8083	05/79	42394	10,14,20,33,48,91,104
8084	05/79	42395	10,14,20,33,48,91,104
8085	05/79	42396	10,14,20,33,48,91,104
8086	05/79	42397	10,14,20,33,48,91,104

Road#	Built	Build#	Notes
8087	05/79	42398	10,14,20,33,48,91,104
8088	05/79	42399	10,14,20,33,48,91,104
8089	05/79	42400	10,14,20,33,48,91,104
8090	05/79	42401	10,14,20,33,48,91,104
8091	05/79	42402	10,14,20,33,48,91,104
8092	05/79	42403	10,14,20,33,48,84,91,104
8093	05/79	42404	10,14,20,33,48,84,91,104
8094	06/79	42405	10,14,20,33,48,84,91,104
8095	06/79	42406	10,14,20,33,48,84,91,104
8096	06/79	42407	10,14,20,33,48,84,91,104
8097	06/79	42408	10,14,20,33,48,84,91,104
8098	06/79	42409	10,14,20,33,48,84,91,104

C30-7   8099 Class   3,000 hp   24 units

7FDL-16G36 engine   91,500 lbs T.E. @ 8.4 mph   395,000 lbs

Road#	Built	Build#	Notes
8099	05/80	42500	10,11,20,33,51,104
8100	05/80	42501	10,11,20,33,51,104
8101	05/80	42502	10,11,20,33,51,104
8102	05/80	42503	10,11,20,33,51,104
8103	05/80	42504	10,11,20,33,51,104
8104	05/80	42505	10,11,20,33,51,104
8105	05/80	42506	10,11,20,33,51,104
8106	05/80	42507	10,11,20,33,51,104
8107	05/80	42508	10,11,20,33,51,104
8108	05/80	42509	10,11,20,33,51,104
8109	05/80	42510	10,11,20,33,51,104
8110	05/80	42511	10,11,20,33,51,104
8111	05/80	42512	10,11,20,33,51,104
8112	05/80	42513	10,11,20,33,51,104
8113	05/80	42514	10,11,20,33,51,104
8114	05/80	42515	10,11,20,33,51,104
8115	05/80	42516	10,11,20,33,51,104
8116	05/80	42517	10,11,20,33,51,104
8117	05/80	42518	10,11,20,33,51,104
8118	06/80	42519	10,11,20,33,51,104
8119	06/80	42520	10,11,20,33,51,104
8120	06/80	42521	10,11,20,33,51,104
8121	06/80	42522	10,11,20,33,51,104
8122	06/80	42523	10,11,20,33,51,104

C30-7   8123 Class   3,000 hp   30 units

7FDL-16 engine   91,500 lbs T.E. @ 8.4 mph   395,000 lbs

Road#	Built	Build#	Notes
8123	05/81	43550	10,11,20,33,51,104
8124	05/81	43551	10,11,20,33,51,104
8125	05/81	43552	10,11,20,33,51,104
8126	05/81	43553	10,11,20,33,51,104
8127	05/81	43554	10,11,20,33,51,104
8128	05/81	43555	10,11,20,33,51,104
8129	05/81	43556	10,11,20,33,51,104
8130	05/81	43557	10,11,20,33,51,104
8131	05/81	43558	10,11,20,33,51,104
8132	05/81	43559	10,11,20,33,51,104
8133	06/81	43560	10,11,20,33,51,104
8134	05/81	43561	10,11,20,33,51,104
8135	06/81	43562	10,11,20,33,51,104
8136	05/81	43563	10,11,20,33,51,104
8137	06/81	43564	10,11,20,33,51,104
8138	06/81	43565	10,11,20,33,51,104
8139	06/81	43566	10,11,20,33,51,104
8140	06/81	43567	10,11,20,33,51,104
8141	06/81	43568	10,11,20,33,51,104
8142	06/81	43569	10,11,20,33,51,104
8143	06/81	43570	10,11,20,33,51,104
8144	06/81	43571	10,11,20,33,51,104
8145	06/81	43572	10,11,20,33,51,104
8146	06/81	43573	10,11,20,33,51,104
8147	06/81	43574	10,11,20,33,51,104
8148	06/81	43575	10,11,20,33,51,104
8149	06/81	43576	10,11,20,33,51,104
8150	06/81	43577	10,11,20,33,51,104
8151	06/81	43578	10,11,20,33,51,104
8152	06/81	43579	10,11,20,33,51,104

8112, Topeka, Kansas, September 26, 1988. *Thomas Chenoweth*

8134, Topeka, Kansas, September 16, 1988. *Thomas Chenoweth*

8154, Chicago, Illinois, March 30, 1991. *George Horna*

C30-7   8153 Class   3,000 hp   14 units

7FDL-16G49 engine   91,500 lbs T.E. @ 8.4 mph   392,500 lbs

Road#	Built	Build#	Notes
8153	01/83	44067	10,11,20,33,51
8154	01/83	44068	10,11,20,33,51
8155	01/83	44069	10,11,20,33,51
8156	01/83	44070	10,11,20,33,51
8157	01/83	44071	10,11,20,33,51
8158	01/83	44072	10,11,20,33,51
8159	01/83	44073	10,11,20,33,51
8160	01/83	44074	10,11,20,33,51
8161	01/83	44075	10,11,20,33,51
8162	01/83	44076	10,11,20,33,51
8163	01/83	44077	10,11,20,33,51
8164	01/83	44078	10,11,20,33,51
8165	01/83	44079	10,11,20,33,51
8166	01/83	44080	10,11,20,33,51

U36C	8736 Class	3,600 hp	27 units
7FDL16-F3 engine	90,600 lbs T.E. @ 11.8 mph		391,500 lbs

Road#	Built	Build#	Notes
8736	06/74	39686	10,14,20,34,48,104,105
8737	06/74	39687	10,14,20,34,48,104,106
8738	06/74	39688	10,14,20,34,48,104,106
8739	06/74	39689	10,14,20,34,48,104,106
8740	06/74	39690	10,14,20,34,48,104,106
8741	06/74	39691	10,14,20,34,48,104,105
8742	06/74	39692	10,14,20,34,48,104,106
8743	06/74	39693	10,14,20,34,48,104,106
8744	06/74	39694	10,14,20,34,48,104,105
8745	06/74	39695	10,14,20,34,48,104,106
8746	06/74	39696	10,14,20,34,48,104,106
8747	06/74	39697	10,14,20,34,48,104,106
8748	06/74	39698	10,14,20,34,48,104,106
8749	06/74	39699	10,14,20,34,48,104,106
8750	06/74	39700	10,14,20,34,48,104,106
8751	07/74	39701	10,14,20,34,48,104,106
8752	07/74	39702	10,14,20,34,48,104,106
8753	07/74	39703	10,14,20,34,48,104,106
8754	07/74	39704	10,14,20,34,48,104,105
8755	07/74	39705	10,14,20,34,48,104,106
8756	07/74	39706	10,14,20,34,48,104,106
8757	07/74	39707	10,14,20,34,48,104,106
8758	07/74	39708	10,14,20,34,48,104,106
8759	07/74	39709	10,14,20,34,48,104,106
8760	07/74	39710	10,14,20,34,48,104,106
8761	07/74	39711	10,14,20,34,48,104,106
8762	07/74	39712	10,14,20,34,48,104,106

SF30C	9500 Class	3,000 hp	70 units
7FDL-16F5 engine	91,500 lbs T.E. @ 9.6 mph		391,500 lbs

Road#	1st#	Built	Rebuilt	Build#	Notes
9500	8721	03/73	04/85	38883	10,11,19,34,51,76
9501	8728	03/73	09/85	38890	10,11,19,34,51,76
9502	8713	07/72	09/85	38468	10,11,19,34,51,76
9503	8733	04/73	10/85	38895	10,11,19,34,51,76
9504	8719	03/73	10/85	38881	10,11,19,34,51,76
9505	8701	06/72	10/85	38456	10,11,19,34,51,76
9506	8718	03/73	10/85	38880	10,11,19,34,51,76
9507	8700	05/72	10/85	38455	10,11,19,34,51,76
9508	8729	03/73	11/85	38891	10,11,19,34,51,76,98
9509	8723	03/73	11/85	38885	10,11,19,34,51,76,99
9510	8725	03/73	11/85	38887	10,11,19,34,51,76,98
9511	8707	06/72	11/85	38462	10,11,19,34,51,76,99
9512	8724	03/73	11/85	38886	10,11,19,34,51,76,98
9513	8703	06/72	11/85	38458	10,11,19,34,51,76,99
9514	8715	03/73	12/85	38877	10,11,19,34,51,76,98
9515	8705	06/72	12/85	38460	10,11,19,34,51,76,99
9516	8717	03/73	12/85	38879	10,11,19,34,51,76,98
9517	8709	06/72	12/85	38464	10,11,19,34,51,76,99
9518	8714	07/72	12/85	38469	10,11,19,34,51,76,98
9519	8734	04/73	01/86	38896	10,11,19,34,51,76,99
9520	8727	03/73	01/86	38889	10,11,19,34,51,76,98
9521	8720	03/73	01/86	38882	10,11,19,34,51,76,99
9522	8710	06/72	01/86	38465	10,11,19,34,51,76,98
9523	8712	07/72	01/86	38467	10,11,19,34,51,76,99
9524	8730	03/73	01/86	38892	10,11,19,34,51,76,98
9525	8711	06/72	02/86	38466	10,11,19,34,51,76,98
9526	8704	06/72	02/86	38459	10,11,19,34,51,76,98
9527	8708	06/72	02/86	38463	10,11,19,34,51,76,99
9528	8716	03/73	02/86	38878	10,11,19,34,51,76,98
9529	8702	06/72	02/86	38457	10,11,19,34,51,76,99
9530	8726	03/73	03/86	38888	10,11,19,34,51,76,98
9531	8731	03/73	03/86	38893	10,11,19,34,51,76,99
9532	8732	03/73	03/86	38894	10,11,19,34,51,76,98
9533	8735	04/73	03/86	38897	10,11,19,34,51,76,99
9534	8765	12/74	03/86	40009	10,11,19,34,51,76,98
9535	8766	12/74	03/86	40010	10,11,19,34,51,76,99
9536	8767	12/74	03/86	40011	10,11,19,34,51,76,98
9537	8768	12/74	04/86	40012	10,11,19,34,51,76,99
9538	8769	12/74	04/86	40013	10,11,19,34,51,76,98
9539	8764	12/74	04/86	40008	10,11,19,34,51,76,99
9540	8790	02/75	04/86	40034	10,11,19,34,51,76,98
9541	8797	02/75	04/86	40041	10,11,19,34,51,76,99
9542	8775	12/74	05/86	40019	10,11,19,34,51,76,98

8758, Topeka, Kansas, September 20, 1989. *Thomas Chenoweth*

9569, Chicago, Illinois, June 7, 1987. *George Horna*

SF30C	9500 Class	Continued

Road#	1st#	Built	Rebuilt	Build#	Notes
9543	8796	02/75	05/86	40040	10,11,19,34,51,76,99
9544	8772	12/74	05/86	40016	10,11,19,34,51,76,98
9545	8773	11/74	05/86	40017	10,11,19,34,51,76,99
9546	8774	12/74	05/86	40018	10,11,19,34,51,76,98
9547	8778	12/74	06/86	40022	10,11,19,34,51,76,99
9548	8771	12/74	06/86	40015	10,11,19,34,51,76,98
9549	8777	12/74	06/86	40021	10,11,19,34,51,76,99
9550	8779	12/74	06/86	40023	10,11,19,34,51,76,98
9551	8793	02/75	07/86	40037	10,11,19,34,51,76,99
9552	8785	01/75	07/86	40029	10,11,19,34,51,76,98
9553	8784	01/75	07/86	40028	10,11,19,34,51,76,99
9554	8783	12/74	07/86	40027	10,11,19,34,51,76,98
9555	8781	12/74	07/86	40025	10,11,19,34,51,76,99
9556	8782	12/74	08/86	40026	10,11,19,34,51,76,98
9557	8791	02/75	08/86	40035	10,11,19,34,51,76,99
9558	8794	02/75	08/86	40038	10,11,19,34,51,76,98
9559	8776	12/74	09/86	40020	10,11,19,34,51,76,99
9560	8792	02/75	09/86	40036	10,11,19,34,51,76,98
9561	8798	02/75	09/86	40042	10,11,19,34,51,76,99
9562	8770	12/74	09/86	40014	10,11,19,34,51,76,98
9563	8786	01/75	10/86	40030	10,11,19,34,51,76,99
9564	8789	02/75	10/86	40033	10,11,19,34,51,76,98
9565	8795	02/75	10/86	40040	10,11,19,34,51,76,99
9566	8780	12/74	10/86	40024	10,11,19,34,51,76,98
9567	8787	01/75	10/86	40031	10,11,19,34,51,76,99
9568	8788	01/75	10/86	40032	10,11,19,34,51,76,98
9569	8799	02/75	10/86	40043	10,11,19,34,51,76

Since May 1985, 394 units have officially left Santa Fe's roster. In reality, more units than this are no longer working for the Santa Fe.

First, there are units badly damaged by derailment, collision, mechanical failure or fire still on the property that in all likelihood will not be returned to active service.

Second, as part of a maintenance/power guarantee transaction with General Electric in early 1990, all of the B36-7s, plus the C30-7s indicated by service records to be less reliable than average, were returned to GE. Though these units haven't returned to the Santa Fe (except as lease units!), they're still shown on Santa Fe's roster. The B36-7s and those C30-7s that left the Santa Fe have worked as lease units for General Electric on a number of Class I railroads. The C30-7s have also been used to fulfill GE's new locomotive service and delivery guarantees with various Class I railroads.

Some locomotive dispositions are not yet accounted for. Some units recently retired had not been disposed of, and were on Santa Fe's property as of this writing. Several units were apparently scrapped by Santa Fe at either Cleburne, Texas, or San Bernardino, California, and no record of their scrapping has yet been unearthed in Santa Fe's records. (There were several files that referred to the "sale of locomotives," with no numbers referenced; these were gondola loads of remains, and though dinosaur hunters may search for bones somewhat successfully, molten steel all looks alike.) Any information that fills in the gaps would be much appreciated.

In this section, the date of retirement is shown, followed by each unit's subsequent owner(s), number(s), and the date of sale. Some intermediate owners which did not operate the locomotive are not shown to conserve space. Locomotives sold to scrappers and dealers such as Pielet Brothers, Erman-Howell, Chrome Crankshaft, Pacific Dismantling, Purdy, Southwest Railroad Car Parts and others are assumed scrapped unless further owners are shown. Abbreviations used in this section are as follows.

Railroads

ABL	Alameda Belt Line	GGSR	Georgia Great Southern Railroad
ADN	Ashley Drew & Northern Railway	GLSR	Gloster Southern Railroad
AR	Aberdeen & Rockfish Railroad	GSWR	Georgia Southwestern Railroad
ATL	AT&L Railroad	GWR	Great Western Railway
AZCE	Arizona Central Railroad	HESR	Huron & Eastern Railway
BAR	Bangor & Aroostook Railroad	HE	Hollis & Eastern Railroad
BMRG	Blue Mountain & Reading Railroad	IAIS	Iowa Interstate Railroad
BPRR	Buffalo & Pittsburgh Railroad	IHRC	Indiana Hi-Rail Corporation
CAGY	Columbus & Greenville Railway	IANR	Iowa Northern Railroad
CALB	Chesapeake & Albemarle Railroad	INRD	Indiana Rail Road
CBRR	Council Bluffs Railroad	JXPT	Jaxport Terminal Railway
CCKY	Chattooga & Chickamauga Railway	KJRY	Keokuk Junction Railway
CLK	Cadillac & Lake City Railway	KLSC	Kalamazoo, Lake Shore & Chicago Railway
CNWR	Carolina Northwestern Railroad	LAJ	Los Angeles Junction Railway
CWRY	Commonwealth Railway	LDRR	Louisiana & Delta Railroad
DGNO	Dallas, Garland & Northern Railroad	LNW	Louisiana & North West Railroad
DSRR	Delta Southern Railroad	MCER	Massachusetts Central Railroad
EIRR	Eastern Illinois Railroad	MSRC	Mid-South Railroad
FCEN	Florida Central Railroad	NERR	Nashville & Eastern Railroad
FMID	Florida Midland Railroad	NEKM	Northeast Kansas & Missouri Railroad
FNOR	Florida Northern Railroad	OCTR	Octoraro Railroad
FWW	Fort Worth & Western Railroad	ORR	Osage Railroad
GCRR	Grand Canyon Railroad	OTR	Oakland Terminal Railway
		PAL	Paducah & Louisville Railway
		PVRR	Pioneer Valley Railroad

The Santa Fe began its long-awaited purge of SD45s in March 1991, though a traffic surge later that year postponed more large-scale retirements of this type from Santa Fe's locomotive fleet. The 5304 Class, which contains almost all of the SD45s, has lost eight units to date, including the 5309, which was idling between road jobs at Chicago on March 21, 1989.
Gary Zuters

RLK	Rail-Link
RRVW	Red River Valley & Western Railroad
RS	Roberval & Saguenay Railway
SCBT	Santa Cruz, Big Trees & Pacific Railway
SCTR	South Central Tennessee Railroad
SDIY	San Diego & Imperial Valley Railroad
SEKR	South East Kansas Railroad
SFSR	Santa Fe Southern Railway
SKOL	South Kansas & Oklahoma Railroad
ST	Springfield Terminal Railway
SWRR	Southwestern Railroad
TKEN	Tennken Railroad
TN	Texas & Northern Railway
TNER	Texas Northeastern Railroad
TNMR	Texas-New Mexico Railroad
TPW	Toledo, Peoria & Western Railway
VCY	Ventura County Railway
WCLR	Waccamaw Coastline Railroad
WCRC	Washington Central Railroad
WTNN	West Tennessee Railroad

Industrial and Contract Switching Companies

BCAS	Boise-Cascade, Wallula, Washington
CPC	Corn Products Company, Stockton, California
DUPX	Dupont, Belle, West Virginia, and Freeport, Texas
ECONO	Econorail, Inc., Beaumont, Texas
GRCO	Green River Coal, Madison, Kentucky
MCHA	Midwest Coal Handlers, Central City, Kentucky
RESCAR	RESCAR, Inc., Longview, Texas
THST	Thomas Steel
WHEV	Wheeler Evans Elevator, White Deer, Texas
WATCO	WATCO Leasing, Pittsburg, Kansas

Locomotive Dealers, Leasing Companies and Scrapyards

ChrCrank	Chrome Crankshaft, San Bernardino, California
BMAL	BMAL Enterprises, Chicago, Illinois
DrumMet	Drumright Metals
Erman	Erman-Howell Division, Kansas City, Kansas
GE	General Electric
Helm	Helm Financial Corp., San Francisco, California
ILS	Independent Locomotive Service, Bethel, Minnesota
ISMP	Illinois Scrap Metal Processing
MDC	Mountain Diesel Corporation, Denver, Colorado
NatMet	National Metals, Phoenix, Arizona
NRE	National Railway Equipment Co., Dixmoor, Illinois
Pielet	Pielet Brothers, Chicago, Illinois
Purdy	Purdy Company, Long Beach, California
Pacific	Pacific Rail Dismantling, Colton, California
Railtex	Railtex, Inc., San Antonio, Texas
Relco	Relco Locomotives, Inc., Minooka, Illinois
RRI	Railroad Inc., Westfield, Maryland
Pinsley	S.M. Pinsley Co., Boston, Massachusetts
Southwest	Southwest Railroad Car Parts, Longview, Texas
VMV	VMV Enterprises, Inc., Paducah, Kentucky
ValRol	Valley Rolling, Inc., Lemoore, California

Museum Abbreviations

| KRM | Kentucky Railroad Museum |

Santa Fe's first 140 Class slugs served the railway for about 15 years following their construction in 1971 and 1972. The last of the class was retired by 1987. The first 140 Class slugs were built from cut-down RSD-5s and RSD-15s at Santa Fe's shops at San Bernardino, California, and Cleburne; Texas. They were the last units on the roster equipped with the obsolescent Alco tri-mount truck. The replacement second-140 Class slugs were built from assorted EMD and GE six-motor units of more modern vintage. At Bedford Park, Illinois, the 144:2 was on its way to the scrapyard on February 28, 1988.
David Fasules

Two GP60Ms, the 148 and 152, are the only Super Fleet units off the roster as of summer 1992. Both were involved in a disastrous head-on collision at Corona, California, on November 7, 1990. On October 6, 1990, a month before its fiery finish, the 152 was leading a hotshot at Romeo, Illinois. *Gary Clark*

GP60M   100 Class   2 units retired

Road#	Built	Build#	Retd.	Disposition
148:2	07/90	886063-49	12/90	Wrecked Corona, CA, 11/7/90, to ChrCrank 01/91
152:2	08/90	886063-53	12/90	Wrecked Corona, CA, 11/7/90, to ChrCrank 01/91

Slug   140 Class (1st)   7 units retired

Road#	1st#	2nd#	3rd#	Built	Rebuilt	Build#	Retd.	Disposition
140:2	2110:1	9850	3950	08/52	08/70	80196	10/85	To ChrCrank 01/86
141:2	9128	9851	3951	04/53	08/71	80412	05/87	Scrapped
142:2	9112	9852	3952	09/52	12/71	80198	10/87	Scrapped 10/87
143:2	9119	9853	3953	10/52	01/72	80205	05/87	Scrapped
144:2	9129	9854	3954	04/53	01/72	80414	05/87	Scrapped
145:2	9805			05/59	02/76	83431	10/85	To ChrCrank 01/86
146:2	9819			06/59	03/76	83478	10/85	To ChrCrank 01/86

Slug   1115 Class   2 units retired

Road#	1st#	2nd#	3rd#	Built	Rebuilt	Build#	Retd.	Disposition
1120:2	2357:1	2407:2	120:2	08/39	04/73	919	07/91	To Railtex 11/91
1121:2	2356:1	2406:2	121:2	08/39	07/73	918	12/86	To NRE 12/86

GP7   1310 Class   1 unit retired

Road#	1st#	Built	Rebuilt	Build#	Retd.	Disposition
1326:2	2793	10/52	12/81	17448	8/91	To Railtex 11/91

SW900   1450 Class   1 unit retired

Road#	1st#	2nd#	Built	Build#	Retd.	Disposition
1453	653	1153:1	06/57	23404	06/87	To BMRG 10/87

SW900 1453 was the last of its kind on the roster, its retirement eliminating every unit that doesn't ride on road trucks from Santa Fe's fleet (the "Switcher," the 1460, rides on Blomberg trucks). A shiny 1453 was working at Atchison, Kansas, on December 20, 1980. *Paul DeLuca*

More than half of the 2000 Class GP7s have left the roster since 1985. Almost all have gone on to new careers on a number of shortlines and regional railroads. The unlucky 2008, however, had an appointment with the torch at Pielet Brothers in McCook, Illinois, six years after it was photographed in the same Chicago suburb on July 16, 1985. *George Horna*

GP7				2000 Class				17 units retired
Road#	1st#	2nd#	Built	Rebuilt	Build#	Retd.	Disposition	
2001	2658		10/50	10/73	13162	03/89	To GWR-2001 05/89, to CBRR-714	
2002	2661		12/50	01/74	13165	10/88	To VMV 10/88, to PAL-8200	
2003	2683		05/51	03/74	13194	10/88	To VMV 10/88, to PAL-8202	
2004	2665		01/51	04/74	13186	03/89	To Helm 07/89, to BAR-24 09/89	
2005	2687		05/51	10/74	13198	10/88	To VMV 10/88, to PAL-2005, to MCHA-2005 11/88	
2006	2668		01/51	11/74	13189	03/89	To IHRC-347 06/89	
2007	2690		05/51	05/76	13201	10/88	To VMV 10/88, to PAL-8201	
2008	2695		05/51	04/77	13206	07/91	To Pielet 10/91	
2013	99	2899:1	03/54	07/81	18789	07/91	To Railtex 11/91, to DGNO-2013	
2015	2805:2		10/52	08/81	17460	04/89	To NRE 08/89	
2018	2700:1		01/52	08/81	15800	07/91	To Pielet 10/91	
2021	2758:1		09/52	09/81	16985	04/87	Wrecked 04/24/87, to ISMP 01/88	
2022	2804:2		10/52	09/81	17459	03/90	To Railtex 08/90, to NEKM-2022, to TNER-2022	
2023	2845:1		12/52	10/81	17706	02/88	To Southwest 05/88, to NRE 07/88, to BAR-21:2 03/89	
2024	2875:1		11/53	10/81	18892	07/89	To NRE 11/89	
2025	2821:1		12/52	10/81	17632	10/88	To VMV 10/88, to PAL-2025	
2027	2728:1		05/52	11/81	16372	06/89	To Railtex 02/90, to GSWR-2027	

Concurrent with its elimination of branch-lines, the Santa Fe has eliminated its branchline locomotives. Over 100 of the 2050 Class GP7s were gone by summer 1992, and like the 2000 Class GP7s, most of them now work for shortlines. Many of these units are now working the very same branchlines they worked for the Santa Fe, but not the 2076, which was scrapped at Southwest Railroad Car Parts in 1988. At Gainesville, Texas, on January 4, 1986, the 2076 is hauling a gondola load of scrap, an omen of its own future. *John Leopard*

GP7			2050 Class			106 units retired
Road#	**1st#**	**Built**	**Rebuilt**	**Build#**	**Retd.**	**Disposition**
2050	2834:1	12/52	11/72	17645	03/89	To RESCAR-2050 07/89
2051	2781:1	09/52	04/73	17008	03/89	To GWR-2051 05/89
2053	2882:1	11/53	07/73	18899	04/89	To Railtex 09/89, to TNMR-2053
2054	2855:1	07/53	07/73	18560	12/87	To NRE 02/88, to NRL, to BPRR 1988, to JXPT-2054
2056	2756:1	09/52	08/73	16983	03/89	To GWR-2056 05/89, to GWR-711
2057	2806:2	10/52	09/73	17461	03/89	To NRE 11/89, to JXPT-2057
2058	2813:2	11/52	10/73	17624	07/91	To Pielet 10/91
2059	2782:1	09/52	11/73	17009	03/89	Sold
2060	2827:1	12/52	11/73	17638	03/89	To RESCAR-2060 04/89
2061	2811:2	10/52	12/73	17466	03/89	To Pielet 06/89
2062	2708:1	01/52	12/73	15808	03/89	To Pielet 06/89, to SCTR-2062
2064	2719:1	02/52	02/74	15819	03/89	To Helm 07/89, to HESR-104 08/89
2065	2774:1	09/52	03/74	17001	03/89	To IHRC-348 06/89
2066	2710:1	01/52	03/74	15810	03/89	To Helm 07/89, to KLSC-86 02/90
2067	2893:1	12/53	04/74	18910	03/89	To Helm 07/89, to KLSC-87 02/90
2069	2832:1	12/52	05/74	17643	03/89	To Helm 07/89, to MCER-2069 09/89
2070	2766:1	09/52	05/74	16993	03/89	To Pielet 06/89, to SCTR-2070
2071	2672	09/52	06/74	16989	03/90	To NRE 1990
2072	2888:1	12/53	06/74	18905	03/89	To GCRR-2072 04/89, to SWRR-2072
2074	2876:1	11/53	07/74	18893	07/91	To Pielet 10/91
2075	2861:1	07/53	07/74	18566	03/92	To SFSR-92 03/92
2076	2701:1	01/52	08/74	15801	02/88	To Southwest 07/88
2077	2761:1	09/52	08/74	16988	03/90	To Railtex 08/90
2078	2755:1	09/52	08/74	16982	03/90	To Railtex 08/90
2081	2768:1	09/52	10/74	16995	03/89	To Relco-1608 07/89
2082	2867:1	11/53	11/74	18884	10/89	Wrecked, Winslow, AZ, 09/24/89, scrapped 10/16/89
2085	2836:1	12/52	12/74	17647	07/91	To GWR-2085 10/91
2086	2727:1	05/52	01/75	16371	07/91	To Pielet 10/91
2088	2745:1	08/52	01/76	16389	07/89	To NRE 11/04/89
2093	2736:1	06/52	03/77	16380	10/88	To VMV 10/88, to PAL-2093
2094	2773:1	09/52	03/77	17000	07/91	To Pielet 10/91
2097	2842:1	12/52	06/77	17703	03/90	To IHRC-2097 1990
2099	2653	12/50	07/77	12199	06/86	Wrecked, Antelope Gap, TX, 06/23/86, scrapped Cleburne
2100:2	2847:1	12/52	07/77	17708	04/89	To Pielet 11/89
2101:2	2783:1	10/52	08/77	17010	07/91	To Pielet 10/91
2105:2	2891:1	12/53	09/77	18908	07/91	To GWR-2105 10/91
2106:2	2706:1	01/52	09/77	15806	07/91	To Pielet 10/91
2111:2	2686	05/51	12/77	13197	10/88	To VMV 10/88, to PAL-2111
2112:2	2880:1	11/53	12/77	18897	07/91	To Pielet10/91
2114:2	2655	09/50	03/78	13159	03/90	To NRE 1990
2118:2	2754:1	09/52	04/78	16981	04/89	To Pielet 11/89
2121:2	2889:1	12/53	07/78	18906	06/89	To NRE 11/89
2126:2	2760:1	09/52	08/78	16987	06/89	To NRE 11/89
2127:2	2733:1	05/52	08/78	16377	03/90	To Railtex 08/90, to GSWR-2127
2128:2	2823:1	12/52	08/78	17634	07/91	To Pielet 10/91
2129:2	2789	03/53	08/78	17016	10/88	To VMV 10/88, to PAL-2129

Road#	1st#	Built	Rebuilt	Build#	Retd.	Disposition
2130:2	2825:1	12/52	09/78	17636	06/89	To Railtex 02/90, to GSWR-2130, to GGSR-2130
2134:2	2881:1	11/53	10/78	18898	03/89	To GCRR-2134 04/89
2139:2	2688	05/51	11/78	13199	07/91	To Pielet 10/91
2144:2	2868:1	11/53	12/78	18885	12/88	To ABL-2144 12/88
2146:2	2863:1	07/53	12/78	18568	10/88	To VMV 10/88, to PAL-1003, to WATCO-1003
2150:2	2887:1	11/53	01/79	18904	04/89	To IHRC-346 08/89, to OCTR-346
2151:2	2871:1	11/53	02/79	18888	03/89	To Railtex 09/89
2152:2	2666	01/51	02/79	13187	12/88	To LNW-53 03/89
2153:2	2682	02/51	03/79	12210	03/89	To Railtex 09/89, to TNER-2153
2154:2	2848:1	03/53	03/79	18085	10/88	To VMV 10/88, to PAL-2154
2155:2	2680	02/51	04/79	12208	03/89	To FCEN-2155 04/89
2156:2	2797:1	10/52	04/79	17452	03/89	To SCTR-2156 05/89
2157:2	2852:1	06/53	05/79	18557	03/89	To FCEN-2157 04/89
2158:2	2751:1	08/52	05/79	16978	03/89	To Railtex 09/89, to CALB-2158
2160	2729:1	05/52	05/79	16373	03/89	To Railtex 09/89, to GSWR-2160
2161	2685	05/51	06/79	13196	06/89	To ValRol 10/89
2162	2667	01/51	07/79	13188	06/89	To Railtex 02/90, to SDIY-2162 06/90
2163	2677	02/51	07/79	12205	01/90	To ILS 02/90, to SWRR-2163
2164	2662	12/50	07/79	13166	01/90	To ILS 02/90, to SWRR-2164
2165	2877:1	11/53	07/79	18894	01/90	To ATL-2165 01/90
2166	2807:1	10/52	08/79	17462	06/89	To NRE 11/89, to TNER-2166
2167	2784:1	10/52	08/79	17011	10/89	To Railtex 07/90, to NEKM-2167 02/90, to IAIS-2167 10/91
2168	2800:2	10/52	08/79	17455	10/89	To Railtex 07/90, to SDIY 2168 06/90
2169	2657	10/50	08/79	13161	01/90	To ATL-2169 01/90
2170	2786	10/52	09/79	17013	04/87	Wrecked 04/24/87, to ISMP 01/88
2171	2660	10/50	10/79	13164	01/90	To ILS 02/90, to SWRR-2171
2173	2818:2	11/52	10/79	17629	02/89	To DrumMet 08/29/89, scrapped
2174	2720:1	02/52	10/79	15820		
2175	2741:1	08/52	11/79	16385	04/87	To NRE 02/88, to BAR-23 03/89
2176	2730:1	05/52	11/79	16374	03/90	To Railtex 08/90
2177	2810:2	10/52	12/79	17465	04/87	Wrecked 04/24/87, to ISMP 01/88
2178	2779:1	09/52	12/79	17006		
2179	2652	10/50	12/79	12198	07/91	To GWR-2179 10/91, to VCY-101 05/92
2180	2799	10/52	01/80	17454	03/90	To NRE in 03/90
2182	2674	02/51	01/80	12202	03/90	To SWRR-2182 08/90
2184	2753:1	02/52	02/80	16980		
2185	2739:1	08/52	02/80	16383	03/89	To Railtex 09/89
2186	2791	04/53	03/80	17018	11/89	To NRE 11/89
2187	2828:1	12/52	03/80	17639		
2188	2767:1	09/52	04/80	16994		
2189	2763	09/52	04/80	16990	03/89	To NRE 09/23/89
2190	2817:2	11/52	04/80	17628	03/89	To Railtex 09/89, to CALB-2190
2191	2790	03/53	04/80	17017		To SKOL-2191
2196	2735:1	06/52	06/80	16379	07/91	To GWR-2196 10/91, to VCY-100 5/92
2197	2840:1	12/52	06/80	17701	12/88	To ABL-2197 12/88, to OTR-2197 12/88
2198	2785:1	10/52	06/80	17012	10/88	To VMV 10/88, to PAL-2198
2202:2	2692	05/51	08/80	13203	04/89	To IHRC-341 08/89, to OCTR-341
2203:2	2778:1	09/52	08/80	17005	04/89	To IHRC-342 08/89
2205:2	2678	02/51	08/80	12206	02/88	To Southwest 05/88, to BAR-20:2 03/89
2206:2	2743:1	08/52	09/80	16387	10/88	To VMV 10/88, to PAL-2206
2207:2	2664	01/51	09/80	13185	07/91	To Railtex 11/91, to DGNO-2207
2210:2	2698	01/52	10/80	15798	06/89	To Railtex 02/90, to NEKM-2210 02/90
2211:2	2663	01/51	10/80	13184	03/90	To SWRR-2211 08/90
2214:2	2748:1	08/52	11/80	16975	10/88	To VMV 10/88, to PAL-2214
2219:2	2849:1	06/53	12/80	18554	06/89	To NRE 11/89, to TNER-2219
2223:2	2738:1	06/52	01/81	16382	04/89	To IHRC-343 08/89
2225:2	2691	05/51	02/81	13202	04/89	To IHRC-344 08/89
2226:2	2759:1	09/52	02/81	16986	04/89	To IHRC-345 08/89
2227:2	2722:1	02/52	02/81	15822	02/88	To NRE 07/87, to BAR-22:2 03/89
2234:2	2744:1	08/52	04/81	16388	07/91	To Railtex 11/91

Road#	1st#	2nd#	Built	Rebuilt	Build#	Retd.	Disposition
2264	718	2918:1	05/56	12/78	21588	02/89	To DrumMet 08/29/89, scrapped
2278	737	2937:1	04/57	07/79	23140	12/88	To AZCE-2278 04/89
2284	715	2915:1	05/56	09/79	21585	02/89	To DrumMet 08/29/89, scrapped

Road#	1st#	Built	Rebuilt	Build#	Retd.	Disposition
2348	3548	08/70	09/84	36584	04/87	Wrecked 04/24/87, to ISMP 01/88

Two large classes of remanufactured loco-motives have been eliminated from the Santa Fe roster so far, the CF7s and SD26s, though the GP7s, SD45s and SDF45s are likely to follow in the near future. There wasn't anything tremendously defective about the CF7s, but the trend away from branchlines and carload traffic left the CF7s without employment. Interestingly, most of the CF7s migrated to shortlines and regionals in the southeast. The 2573, at Barstow, California, on February 4, 1987, is typical, becoming Mid-South-7009 after leaving the Santa Fe 11 months later. *George Horna*

| **CF7** | | | | **2417 Class** | **132 units retired** |

Road#	1st#	2nd#	Rebuilt	Retd.	Disposition
2441	287C		09/77	11/85	To WATCO-2441 11/85
2449	259L		07/77	08/86	To TKEN-2449 08/86, to NERR-2449 09/86
2452	258C		06/77	04/86	To ECONO-2452 04/86
2473	301C	345C	12/76	03/86	To ECONO-2473 04/86
2474	281C		11/76	01/87	To FCEN-47 01/87
2475	263L		10/76	08/86	To TKEN-2475 08/86, to NERR-2475 09/86, to RLK-2475
2476	207C		08/76	06/87	To NRE 06/88, to DSRR-103
2477	225C		07/76	07/86	To TKEN-2477 08/86, to NERR-2477 09/86, to RLK-2477, to CNWR-477
2478	226C		06/76	04/86	To ECONO-2478 04/86
2479	286C		03/76	11/86	To THST-2479 11/86
2480	286L		02/76	01/86	To BMRG-2480 09/86, to WCLR-2480 08/88
2482	284L		01/75	06/87	To NRE 01/88, to CAGY-810 02/88
2483	224C		01/75	06/87	To NRE 01/88, to CAGY-808 02/88
2484	241L		01/75	06/87	To NRE 07/87, to MCER-484 10/87
2485	289C		01/75	03/86	To INRD-2485 04/86, wrecked 03/87
2486	259C		01/75	08/86	To BMRG-2486 09/86, to AR-2486 08/88
2487	342L		12/74	03/86	To GLSR-1501 04/86
2488	337L		12/74	06/87	To NRE 06/88, to KJRY-488
2489	206C		12/74	12/85	To RRI 03/86, to CLK-48 03/86, to MDC, to LDRR-1504 07/90
2490	32C	314C	12/74	03/86	To ADN-1513 04/86
2491	37C	312L	12/74	12/85	To WHEV-2491 09/86, to ATL-2491
2492	301L		11/74	11/85	To GRCO-2492 11/85, to MCHA-2492
2493	300L		11/74	01/87	To IANR-2493 02/87
2494	311L		11/74	12/85	To RRI 12/85, to Pinsley, to FCEN-2494 11/86, to FCEN-49
2495	44L	310L	10/74	12/85	To GRCO-2495 11/85, to MCHA-2495
2496	253C		10/74	06/87	To NRE 07/87, to MSRC-7001 07/87, to EIRR-7001
2501	262L		09/74	06/87	To NRE 12/87, to TN-992 02/88
2503	268C		09/74	09/87	To ECONO-2503 10/87, to FCEN-2503 10/87
2504	284C		08/74	06/87	To NRE 07/87, to MSRC-7007 12/87
2505	239C		08/74	06/87	To NRE 01/88, to CAGY-807 02/88
2506	203L		08/74	03/86	To INRD-2506 04/86
2507	313L		08/74	01/87	To RESCAR-2507 02/87
2508	314L		08/74	01/86	To Pinsley 01/86, to GRCO-2508 04/86, to MCHA-2508
2509	224L		08/74	12/85	To RRI 03/86, to CLK-2509 03/86, to CLK-50, to FNOR-50
2510	217C		07/74	06/86	To ECONO 07/86 for parts
2511	232L		07/74	11/85	To GRCO-2511 11/85, to MCHA-2511
2512	304L		07/74	08/86	To TKEN-2512 08/86, to NERR-2512 09/86, to CWRY-512
2515	287L		07/74	03/86	To INRD-2515 04/86
2516	272C		06/74	03/86	To ECONO-2516 06/86
2517	315L		06/74	08/86	To TKEN-2517 08/86, to NERR-2517 09/86, to RLK-517, to CWRY-517
2518	36C	312C	06/74	08/86	To TKEN-2518 08/86, to NERR 09/86, to TKEN-2518
2520	282C		05/74	01/87	To RESCAR-2520 02/87, to HE-2520 1987
2522	255C		05/74	03/86	To ADN-1514 04/86
2523	277L		04/74	08/86	To TKEN-2523 08/86, to NERR-2523 09/86, to RLK-523
2525	344L		04/74	08/86	To TKEN-2525 08/86, to NERR-2525 09/86
2526	251C		04/74	04/86	To ECONO-2526 04/86
2527	308L	327L	03/74	03/86	To INRD-2527 04/86, to INRD-200
2528	239L		03/74	03/86	To INRD-2528 04/86
2529	276L		03/74	08/86	To TKEN-2529 08/86, to NERR-2529 09/86
2530	209L		03/74	06/87	To NRE 12/87, to TN-993 02/88
2532	266C		02/74	03/86	To INRD-2532 04/86
2533	255L		02/74	11/85	To WATCO-2533 11/85
2534	309L		02/74	03/86	To ECONO-2534 04/86
2535	304C		02/74	01/87	To RESCAR-2535 02/87

Road#	1st#	2nd#	Rebuilt	Retd.	Disposition
2536	242L		01/74	08/86	To TKEN-2536 08/86, to NERR-2536 09/86
2537	233C		01/74	09/86	Scrapped
2538	307L		01/74	06/87	To NRE 07/87, to MSRC-7012 07/87
2539	221C		12/73	03/86	To INRD-2539 04/86, to INRD-201
2541	240L		12/73	09/86	To ECONO-2541 02/87
2542	218C		11/73	01/87	To WATCO-2542 02/87, to SEKR-1000 04/87, to ORR-1000
2543	46C	300C	11/73	03/86	To INRD-2543 04/86
2544	249C		11/73	01/87	To WATCO-2544 02/87, to SEKR-1001 04/87
2545	256C		11/73	09/86	Scrapped
2546	229L		11/73	03/86	To INRD-2546 04/86, to KRM
2547	231L		10/73	08/86	To TKEN-2547, 08/86, to NERR-2547 09/86, to RLK-547
2548	257L		10/73	06/87	To NRE 01/88, to CAGY-808 02/88, to CCKY-101
2549	208C		10/73	01/87	To WATCO-2549 02/87, to SEKR-1002 04/87
2550	278C		10/73	06/87	To NRE 12/87, to TN-994 02/88
2551	336L		09/73	03/86	To INRD-2551 04/86
2552	243C		09/73	10/85	Scrapped
2553	257C		09/73	08/86	To TKEN-2553 08/86, to NERR-2553 09/86
2555	207L		08/73	08/86	To TKEN-2555 08/86, to NERR-2555 09/86, to WTNN-55 05/88, to RLK-555
2559	47C	303C	08/73	08/86	To TKEN-2559 08/86, to NERR-2559 09/86
2560	240C		07/73	04/86	To ECONO-2560 03/87
2561	230C		07/73	10/86	To NRE 01/88, to MSRC-7010 01/88
2563	228L		07/73	02/86	To LAJ-2563 03/86
2564	38C	305C	07/73	01/88	To NRE 01/88, to MSRC-7004:2 01/88
2565	34L	302C	06/73	12/85	To Pinsley 06/86, to PVRR-2565
2566	216C		06/73	01/88	To NRE 01/88, to MSRC-7013 01/88
2568	226L		06/73	02/86	To LAJ-2568 03/86
2569	213C		05/73	04/86	To ECONO-2569 03/87, to FWW-2569
2570	242C		05/73	06/87	To NRE 06/88, to DSRR-100
2571	202L		05/73	02/86	To LAJ-2571 03/86
2572	206L		05/73	04/86	To ECONO-2572 03/87, to DUPX-2572 10/87
2573	248C		04/73	01/88	To NRE 01/88, to MSRC-7009 01/88
2575	233L		04/73	04/86	To ECONO-2575 03/87, to DUPX-2575 10/87
2577	204L		04/73	01/88	To NRE 01/88, to MSRC-7008 12/87
2578	230L		04/73	06/87	To NRE 11/87, to WCRC-401 10/87
2579	221L		03/73	04/86	To ECONO-2579 03/87, to DUPX-2579 10/87
2580	276C		03/73	04/86	To ECONO-2580 03/87
2581	267L		02/73	04/86	To ECONO-2581 03/87
2582	250C		02/73	04/86	To ECONO-2582 03/87
2585	264C		01/73	06/87	To NRE 06/88, to DSRR-101
2586	244C		01/73	10/86	To NRE 12/87, to MSRC-7006 12/87
2589	243L		12/72	06/87	To NRE 01/88, to MSRC-7014 01/88
2591	235L		12/72	10/86	To NRE 12/87, to MSRC-7005 12/87
2593	214C		11/72	03/87	To ECONO-2593 04/86
2596	212C		11/72	01/88	To NRE 01/88, to MSRC-7015 01/88
2598	254L		10/72	03/87	To MDC 02/87, to CPC-2598 03/87
2600	248L		10/72	10/86	To SCBT-2600 10/86
2602	234C		09/72	04/86	To ECONO-2602 03/87
2604	278L		09/72	03/86	To ECONO-2604 04/86
2605	260L		09/72	06/85	To NRE 06/88, to DSRR-105
2606	220C		09/72	04/87	To WATCO-6 04/87, leased to BCAS
2607	274L		08/72	06/87	To NRE 06/88, to DSRR-106
2608	211L		08/72	04/86	To ECONO-2608 03/87
2609	29L		08/72	10/86	To NRE 12/87, to MSRC-7002 12/87
2612	272L		07/72	03/86	To GLSR-1502 04/86
2614	33L		07/72	06/87	To NRE 07/87, to RRVW-309 09/87
2616	16C		06/72	06/87	To NRE 07/87, to MSRC-7004:1 07/87, to MSRC-7011
2617	31L		06/72	03/86	To INRD-2617 04/86, cannabalized
2618	27C		06/72	06/87	To NRE 12/87, to LDRR-1500 12/87
2619	201C		05/72	06/87	To NRE 07/87, to LAJ 10/87 for parts
2621	227L		05/72	06/87	To NRE 07/87, to MSRC-7003 07/87
2622	19L		05/72	06/87	To NRE 12/87, to LDRR-1501 12/87
2623	24L		04/72	01/87	To RESCAR-2623 02/87
2624	35C		04/72	09/86	Scrapped
2626	22C		03/72	06/85	To NatMet 06/85, scrapped
2627	21L		03/72	11/85	To GRCO-2627 11/85, to MCHA-2627
2629	20L		02/72	06/87	To NRE 06/88, to DSRR-105
2631	34C	313C	12/71	04/86	To ECONO-2631 04/86
2633	312L		11/71	04/87	To WATCO-7 05/87, leased to BCAS
2636	31C		08/71	06/87	To NRE, to WCRC-402 10/87
2637	246C		07/71	10/86	To Pinsley, to FCEN-2637 10/86, to FMID-2637 11/87
2640	310L		03/71	06/87	To NRE 06/88, to DSRR-107
2641	222L		03/71	10/86	To SCBT-2641 10/86
2642	27L		02/71	04/86	To ECONO-2642 03/87
2643	270L		01/71	01/87	To FCEN-2643 01/87, to FMID-2643 11/87
2644	222C		11/70	06/87	To NRE 01/88, to CAGY-809 02/88
2646	200C		09/70	10/86	To NRE 12/87, to TN-995 02/88
2647	210L		08/70	12/85	To Pinsley 06/86, to PVRR-2647
2648	203C		07/70	01/86	To WATCO 02/87, to SEKR-1003 04/87

Aside from four GP20s scrapped due to wreck damage, only 19 3000 Class GP20s have left the Santa Fe to date, all of which were included in the sale of the Toledo, Peoria & Western in February 1989. The 3014:2, which became TP&W-2009, was working in TP&W territory at East Peoria, Illinois, on November 11, 1987. The GP20s lost their attractive one-piece windshields when they were remanufactured at San Bernardino, California.
George Horna

GP30 — 2700 Class — 2 units retired

Road#	1st#	2nd#	Built	Rebuilt	Build#	Retd.	Disposition
2733:2	1233	3233	06/62	10/81	27220	04/87	Wrecked 04/24/87, to ISMP 01/88
2752:2	1252	3252	03/63	02/84	28075		

GP35 — 2800 Class — 8 units retired

Road#	1st#	2nd#	Built	Rebuilt	Build#	Retd.	Disposition
2846:2	1346	3346	06/64	12/82	28743	02/88	Wrecked Pico Rivera, CA 01/28/88, to Purdy 07/88
2856:2	1356	3356	05/65	03/83	30070	02/88	Wrecked Pico Rivera, CA 01/28/88, to Purdy 07/88
2879:2	1379	3379	06/65	11/81	30093	02/88	Wrecked Pico Rivera, CA 01/28/88, to Purdy 07/88
2881:2	1381	3381	06/65	06/84	30095	08/90	
2900:2	1400	3400:1	07/65	09/81	30545	02/88	Wrecked Pico Rivera, CA 01/28/88 to Purdy 07/88
2939:2	1439	3439:1	10/65	06/84	30584	10/89	
2945:2	1445	3445:1	10/65	05/84	30590	02/88	Wrecked Pico Rivera, CA 01/28/88, to Purdy 07/88
2964	TP&W-1000	ATSF-3461	05/69	08/84	35054	02/88	Wrecked Pico Rivera, CA 01/28/88, to Purdy 07/88

GP20 — 3000 Class — 19 units retired

Road#	1st#	2nd#	Built	Rebuilt	Build#	Retd.	Disposition
3003:2	1103:1	3103:1	05/60	11/80	25576	02/89	To TPW-2003 02/89
3004:2	1104:1	3104:1	05/60	11/80	25577	02/89	To TPW-2005 02/89
3013:2	1113	3113:1	06/60	10/80	25586	02/89	To TPW-2016 02/89
3014:2	1114	3114:1	06/60	11/79	25587	02/89	To TPW-2009 02/89
3015:2	1115:1	3115:1	06/60	02/80	25588	02/89	To TPW-2015 02/89
3016:2	1116:1	3116:1	06/60	12/80	25589	02/89	To TPW-2007 02/89
3019:2	1119:1	3119:1	07/60	07/79	25592	02/89	To TPW-2012 02/89
3022	1122	3122:1	07/60	09/79	25595	02/89	To TPW-2014 02/89
3034	1134	3134:1	09/61	02/80	26840	02/89	To TPW-2018 02/89
3039	1139	3139:1	09/61	09/79	26845	02/89	To TPW-2002 02/89
3040	1140:1	3140:1	09/61	01/81	26846	02/89	To TPW-2010 02/89
3051	1151	3151:1	10/61	12/79	26857	02/89	To TPW-2008 02/89
3053	1153	3153	11/61	08/80	26859	02/89	To TPW-2011 02/89
3059	1159	3159:1	11/61	02/81	26865	02/89	To TPW-2017 02/89
3063	1163	3163:1	11/61	12/80	26869	02/89	To TPW-2019 02/89
3068	1168	3168	12/61	11/79	26874	02/89	To TPW-2013 02/89
3071	1171	3171	12/61	09/80	26877	02/89	To TPW-2004 02/89
3073	1173	3173	12/61	07/80	26879	02/89	To TPW-2006 02/89
3074	1174	3174	12/61	12/79	26880	02/89	To TPW-2001 02/89

GP39-2 — 3683 Class — 1 unit retired

Road#	1st#	2nd#	Built	Build#	Retd.	Disposition
3691:2	3691:1	3189	05/79	786224-9	08/86	Wrecked Valley Falls, KS, 07/01/86, scrapped

Road#	1st#	2nd#	Built	Rebuilt	Build#	Retd.	Disposition
4600	900	4500	05/59	10/74	25167	01/87	To ST-615 02/87
4601	901	4501	05/59	07/74	25168	01/87	To ST-616 02/87, retired
4603	903	4503	05/59	11/73	25170	01/87	To ST-617 02/87, retired
4604	904	4504	05/59	10/73	25171	01/87	To ST-618 02/87, retired
4605	905	4505	05/59	09/74	25172	01/87	To ST-619 02/87
4606	906	4506	05/59	09/73	25173	01/87	To ST-610 02/87
4607	907	4507	05/59	06/73	25174	01/87	To ST-621 02/87
4612	912	4512	06/59	07/74	25179	01/87	To ST-622 02/87
4613	913	4513	06/59	01/75	25180	01/87	To ST-623 02/87, retired
4617	917	4517	06/59	12/74	25184	01/87	To ST-624 02/87, retired
4618	918	4518	06/59	12/73	25185	01/87	To ST-625 02/87, retired
4627	927	4527	06/59	03/74	25194	01/87	To ST-626 02/87, retired
4640	940	4540	06/59	11/73	25337	01/87	To ST-627 02/87
4641	941	4541	06/59	03/77	25338	01/87	To ST-628 02/87, retired
4644	944	4544	06/59	11/77	25341	01/87	To ST-629 02/87, retired
4645	945	4545	05/60	09/76	25855	01/87	To ST-630 02/87, retired
4646	946	4546	05/60	01/74	25856	01/87	To ST-631 02/87, retired
4648	948	4548	05/60	01/74	25858	01/87	To ST-632 02/87, retired
4650	950	4550	05/60	03/77	25860	01/87	To ST-633 02/87
4652	952	4552	05/60	07/73	25862	01/87	To ST-634 02/87, retired
4655	955	4555	05/60	07/73	25865	01/87	To ST-635 02/87, retired
4657	957	4557	05/60	07/73	25867	01/87	To ST-636 02/87, retired
4661	961	4561	06/60	07/73	25871	01/87	To ST-637 02/87, retired
4665	965	4565	06/60	07/73	25875	01/87	To ST-638 02/87, retired
4667	967	4567	06/60	07/73	25877	01/87	To ST-639 02/87
4668	968	4568	06/60	07/73	25878	01/87	To ST-640 02/87, retired
4669	969	4569	06/60	07/73	25879	01/87	To ST-641 02/87, retired
4670	970	4570	06/60	07/73	25880	01/87	To ST-642 02/87, retired
4673	973	4573	06/60	07/73	25883	01/87	To ST-643 02/87
4674	974	4574	06/60	07/73	25884	01/87	To ST-644 02/87
4675	975	4575	06/60	07/73	25885	01/87	To ST-645 02/87, retired
4676	976	4576	06/60	07/73	25886	01/87	To ST-646 02/87, retired
4677	977	4577	06/60	07/73	25887	01/87	To ST-647 02/87
4678	978	4578	06/60	07/73	25888	01/87	To ST-648 02/87, scrapped 10/91
4679	979	4579	07/60	07/73	25889	01/87	To ST-649 02/87, retired

The least successful of Santa Fe's big remanufacturing program was the SD26 program, which was an effort to remedy the problems that plagued Santa Fe's SD24s. Fifty-five of the SD26s were traded-in to EMD in 1985 for GP50s. The remaining 35 left storage at Barstow, California, in February 1987, and were exiled to the Springfield Terminal. Most of them, like the 4646, didn't find better luck in the Northeast, and have since been retired. The 4646 was in copper ore service at Santa Rita, New Mexico, on April 4, 1980. This line is now operated by the Southwestern Railroad. *Alan Burns*

SD40 — 5000 Class — 1 unit retired

Road#	1st#	Built	Rebuilt	Build#	Retd.	Disposition
5015	1715	03/66	03/81	32051	03/86	Wrecked Levy, NM, 01/28/86, rebuilt to slug 141:2

SD40-2 — 5200 Class — 1 unit retired

Road#	Built	Build#	Retd.	Disposition
5208	10/78	786153-9	07/86	Wrecked C.A. Jct., MO, 07/03/86, rebuilt to slug 142:2

SD45 — 5300 Class — 1 unit retired

Road#	1st#	2nd#	Built	Rebuilt	Build#	Retd.	Disposition
5302	1868	5568	12/66	04/80	32544	12/89	To Pacific 03/91

SD45 — 5304 Class — 8 units retired

Road#	1st#	2nd#	Built	Rebuilt	Build#	Retd.	Disposition
5309	1878	5578	12/66	09/81	32554	07/91	
5313	1812	5512	06/66	11/81	32068	07/91	
5314	1846	5546	11/66	12/81	32522	07/91	
5316	1862	5562	12/66	10/81	32538	03/90	To SWRR-5316 08/90
5322	1879	5579	12/66	02/82	32555	07/91	
5324	1831	5531	10/66	02/82	32507	03/91	To Pacific 03/91
5340	1847	5547	11/66	10/82	32523		
5363	1838	5538	10/66	07/83	32514	12/90	Wrecked Corona, CA, 11/07/90, to ChrCrank 01/91

SD45 — 5426 Class — 4 units retired

Road#	1st#	2nd#	Built	Rebuilt	Build#	Retd.	Disposition
5426	1872	5572	12/66	05/80	32548	03/91	To Pacific 09/91
5427	1850	5550	11/66	05/80	32526	03/91	To Pacific 09/91
5428	1882	5582	12/66	06/80	32558	03/91	To Pacific 09/91
5429	1813	5513	06/66	06/80	32073	03/91	To Pacific 09/91

SD45 — 5430 Class — 4 units retired

Road#	1st#	2nd#	Built	Rebuilt	Build#	Retd.	Disposition
5430	1805	5505	06/66	03/81	32061	03/91	Scrapped
5431	1801	5501	06/66	04/81	32057	03/91	Scrapped
5432	1845	5545	11/66	05/81	32521	03/91	Scrapped
5433	1889	5589	12/66	06/81	32565	03/91	Scrapped

SD45B — 5500 Class — 1 unit retired

Road#	1st#	2nd#	Built	Rebuilt	Build#	Retd.	Disposition
5502:1	1823	5523	08/66	12/83	32079	07/87	Wrecked C.A. Jct, MO, 07/03/86, scrapped San Bernardino

The four 5426 Class SD45s were built as prototypes for the SD45 remanufacturing program in May 1980, using new 16-645F3 engines in place of the troublesome 20-645E3 engines which originally equipped the SD45s. The 16-cylinder engines were subsequently deemed as providing benefits too limited compared to the exorbitant expense of their purchase from EMD, and subsequent program SD45s reused their original 20-cylinder engines. The 5426 Class units weren't successful, and all were retired and scrapped in March 1991, only ten years after their remanufacture. The 5426 was at Barstow, California, on February 4, 1987. *George Horna*

General Electric's U-series locomotives have not been noted for longevity in Santa Fe's fleet, as very few have worked for the Santa Fe longer than 15 years. The U23Bs beat the average by several years, most lasting 17 to 18 years before the class was cleaned out in a sale to GE in 1988. This eliminated low-horsepower U-series locomotives from Santa Fe's roster, leaving SF30B 6419 and their newer cousins, the B23-7s, as the only low-horsepower GEs on the Santa Fe. The 6335, at Chicago on May 18, 1978, was one of 33 U23Bs banished to GE's boneyard during September 1988. *George Horna*

U23B — 6300 Class — 34 units retired

Road#	Built	Build#	Retd.	Disposition
6300	06/70	37491	08/88	To GE 09/88
6304	07/70	37495	08/88	To GE 09/88, to Pielet 01/92
6305	07/70	37496	08/88	To GE 09/88
6309	07/70	37500	08/88	To GE 09/88
6311	08/70	37502	08/88	To GE 09/88
6313	08/70	37504	08/88	To GE 09/88
6314	08/70	37505	08/88	To GE 09/88, to Pielet 11/91
6315	08/70	37506	08/88	To GE 09/88
6316	08/70	37507	08/88	To GE 09/88
6317	08/70	37508	08/88	To GE 09/88
6318	09/70	37509	08/88	To GE 09/88
6319	09/70	37510	08/88	To GE 09/88, to Pielet 01/92
6322	09/70	37513	08/88	To GE 09/88
6323	09/70	37514	08/88	To GE 09/88
6325	10/70	37516	08/88	To GE 09/88
6326	10/70	37517	08/88	To GE 09/88
6327	10/70	37518	08/88	To GE 09/88
6328	10/70	37519	08/88	To GE 09/88
6329	10/70	37520	08/88	To GE 09/88
6330	11/70	37521	08/88	To GE 09/88
6332	12/70	37523	09/86	Wrecked, rebuilt as SF30B 7200
6333	12/70	37524	08/88	To GE 09/88, to Pielet 11/91
6334	12/70	37525	08/88	To GE 09/88, to Pielet 01/92
6335	12/70	37526	08/88	To GE 09/88
6336	12/70	37527	08/88	To GE 09/88, to Pielet 11/91
6337	12/70	37528	08/88	To GE 09/88, to Super 7-23B RS-50
6338	01/71	37529	08/88	To GE 09/88, to Super 7-23B RS-51
6340	01/71	37531	08/88	To GE 09/88
6342	01/71	37533	08/88	To GE 09/88
6343	01/71	37534	08/88	To GE 09/88
6344	01/71	37535	08/88	To GE 09/88, to Pielet 11/91
6345	02/71	37536	08/88	To GE 09/88
6347	02/71	37538	08/88	To GE 09/88
6348	02/71	37539	08/88	To GE 09/88, to Pielet 11/91

C30-7 — 8010 Class — 2 units retired

Road#	Built	Build#	Retd.	Disposition
8044	06/78	41711		
8050	06/78	41717	03/89	Wrecked, to DrumMet

C30-7 — 8064 Class — 1 unit retired

Road#	Built	Build#	Retd.	Disposition
8067	05/79	42378	05/88	Wrecked C.A. Junction, MO, 07/03/86, to Erman 05/88

As of May 14, 1992

Model	Class	#Series	HP	Active	Retired
SDFP45	90 Class	90-98	3,600 hp	8 units	0 units
GP60M	100 Class	100-162	3,800 hp	61 units	2 units
GP60B	325 Class	325-347	3,800 hp	23 units	0 units
DASH 8-40BW	500 Class	500-539	4,000 hp	40 units	0 units
DASH 8-40BW	500 Class	540-559	3,800 hp	20 units	0 units
DASH 8-40BW	560 Class	560-582	3,800 hp	23 units	0 units
DASH 8-40CW	800 Class	800-866	4,000 hp	34 units	0 units
Slug	1101 Class	1101-1109	N/A	9 units	0 units
Slug	1115 Class	1115-1125	N/A	8 units	2 units
Slug	1126 Class	1126-1129	N/A	4 units	0 units
Slug	1140 Class	1140-1146	N/A	7 units	0 units
GP7	1310 Class	1310-1329	1,500 hp	19 units	1 unit
Switcher	1460 Class	1460	1,500 hp	1 unit	0 unit
SD39	1556 Class	1556-1575	2,500 hp	20 units	0 units
GP7	2000 Class	2000-2026	1,500 hp	11 units	16 units
GP7	2050 Class	2050-2243	1,500 hp	81 units	113 units
GP9	2244 Class	2244-2299	1,750 hp	50 units	6 units
GP38	2300 Class	2300-2360	2,000 hp	58 units	3 units
GP38-2	2370 Class	2370-2380	2,000 hp	11 units	0 units
GP30	2700 Class	2700-2785	2,500 hp	78 units	8 units
GP35	2800 Class	2800-2963	2,500 hp	150 units	14 units
GP20	3000 Class	3000-3072	2,000 hp	52 units	21 units
GP39-2	3400 Class	3400-3449	2,300 hp	50 units	0 units
GP39-2	3600 Class	3600-3616	2,300 hp	17 units	0 units
GP39-2	3640 Class	3640	2,300 hp	1 unit	0 units
GP39-2	3669 Class	3669-3682	2,300 hp	13 units	1 unit
GP39-2	3683 Class	3683-3695	2,300 hp	11 units	2 units
GP39-2	3696 Class	3696-3705	2,300 hp	10 units	0 units
GP40X	3800 Class	3800-3809	3,500 hp	10 units	0 units
GP50	3810 Class	3810-3839	3,500 hp	30 units	0 units
GP50	3840 Class	3840-3854	3,600 hp	15 units	0 units
GP60	4000 Class	4000-4039	3,800 hp	40 units	0 units
SD40	5000 Class	5000-5019	3,000 hp	18 units	2 units
SD40-2	5020 Class	5020-5057	3,000 hp	37 units	1 unit
SD40-2	5058 Class	5058-5070	3,000 hp	13 units	0 units
SD40-2	5071 Class	5071-5124	3,000 hp	54 units	0 units
SD40-2	5125 Class	5125-5169	3,000 hp	45 units	0 units
SD40-2	5170 Class	5170-5192	3,000 hp	23 units	0 units
SD40-2	5200 Class	5200-5213	3,000 hp	13 units	1 unit
SDF40-2	5250 Class	5250-5267	3,000 hp	18 units	0 units
SD45	5300 Class	5300-5303	3,600 hp	3 units	1 unit
SD45	5304 Class	5304-5408	3,600 hp	97 units	8 units
SD45	5430 Class	5434-5437	3,500 hp	4 units	0 units
SD45B	5500 Class	5501-5502	3,600 hp	2 units	1 unit
SD45-2B	5510 Class	5510-5517	3,600 hp	8 units	0 units
SD45-2	5705 Class	5705-5714	3,600 hp	9 units	1 unit
SD45-2	5800 Class	5800-5868	3,600 hp	69 units	0 units
SDF45	5950 Class	5950-5989	3,600 hp	40 units	0 units
B23-7	6350 Class	6350-6363	2,250 hp	14 units	0 units
B23-7	6364 Class	6364-6389	2,250 hp	26 units	0 units
B23-7	6390 Class	6390-6418	2,250 hp	29 units	0 units
SF30B	6419 Class	6419	3,000 hp	1 units	0 units
B39-8	7400 Class	7400-7402	3,900 hp	3 units	0 units
DASH 8-40B	7410 Class	7410-7449	4,000 hp	40 units	0 units
B36-7	7484 Class	7484-7499	3,600 hp	16 units	0 units
C30-7	8010 Class	8010-8057	3,000 hp	46 units	2 units
C30-7	8058 Class	8058-8063	3,000 hp	6 units	0 units
C30-7	8064 Class	8064-8098	3,000 hp	34 units	1 unit
C30-7	8099 Class	8099-8122	3,000 hp	24 units	0 units
C30-7	8123 Class	8123-8152	3,000 hp	30 units	0 units
C30-7	8153 Class	8153-8166	3,000 hp	14 units	0 units
U36C	8736 Class	8736-8762	3,600 hp	27 units	1 unit
SF30C	9500 Class	9500-9569	3,000 hp	70 units	0 units

792 EMD B-B units:
1	Switcher
111	GP7
50	GP9
52	GP20
78	GP30
150	GP35
58	GP38
11	GP38-2
102	GP39-2
10	GP40X
45	GP50
40	GP60
61	GP60M
23	GP60B

212 GE B-B units:
69	B23-7
1	SF30B
16	B36-7
3	B39-8
40	DASH 8-40B
83	DASH 8-40BW

481 EMD C-C units:
20	SD39
18	SD40
104	SD45
2	SD45B
40	SDF45
8	SDFP45
185	SD40-2
18	SDF40-2
78	SD45-2
8	SD45-2B

285 GE C-C units:
70	SF30C
27	U36C
154	C30-7
34	DASH 8-40CW

Total: 1,770 units, 28 slugs